ENGLISH WORKSHOP

FIRST COURSE

HOLT, RINEHART AND WINSTON
Harcourt Brace & Company
Austin • New York • Orlando • Atlanta • San Francisco
Boston • Dallas • Toronto • London

ACKNOWLEDGMENTS

We wish to thank the following teachers who reviewed materials for *English Workshop*, either in manuscript or in field tests.

Gail Craig
LaSalle Springs Middle School
Glencoe, MO 63038-2201

Cindy Hamlin
Bailey Middle School
Austin, TX 78739

Claire Miner
Burnt Hills Middle School
Burnt Hills, NY 12027

Janet Peña-Davis
Dodge School
Chicago, IL 60612

Conrad Pepin
Fairgrounds Junior High School
Nashua, NH 03060

Mary Schultz
Our Lady of the Greenwood
Greenwood, IN 46143

Executive Editor: Mescal Evler

Managing Editor: Robert R. Hoyt

Project Editor: Suzanne Thompson

Editorial Staff: Laura Britton, Tara Ellis, Karen Forrester, Karen Hoffman, Guy Holland, Christy McBride, Michael Neibergall, Marie Price, Patricia Saunders, Amy Simpson, Atietie Tonwe

Editorial Support Staff: Carla Beer, Stella Galvan, Margaret Guerrero, Ruth Hooker, Pat Stover

Editorial Permissions: Ann Farrar

Design, Photo Research, and Production: Pun Nio, *Senior Art Director;* Rebecca Byrd-Bretz, *Cover Design;* Beth Prevelige, *Production Manager;* Joan Eberhardt, *Production Assistant;* Linda Moyer, *Production Coordinator;* Debra Saleny, *Photo Research Manager;* Mavournea Hay, *Photo Researcher;* Carol Martin, *Electronic Publishing Manager;* Debra Schorn, *Electronic Publishing Senior Coordinator*

Printed in the United States of America

ISBN 0-03-097174-8

20 21 22 054 09 08 07 06

TABLE OF CONTENTS

PREWRITING: JOURNALS AND FREEWRITING

Your unique interests, observations, and experiences are waiting to be shared with a reader. The following prewriting techniques can help you to unlock your ideas for writing.

WRITER'S JOURNAL

A ***writer's journal*** can serve as a record of your thoughts about what you see, hear, feel, and do. Choose a notebook or folder especially for your writer's journal. Set aside a time to write each day. Write about something that is truly interesting and enjoyable to you.

- Let your imagination soar as you write about dreams, daydreams, and hopes for the future.
- Try creating songs, poems, or stories. If you enjoy drawing, you can even include sketches or cartoons in your journal.

FREEWRITING

Freewriting is thinking about a subject and then writing whatever ideas pop into your head.

- Focus on a topic that interests you, such as your memory of an exciting experience or a special person or place you would like to describe on paper.
- Get a paper and pencil. Then set a time limit of three to five minutes. Let your thoughts and ideas flow freely from your mind to your paper.
- Let yourself go! Try to keep your pen or pencil moving during your time limit. Jot down all the ideas that come to you. Don't stop to make corrections.

EXERCISE 1 Using Prewriting Techniques

You have been asked to write a paragraph about something that you have done that made you proud or happy. To find and develop your ideas, choose one of the prewriting techniques described above. On your own paper, write a page for your writer's journal or freewrite for three to five minutes.

PREWRITING: BRAINSTORMING AND CLUSTERING

BRAINSTORMING

When you ***brainstorm***, you free your mind to think of ideas as quickly as possible.

- Start by writing a word on a sheet of paper. Then quickly jot down every idea or word that comes to mind.
- Don't stop to judge the ideas. You can do that later.

Brainstorming can also be done in a group. When brainstorming in a group, encourage everyone to share ideas. Listen carefully to each speaker and take notes. Again, don't pause to judge the ideas that people suggest. Save your reactions for later.

CLUSTERING

Clustering is a way to break a subject or a topic into smaller parts. When you cluster, follow these guidelines.

- Write your subject in the center of the paper. Draw a circle around the subject.
- Write related ideas around the subject. Circle each idea, and draw a line from each one to the subject.
- Continue writing down related ideas, circling them, and connecting them with lines until you run out of ideas.

EXERCISE 2 **Brainstorming and Clustering**

Choose a partner. Then, work with your partner to agree on one of the subjects below for a piece of writing. Once you have picked your subject, work separately to create cluster charts on it. Then, meet with your partner to compare cluster charts. Next, brainstorm with your partner to create a list of details that could be included in the piece of writing.

1. a great moment in sports
2. a Saturday adventure
3. a music group
4. a peaceful place
5. what makes a good pet
6. what makes a good friend

PREWRITING: ASKING QUESTIONS

5W-HOW? QUESTIONS

Asking questions that begin with *who, what, where, when, why,* and *how* can help you find information on many different subjects.

- *Who?* (Who were the Maya people?)
- *What?* (What did they accomplish as a civilization?)
- *Where?* (Where did they live in the Americas?)
- *When?* (When did they begin studying astronomy?)
- *Why?* (Why are their buildings considered magnificent?)
- *How?* (How did the Maya people communicate?)

"WHAT IF?" QUESTIONS

If you are planning a piece of creative writing, such as a short story, "What if?" questions are useful. The following questions are examples of "What if?" questions you could ask yourself.

- *What if I could change one thing in my life?* (What if I lived in a different country?)
- *What if some common thing were uncommon?* (What if trees were the rarest plants on earth?)
- *What if one situation in the world could be changed?* (What if cities could be built under the sea?)

EXERCISE 3 Using *5W-How?* Questions

You are writing an informative article for the school newspaper. Choose a topic that you think is interesting from the list below. On your own paper, make a list of *5W-How?* questions that you can use to gather information about the topic.

1. the class picnic or party
2. a new teacher
3. a class or team fund-raising event
4. a local park or teen center
5. a new music group or hit album

EXERCISE 4 Using "What if?" Questions

Work with a partner to plan a short story. Base your story on one of the following situations. With your partner, write on the lines below at least ten "What if?" questions to gather ideas for this story.

1. While flying for the first time, Lita notices someone walking on the wing of her airplane.
2. Your word-processing screen starts to cry while you're keying in a sad poem.
3. Two brothers wake up one morning, get out of bed, and find themselves standing in a strange room.

EX. You and a friend are walking along a city street when you hear an explosion.

What if your friend said she didn't hear the noise?

What if, a minute later, dozens of parakeets were flying from the direction of the noise?

PREWRITING: ARRANGING IDEAS

After gathering ideas for a piece of writing, the next step is to arrange them in a sensible order.

WAYS TO ARRANGE IDEAS	
Type of Order	**Definition**
Chronological	Describes events in the order that they happen
Spatial	Describes objects according to location (near to far, left to right, and so on)
Importance	Gives details from least to most important or from most to least important
Logical	Groups related details together

EXERCISE 5 Arranging Ideas

Read the following descriptions of writing situations, and think about the ideas and details you would use. Then choose an appropriate order for each situation. Identify the order you have chosen on the line before each sentence.

_______________ 1. In an article for your school newspaper, you list the events of the weekly student council meeting.

_______________ 2. You are writing an essay to describe a town you recently visited.

_______________ 3. You've chosen to write a research report about the many kinds of animals that live in the ocean.

_______________ 4. Your school is no longer going to offer sports competitions after school. You write an article for the town newspaper and list four reasons why an after-school sports program is valuable.

WRITING A FIRST DRAFT

After finding ideas and arranging them, you will be ready to shape your first draft.

- Use your prewriting plans as a guide.
- Feel free to include new ideas as you write.
- Don't edit your work at this point. Getting all your ideas down on paper is more important.
- You can write as fast as your ideas will flow, or you can draft slowly, thinking about each paragraph. Either method is useful. Choose the one that is right for you.

The paragaraph draft below is about Marion Wright Edelman, founder of the Children's Defense Fund. Notice the brackets around the questions and notes. The writer will need to return to the prewriting stage to find more information before creating a final draft. Also notice that this paragraph is not as polished as it will be in the final draft. Problems with content, organization, and mechanics can be fixed at a later stage.

> Marian Wright Edelman was born on June 6, 1939 [1940? check date] in Bennettsville, SC. She attended ~~callege~~ college in Atlanta, Georgia. [name of college?] She received a degree. ~~and~~ Then she went to Yale Law School in New Haven, CT. She became the first African American woman to be a practicing lawyer in Mississippi. [What year was this?] As a lawyer, she focused on Civil Rights cases. ~~She later concentrated on protecting the rights of children. [more specific details here?]~~ Eventually she founded and became the president of the Children's Defense Fund. [year it began?] This organization is devoted to protecting the rights of children. [specific details?]

EXERCISE 6 Writing a First Draft

Using what you learned in Exercise 5, draft a description of a room or space in your school. This place might be your classroom, the art or band room, the locker room, or the gymnasium. Write your draft on your own paper. Include concrete details to make the place real to someone who has never been there. Share your draft with others in your class.

EVALUATING

After writers finish their drafts, they ***evaluate*** them. They judge what's good about the draft and what needs to be improved. They use four ***standards***, or rules, for good writing.

- The writing is interesting. It grabs and holds the reader's attention.
- The writing has a clear main idea.
- The main idea is supported with details.
- The ideas and details are presented in a clear and reasonable order.

Evaluating is often a two-step process. First, the writer evaluates what he or she has written. Second, to get some valuable feedback, the writer asks someone else to evaluate it, too. This person is the writer's ***peer***, someone who is the writer's equal, like a classmate. Here are some tips to follow as you evaluate a piece of writing, your own or that of a peer.

GUIDELINES FOR EVALUATION	
Self-Evaluation	**Peer Evaluation**
1. Put your draft away for a while before evaluating it. You will be able to think about it more clearly when your mind is fresh. 2. Read your paper two or three times. Each time you read it, focus on one of the standards listed above. 3. Read your draft aloud. Listen for awkward or unclear spots that need attention.	1. Always tell the writer something good about the paper. 2. Focus on the content of the paper and the order of the ideas and details. Don't point out errors in spelling and grammar at this point. 3. Ask helpful questions such as "Can you use an easier word here?" or "Can you add details to make this idea clearer?" 4. Make your suggestions specific.

EXERCISE 7 Practicing Peer Evaluation

Practice your peer-evaluation skills by evaluating the paragraph below. Use the four standards for good writing listed at the top of the previous page. Write your evaluation on the lines below. Begin with a comment on what's good about the paragraph. Then write helpful questions or suggestions about what needs to be improved.

> Whenever I need to have some quiet time alone to think or just get my thoughts together, I walk to Banneker Park. It was named for Benjamin Banneker. The park is green and shady, with a fountain and benches. He lived about two hundred years ago. Somehow it's easy to think there. It's easy to feel peaceful. There are hardly any sounds, except the birds and the sound of water splashing in the fountain.

REVISING

Revising means making the changes that are needed to improve a piece of writing. Whether you make changes by hand or on a typewriter or word processor, you'll use four basic revision techniques: *adding, cutting, replacing, and reordering.*

REVISION TECHNIQUES	
Add	Adds new words, sentences, or paragraphs
Cut	Takes out unnecessary or repeated ideas
Replace	Replaces weak or unclear wording with precise words or details
Reorder	Moves words, sentences, and paragraphs for clear order

EXAMPLE

One of the most interesting [and beautiful] countries in Central America is Belize. Known for its ~~beautiful scenery~~ [beaches, mountains, and tropical jungles], this tiny country attracts many tourists from the United States. ~~The country isn't very big, but it is beautiful.~~ Tourists ~~go~~ [travel] to Belize to see its Mayan ruins. ~~They~~ [Tourists] also [visit] ~~go to~~ Belize for its wonderful snorkeling and scuba diving. The Mayans ruled in Belize from about 300 B.C. to A.D. 900 and left behind many impressive temples and other buildings.

EXERCISE 8 Revising a Piece of Writing

Read the description you wrote for Exercise 6. Then, evaluate your draft. Next, revise it, using the basic revision techniques. Make your changes directly on your draft by hand. Finally, rewrite your revised paragraph on your own paper.

PROOFREADING AND PUBLISHING

PROOFREADING

Proofreading is a careful search to find mistakes in grammar, spelling, capitalization, and punctuation. When you allow enough time to put your paper aside for a while, you can usually find mistakes more easily.

Proofreading with a classmate can be helpful, too. Exchange papers with a partner, and try to find errors in each other's papers. When you proofread, use the following guidelines.

Guidelines for Proofreading
1. Have you avoided sentence fragments and run-ons?
2. Are capitalization and punctuation correct throughout?
3. Do verbs agree with their subjects?
4. Are verb forms and verb tenses correct throughout?
5. Are adjective and adverb forms used correctly?
6. Are all pronouns used correctly?
7. Is each word spelled correctly?

Symbols for Revising and Proofreading	
Capitalize	president lincoln
Delete	For many, many years
Change order	thier
Begin new paragraph	¶ After the war, . . .
Insert	univrsity

EXERCISE 9 Proofreading a Paragraph

Proofread the following paragraph to find ten mistakes in grammar, mechanics, spelling, or capitalization. If you need help, you can use a dictionary and the lessons on grammar, usage, and mechanics (pages 87–302 in this book). Use proofreading symbols to mark the errors.

My grandmother who was born in Russia visited their after the fall of the Soviet union. She brung back an intresting toy that she called a nesting doll. When she opened the doll, there was anothr doll inside. Within that doll, was smaller doll. Altogether, there was six dolls, one inside the other. The smallest was the size of a peanut

PUBLISHING

After revising and proofreading your paper, share it with someone. Remember that the main purpose of most writing is to communicate with a reader, and there are many ways to publish your paper.

Guidelines for Publishing

- Submit the writing to your school newspaper, yearbook, or literary magazine.
- Check to see what kinds of writing appear in your local newspaper. The newspaper may be a good place to publish a letter to the editor.
- Read your piece aloud to your family, classmates, or friends.
- Try posting items on a bulletin board at school or in your local library.

Guidelines for Manuscript Form

1. Use only one side of a sheet of paper.
2. Write in blue or black ink, or use a typewriter or a word processor.
3. Leave margins of about one inch at the top, sides, and bottom of each page.
4. Follow your teacher's instructions for placing your name, the date, and the title on the paper.
5. Indent the first line of each paragraph.
6. Keep your paper neat and clean.

EXERCISE 10 Finding Ideas for Publishing

Read the following descriptions of types of writing. On the lines after each description below, list one or two publishing ideas.

1. a review of a musical that took place at a local theater ______________

____

2. a letter trying to convince students to attend student council meetings ____

____

3. an essay describing four or five excellent fiction books ______________

____

4. an original short story or poem ______________________________

____

EXERCISE 11 Preparing a Final Copy

Proofread the draft that you revised for Exercise 8. Then prepare a clean final copy of your paper. Share it with your classmates by reading it aloud in a small group or posting it on your classroom bulletin board.

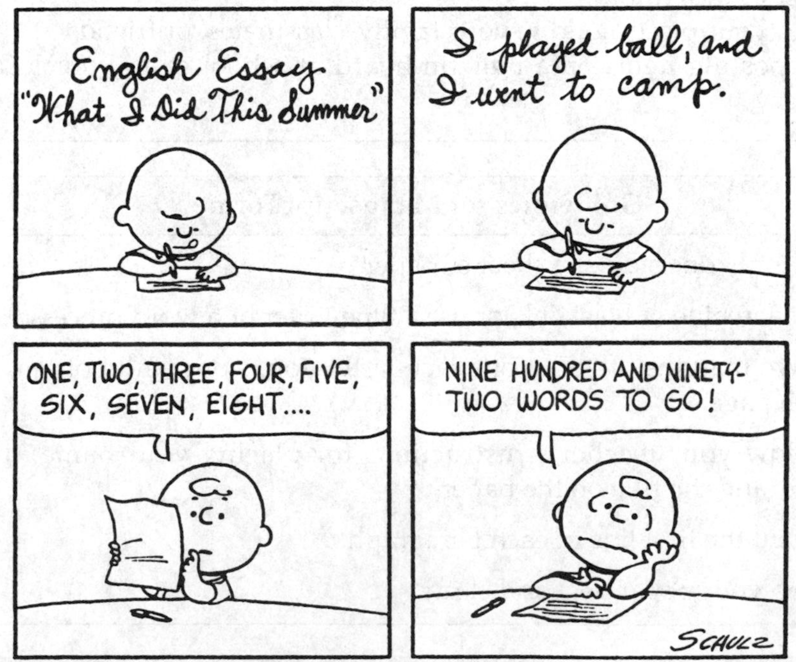

Peanuts reprinted by permission of UFS, Inc.

MAIN IDEAS AND TOPIC SENTENCES

A paragraph usually has a single ***main idea.*** This main idea is what the paragraph is about. Sometimes the main idea is stated in a single sentence called the ***topic sentence.*** A topic sentence can be placed anywhere in a paragraph—at the beginning, in the middle, or at the end. In the following paragraph, the topic sentence comes at the beginning.

> **Besides state flags, most states have other symbols as well.** For example, many states have state birds and state flowers. Several have state colors and state grasses. Milk is the state drink of more than ten different states. One state, Maine, even has a state cat. It is the Maine coon cat.

A paragraph that relates a series of events, tells part of a story, or gives a description often does not have a topic sentence. Read the following paragraph. It has no topic sentence, but it does have one main idea—what ancient Mayan manuscripts looked like.

> The manuscript was covered with line drawings of people and mythical creatures. The pictures were arranged in different scenes. A series of dots and dashes appeared among the pictures. These dots and dashes stood for numbers.

EXERCISE 1 Identifying Main Ideas and Topic Sentences

Each of the following paragraphs has a main idea. On the lines after each paragraph, write the main idea in your own words. Then look for a topic sentence. If the paragraph has one, underline it.

1. In fifth grade, Pilar started playing the piano. In sixth grade, she appeared in a play. This spring she was the goalie on our soccer team. She also loves to write stories and draw cartoons. Pilar is definitely a person of many talents.

   Main Idea: ____

   ____

2. Salim looked up at the heavy rope and frowned. Climbing it could be difficult. He hesitated a moment and then clamped his hands on the rope. Next, he pulled himself up a few inches and locked his legs around the rope. "That wasn't too bad," Salim thought. Then he reached up another few inches and grasped the rope. Again, he pulled. Slowly, he rose toward the top of the gymnasium.

Main Idea: ____

____

3. Many important food crops were first grown in the Americas. Maize, or corn, was first grown in Mexico. Later, Christopher Columbus introduced it to Europe. Potatoes originated in Peru, Chile, and Bolivia, and Spaniards took them to Europe in the 1500s. Other foods from the Americas include tomatoes, chili peppers, and peanuts.

Main Idea: ____

____

4. Many Spanish girls have names that are also words in the Spanish language. My first name, *Milagros*, means "miracles" in Spanish. The name *Soledad* means "solitude,"and the name *Dolores* means "sorrows." *Esperanza*, which is my best friend's name, means "hope."

Main Idea: ____

____

UNITY AND COHERENCE

UNITY

A paragraph has ***unity*** when all the sentences tell about the main idea. Read the following paragraph, and notice how the sentences work together.

> Even though stars seem to twinkle, they actually give a steady light. This light is affected as it passes through earth's atmosphere. The movement of hot and cold air creates ripples in the atmosphere. These ripples cause the starlight to flicker. On earth the star appears to be twinkling.

Every sentence tells something about why stars seem to twinkle. Suppose you added a sentence about how pretty certain stars are. That sentence would not fit into the paragraph. It would destroy the unity.

EXERCISE 2 **Identifying Sentences that Destroy Unity**

Each paragraph below has one sentence that destroys the unity of the paragraph. Find that sentence, and draw a line through it.

1. Shogi is much more fun to play than chess. In chess, each game piece has one rank. In other words, a castle is always a castle. At a museum I saw a chess set that had castles shaped like real fortresses. In shogi a game piece can be promoted. It can gain greater powers as the game goes on. Game pieces in chess leave the game if they are captured. In shogi they can return to the game. However, they return to serve the other player and battle against their old owner.

2. This city has a wonderful system of public transportation. The buses are clean and inexpensive, and they are reliable. They run on time, and they have ramps for wheelchairs. Within the downtown area, bus rides are free. Outside of this area, passengers can use season tickets instead of money. The subways work as well as the buses do. They are also clean and easy to use. The subways and buses run all night long, so people have no need to use their cars. The city's parks and museums are also exceptional.

COHERENCE

A good paragraph has ***coherence.*** In other words, all the ideas in a coherent paragraph are connected. One way you can create coherence is to use transitional words and phrases to connect ideas. The following chart lists some common words and phrases used to make transitions.

Comparing and Contrasting Ideas	also, although, and, another, but, however, instead, similarly, too, yet
Showing Cause and Effect/Narration	as a result, because, consequently, for, since, so, so that, therefore
Showing Time/ Narration	after, at last, before, finally, first, next, often, then, until, when
Showing Place/ Description	above, around, before, beneath, beside, down

The following paragraph has coherence. The writer has used transitional words to show how the details in the paragraph are related.

After lunch our guide drove the jeep down a hot, dusty road that ran through the middle of the wildlife park. Soon we came to a large, open, grassy area—the savannah. In the distance, a pride of lions was sleeping beneath an acacia tree. Beside one of the female lions, we could see two small cubs. These were the first lions I had ever seen in the wild.

EXERCISE 3 Identifying Transitional Words and Phrases

Underline the transitional words and phrases in the following paragraph. Use the chart above as a guide.

With a few simple steps, you can make a healthful, nutritious omelet. First, chop some vegetables, such as green peppers and onions. Next, separate the whites from the yolks of three eggs. Place the whites in a medium-sized bowl, and whip them. Then pour the egg whites into a pan coated with a little olive oil. Cook them for a minute or two. Finally, add your chopped vegetables and fold half of the egg-white mixture over them. Cook the omelet thoroughly.

USING DESCRIPTION AND NARRATION

DESCRIPTION

Have you ever tried to tell someone what your home looks like? To do that, you use ***description***. You include specific sensory details to help someone else recognize what you are describing. ***Sensory details*** are words that appeal to one of the five senses—sight, sound, touch, taste, and smell. The following paragraph uses details of sight to describe an abandoned house.

The house looked as if no one had lived there for an extremely long time. Near the street was a moss-covered stone wall, parts of which had tumbled to the sidewalk. Beyond the wall, the lawn bristled with weeds—Queen Anne's lace, dandelions, sumac, and poison ivy. Next to the house itself, shrubs grew out of control, covering parts of the front door, with its rusted screen. Many bushes reached almost to the tops of the broken windows on the first floor.

When you write a description, you often use spatial order. ***Spatial order*** arranges details according to their location. For example, the paragraph above describes the wall, the lawn, and the house from near to far. A different paragraph might arrange details from top to bottom, from left to right, or from far to near.

EXERCISE 4 **Collecting and Arranging Sensory Details**

Choose one of the subjects below. On your own paper, make a list of sensory details that describe it. Keep listing details until you run out of ideas. After you have completed your list of details, arrange them in spatial order. Then find a classmate who chose the same subject, and compare your lists. How are they alike or different?

1. your best friend
2. a football field at the moment a touchdown is scored
3. the school lunchroom at noon
4. the setting of your favorite short story
5. the best-looking bicycle that you have ever seen

NARRATION

"What did you do over the weekend?" When you answer that question, you are using narration. ***Narration*** tells about an event or action that happens over time. Narration often uses ***chronological order,*** or time order. You can use narration to tell a story or to explain a process.

TELLING A STORY

Erik peered beneath the rock and saw a small stone. The stone had a metal ring attached to its center. Erik tugged at the ring and felt the stone move. He pulled harder. Suddenly, the rock lifted. Below it was a dark hole. Erik dropped a pebble down the hole and listened. He heard nothing.

EXPLAINING A PROCESS

Lay the square egg-roll skin on a table with one corner pointing toward you. Put a few spoonfuls of filling in the center. Then, take the corner of the skin that is closest to you and fold it over the filling. Next, fold the two side corners inward, using both hands. Then, brush a little beaten egg onto the unfolded corner. Finally, roll the filled part up and over the last corner.

EXERCISE 5 Arranging Details in Chronological Order

Choose two of the following topics—one story topic and one process topic. On your own paper, list at least four events for the story and at least four steps for the process. Then arrange each list in chronological order.

1. You fall asleep on a bus or a subway and miss your stop. Then what happens? (story)
2. You find a small dinosaur eating your trash. And that is only the beginning. (story)
3. A mysterious stranger arrives in your town. People find this stranger frightening. (story)
4. You tell your brother how to set a digital clock. (process)
5. Tell a friend how to disguise herself for a costume party. (process)
6. Explain how to pitch a softball. (process)

USING COMPARISON/CONTRAST AND EVALUATION

COMPARISON AND CONTRAST

When you show how two things are alike, you are ***comparing*** them. You are ***contrasting*** them when you show how they are different. A paragraph may be developed with comparison only, with contrast only, or with both comparison and contrast.

Logical order is a good way to organize ideas when you are comparing and contrasting. If something is logical, it makes sense. Notice the logical order in the following paragraph. First, the writer compares; then she contrasts.

COMPARISON The tomatoes we buy in our grocery stores today look very much like the tomatoes of fifty years ago. They are round and red and smooth. However, many **CONTRAST** people think that appearance is where the similarity ends. Years ago, tomatoes were available only when they were in season locally. Now they are shipped all over the country, so people can eat them throughout the year. As a result, today's tomatoes have to be firm and solid enough for shipping and handling. In the old days, tomatoes were softer, and they didn't travel well. Also, the tomatoes we find today don't taste as good as the ones of fifty years ago. They may be firmer, but they aren't better.

EXERCISE 6 Comparing and Contrasting Features

Here are some pairs of subjects for comparison and contrast. With a partner, choose one of the subject pairs. On your own paper, write two headings: *Similarities* and *Differences*. Then brainstorm with your partner to identify features or details for the subject pair. List at least three features or details that are alike and at least three that are different.

1. families in television and families in real life
2. fast food and home-cooked food
3. individual sports and team sports
4. audiocassettes and CDs

EVALUATION

You are ***evaluating*** when you tell whether you think something is good or bad. For example, you are evaluating when you say that walking is the best form of exercise. To make your evaluation believable to your audience, you need to give reasons that support your thinking.

One way to organize your reasons is ***order of importance.*** For example, you might start with your most important reason. Then you would give the next most important reason, and so on. Or you might start with your least important reason and end with your most important. The following paragraph uses order of importance.

EVALUATION	There are several good reasons for building a new commuter railway in our city.
REASON	First, such a railway would reduce the air pollution and noise pollution, which have reached alarming and dangerous levels.
REASON	Second, the railway would decrease our parking problems and the traffic jams leading into the city.
REASON	Third, building and staffing the railway would create some new jobs for the city's workers.

EXERCISE 7 Developing an Evaluation

Choose one of the following subjects to evaluate. On the lines below, write one sentence stating your evaluation of the subject. Then list two reasons to support your thinking.

EX. Evaluation: Jurassic Park is one of the best movies of the 1990s.
Reason 1: The dinosaurs look real.
Reason 2: This movie is full of fast-paced action.

1. rap music
2. school sports
3. video games

Evaluation: ______________________________

____

Reason 1: ______________________________

Reason 2: ______________________________

CHAPTER 3: COMPOSITION WORKSHOPS

PLANNING A COMPOSITION

Writing a composition takes some planning. First, you need to decide on a main idea and collect information or details about it. (See pages 1–4, "Finding Ideas.") Then you have to find a way to put all your ideas together. A good plan can help you find your way.

EARLY PLANS

An ***early plan,*** sometimes called an ***informal outline,*** is a way to organize your ideas. First, put your ideas into related groups. Then arrange the groups in an order that will make sense to the reader.

GROUPING. Look at the information you have. Group notes that have something in common. Write a heading that identifies what each group of notes has in common.

ORDERING. There are many ways to order ideas in compositions. ***Chronological,*** or time, ***order*** presents events in the order that they happened. You could use chronological order to tell about the process of taking a photograph or baking a cake. ***Spatial order*** presents details according to their location. You could use spatial order to describe a limestone cave or an amusement park. ***Logical order*** presents related ideas together. For example, you could use logical order to organize information about dinosaurs. First, you could tell about the plant-eaters, and then you could tell about the flesh-eaters.

EXERCISE 1 Making an Early Plan

Working with a partner, use logical order to organize the following notes on forest fires by putting the notes into three groups. Then, on your own paper, write a heading for each group, and arrange the notes within the groups in a way that makes sense.

lightning, another cause of fire

people carelessly flipping lighted matches into wooded areas

loss of many birds' and animals' lives in fires

people—cause of 90 percent of all forest fires

lack of food, wildlife die

some fires deliberately set

teach people to appreciate the value of their forests

smoldering campfires left by campers

fish poisoned by streams clogged with ashes

could increase the number of lookout towers

train more firefighters

FORMAL OUTLINES

A ***formal outline*** is more structured than an early plan. It uses letters and numbers to label main headings and the ideas that belong below the headings. A formal outline can have either topics (single words or phrases) or complete sentences. Here is a topic outline for a composition.

Title: The Life of Julia Ward Howe

Main Idea: Julia Ward Howe was one of the great women of the nineteenth century.

I. Her life
   A. Born in New York, New York, 1819
   B. Educated at home and in private schools
   C. Married head of the Perkins Institute for the Blind
   D. Died in Newport, Rhode Island, 1910

II. Her writing
   A. Wrote books of poetry
   B. Wrote two plays
   C. Wrote "The Battle Hymn of the Republic"
   D. Wrote nonfiction books about women

III. Her other achievements
   A. Founded New England Woman Suffrage Association
   B. Became president of Association for the Advancement of Women
   C. Elected to American Academy of Arts and Letters

EXERCISE 2 Making a Formal Outline

Using the early plan you made in Exercise 1, make a formal topic outline on your own paper. Be sure to use letters and numbers to label the main headings and ideas.

WRITING INTRODUCTIONS

The first part of a composition is the ***introduction.*** It's a little bit like the topic sentence in a paragraph. The introduction serves two important functions.

1. **CAPTURING THE READER'S INTEREST.** A good introduction grabs the reader's attention. It makes the reader want to read the rest of the composition.

2. **STATING THE MAIN IDEA.** A good introduction also states the main idea. It tells the reader what the composition will be about.

WAYS TO WRITE INTRODUCTIONS

There are many ways to make an introduction interesting.

- **Ask a question.** The writer asks a question and then answers it.

Why did dinosaurs die out? Some scientists think that a huge meteor crashed into earth, sending up clouds of dust that blotted out the sun for years. Plants died, and so did the animals that fed on plants.

- **Tell an anecdote.** An *anecdote* is a short, interesting or humorous story. Most people like stories, so starting a composition with a brief story is an excellent way to capture the reader's attention.

Not long ago, a German shepherd disappeared from a campsite near Tucson, Arizona. After searching the area for two weeks, the dog's owner gave up and left. Four months later, the dog limped into its owner's yard. The owner lives in Selah, Washington, one thousand miles from Tucson. The Dog is just one of many animals that have traveled amazing distances to return home.

- **State an interesting or startling fact.** Curiosity also makes a reader want to read on. An exciting statement of fact creates curiosity.

Arctic terns can travel more than half a million miles during their lifetimes. They nest in the Arctic area and fly south to Antarctica in the fall. The distance between their summer and winter homes is eleven thousand miles.

EXERCISE 3 Identifying Types of Introductions

On the line below each introduction, write the technique used to get your attention.

1. You might say that a crocodile's toothbrush is a small flock of birds. While people clean their teeth with toothbrushes and toothpaste, crocodiles use a different method. After a meal, a crocodile opens its mouth wide. Small birds, called plovers, enter the crocodile's mouth and pick food from between its teeth.

   ____

2. Have you ever flown a kite on a windy day? If you have, you probably learned something about wind currents.

   ____

3. At least one flower makes noise when it blooms. The yellow evening primrose, which opens only at night, makes a popping sound because it opens so quickly. This story is one of many that I heard from my grandfather, who owned a flower shop in Boston's North End.

   ____

4. Dwayne opened one eye and glanced at the alarm clock. It was 7:45 A.M.! School began in fifteen minutes. He leaped out of bed and scurried to find his clothes. In his rush to get dressed, he broke a shoelace and had to look for another one. Then, on his way to school, Dwayne took a shortcut through a vacant lot, ran over a broken bottle, and ruined a tire of his bicycle. Dwayne's story may sound exaggerated, but it's not. Being in a hurry frequently causes accidents.

   ____

CHAPTER 3: COMPOSITION WORKSHOPS

WRITING CONCLUSIONS

The *conclusion* is the last part, the ending, of a composition. It should make your readers feel that your composition is complete. In your conclusion you need to tie together the ideas in the composition and connect them to your main idea.

WAYS TO WRITE CONCLUSIONS

- **Refer to your introduction.** In the introduction about pets that travel amazing distances, the writer refers to the distance the German shepherd traveled.

Introduction: Not long ago, a German shepherd walked to his home in Selah, Washington, from a campsite in Tuscon, Arizona, one thousand miles away.
Conclusion: The bond between pets and their owners is sometimes so strong that nothing—not even a trip of a thousand miles—will keep them apart!

- **Close with an interesting comment.** Another way to end your composition is to leave your readers with an interesting statement that clearly signals the end.

Meat-eating plants are interesting, but they are not at all dangerous to people. Plants big enough to swallow people are the stuff of science fiction and musicals like *The Little Shop of Horrors*.

- **Restate your main idea.** One direct way to wrap up a composition is to restate your main idea in different words. The following conclusion restates the idea that the dinosaurs died out when a giant meteor crashed into earth.

Did a great disaster cause the dinosaurs to die out? While there are still many unanswered questions, the evidence connecting a huge meteor and the extinction of the dinosaurs is strong. Maybe someday soon this connection will be confirmed.

EXERCISE 4 Writing a Conclusion

Read the introduction and the body of the following composition. On your own paper, write a conclusion by using one of the techniques on the previous page. Then get together with two of your classmates and discuss your conclusions. Why did you choose one technique over another? Which technique do you think creates the best conclusion for the composition?

What did English children in 1662 enjoy watching that children of today also enjoy? They enjoyed watching the comic actions of puppets in puppet shows. The stars of those early English puppet shows were known as Punch and Judy. Today, children around the world enjoy the performances of several different kinds of puppets, including hand puppets, rod puppets, and marionettes.

The most familiar kind of puppet is the hand puppet. Finger puppets, glove puppets, and Muppets are all hand puppets. For a finger puppet, the puppeteer uses two fingers to represent the puppet's legs. To operate a glove puppet, the puppeteer slips the body of the puppet figure over his or her hand. The puppeteer's thumb goes into one arm and a finger or two goes into the other arm. Muppets are familiar to any child who has ever seen the television show Sesame Street. The puppeteer puts his or her fingers into the Muppet's upper face and a thumb into the Muppet's jaw. A glove hides the puppeteer's other hand and forms the Muppet's body.

Another kind of puppet is the rod puppet. Rod puppets are controlled by rods or sticks attached to various parts of the puppet's figure. The puppeteer is usually below the stage and unseen by the audience. Rod puppets are part of a traditional form of entertainment known in Japan as doll theater. The rod puppets of doll theater are about four feet tall. They are controlled by puppeteers who appear on stage dressed from head to toe in black.

A third kind of puppet is the marionette. The movements of marionettes are controlled by strings. To work the marionette, the puppeteer moves a wooden frame to which the strings are attached. The strings lead to the puppet's head, shoulders, hands, and knees. By moving the strings, the puppeteer can make a marionette walk, sit, dance, and even kick a soccer ball.

A JOURNAL ENTRY

Sometimes you want to share your experiences with others. However, when you write in a journal or a diary, you write just for yourself. Of course, whenever you put something in writing, there is always the chance that someone else might read it. As you read the following journal entry, think about the change the writer is facing.

> We're going to move! Dad has a new job in a big city. I feel bad about leaving my friends. I'll sure miss them a lot. Summer will be really hard because I'll remember all of us at the lake. Boy, did we yell and scream when we jumped off the pier and hit the icy water! Sometimes, I just liked to sit and feel the cool breeze. I liked the way it rippled the water and made the oak leaves rattle. Later, I might feel excited about the move. But right now I think about the lake and just feel lonely.

Thinking About the Model

The writer of the model entry uses it to discover and explore important things about herself. To learn how she does this, answer the following questions. Use the lines provided to write your responses.

1. Details in a journal can be about people, places, and events. They can also be about thoughts and feelings. Which kinds of details are included in the model entry?

____

____

2. How does this writer feel about the changes in her life? What details will help her remember those feelings as she rereads her diary ten years from now?

____

____

ASSIGNMENT: WRITING A JOURNAL ENTRY

Write a journal entry about a major change that occurred in your life. Use details that will help you recall your thoughts and feelings when you reread the entry.

Prewriting and Writing

Step 1: What changes have you experienced in your life? Have you had to move to a new home or a new city? Have you made a new friend or become a brother, sister, uncle, or aunt? In the space below, brainstorm a list of changes in your life. When you've run out of ideas, read what you have written. Then choose one idea that is important to you. Since someone else may read this entry, be certain that you won't mind sharing your thoughts and feelings.

Step 2: A journal or diary can be anything you write. If you already have a journal or diary, you can write this entry in it. Or you can write in the space below. As you write, don't worry about keeping ideas in order. Just write whatever comes to mind.

Evaluating and Revising

Journals of famous people, such as writers or actors, are sometimes published. Usually, though, you write a journal just for yourself. Then you don't have to evaluate it or revise it. However, if you plan to share your entry with someone else, you may want to evaluate it first. You might have to add more details to help your reader understand the importance of this change in your life. Write your revision on your own paper.

Proofreading and Publishing

You might want to share your journal entry with a friend or family member. Or you can put it away in a scrapbook or a folder to look at from time to time. You might be surprised by what you learn about yourself.

FOR YOUR PORTFOLIO

Check in your library for journals written by young writers, such as *The Diary of Anne Frank* or *Go Ask Alice*. Make a copy of a favorite journal entry to keep with your own entry.

Calvin and Hobbes **by Bill Watterson**

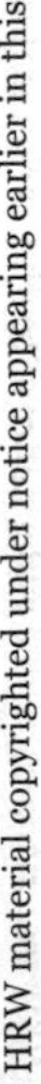

A CHILDHOOD MEMORY

Have you ever wanted to share your experiences with others? One way you can share experiences is to write about them. In the following selection, the writer tells about riding on a snow sled for the first time.

You can't break the law of gravity. I know because I tried to the day my grandparents told me that I could ride my dad's old sled. I could see myself flying down the short slope alongside my grandparents' house. I imagined my hair blowing straight back and my eyes squinted against the cold. I thought it would be easy.

The snow crunched as I carried the sled out to the hill. The sled had a smooth metal frame that curled up at the front and thick wood slats that made a seat. Without wasting time, I climbed onto the sled and pushed off the slope.

What a ride! I got butterflies in my stomach. The wind was so cold I couldn't breathe. It was great! Just then the sled stopped, really stopped. Only I didn't. The next thing I knew, I was over the top. I felt like an astronaut, weightless. That would have been fine if I hadn't thudded into the snow a second later.

I never found out why I crashed, but at least I was only bruised. I did learn something, though. Sledding is not as easy as it looks.

Thinking About the Model

Now that you've read the model childhood memory, are you curious about how the writer recreates the event? Find out by writing answers to the following questions on the lines provided.

1. Does the beginning grab your interest? Explain why.

____

____

2. Does the writer offer any background information? How does this information help you understand the experience?

3. How do you know what the writer saw, heard, or touched during the experience? List some words or phrases that have to do with the writer's senses (sight, hearing, touch).

4. What clues tell you that this experience was important to the writer?

ASSIGNMENT: WRITING ABOUT A CHILDHOOD MEMORY

Write a short narrative about a memory from your childhood. Make the experience come alive for your readers, and be sure to tell why the event is important to you.

Prewriting

What childhood memory might you write about? The steps that follow will help you discover an appropriate memory.

Step 1: In the space below, brainstorm experiences from your childhood that you might want to write about. What has happened to you that has changed your life? What events have changed the way you feel about yourself or about others? What experiences have you had that you could describe as exciting, unforgettable, or frightening? List every idea that comes to your mind. Don't stop to judge any of the ideas now. Keep going until you run out of ideas. (Use your own paper if you need more space.)

Step 2: Choose one experience from your brainstorming list that you would like to write about. The following questions will help you decide whether the event would make a good subject for your narrative.

- Is the experience one that you can share?
- Is the experience important to you? It doesn't have to be a big adventure—just an experience that means something to you.
- Is the experience one that you remember in detail? If it is, you will be able to recreate the experience for your readers.

If the answer to any of these questions is "no," select another idea from your brainstorming list, or brainstorm for additional memories. On the line below, identify the experience you intend to write about.

____

Step 3: Once you have chosen the memory or experience, "replaying" the event in your mind will help you collect details. Try to remember details about what happened, about what you noticed with your five senses, about where the event took place, and about who was there. Answer the questions below.

1. What happened?

____

____

2. What did you hear? see? smell? taste? touch?

____

____

3. Where were you? Describe the place.

____

____

4. Who else was there? What did he or she look like?

____

____

Writing

Use the information from your prewriting notes to write a draft of your narrative about a childhood memory. Your draft might be one paragraph or several. You can use the following plan to help you write your draft.

Beginning	• Grabs the reader's interest • Gives some background information • Hints at the meaning of the experience

Middle	• Tells about the events in the order in which they happened. To help your reader follow this time order, you may use transitional words and phrases such as *first, second, then, at least,* and *finally*. • Gives the reader details that make the event seem real.

Ending	• Tells how the experience turned out • Tells why it was important to you

Some students like to write on every other line in their drafts to leave room for corrections.

Evaluating and Revising

When you evaluate your writing, you judge what's good about it and what needs to be improved. To evaluate your narrative about a childhood memory, you and a classmate will use the **Questions for Evaluation** below.

QUESTIONS FOR EVALUATION

1. Does the beginning grab the reader's interest? If not, what can be added or changed?
2. Does the narrative contain enough background information to understand the events? If not, what can be added?
3. Does the order of events make sense? If not, how could the events be reordered?
4. Do details about sights, sounds, smells, tastes, or texture make the experience seem real? If not, what specific words might be added?
5. Does the narrative tell how the event turned out and explain why the experience was important? If not, what can be added or changed?
6. Does the narrative have a satisfying outcome? If not, what needs to be added or replaced?

Shoe, by Jeff MacNelly, reprinted by permission: Tribune Media Services.

Peer Evaluation

Give your rough draft to a classmate for review. Ask your classmate to follow these steps.

Step 1: Read the rough draft carefully.

Step 2: Complete the **Questions for Evaluation** on a separate sheet of paper.

Self-Evaluation

Next, complete your own evaluation of your rough draft. Follow these steps.

Step 1: Read the peer evaluation written by your classmate. Circle any comments that you plan to make use of as you revise.

Step 2: Reread your draft and write your answers to the **Questions for Evaluation** on page 36 on your own paper.

Now revise your draft. Use your classmate's suggestions and your answers to the **Questions for Evaluation**. You can make corrections directly on your draft; you can rewrite your draft; or you can start all over again with prewriting.

Proofreading and Publishing

Step 1: Check your paper for errors in spelling. Think about each word. If you are not sure of a word, look it up in a dictionary. Then correct any spelling errors in your paper. (Hint: To be a good proofreader, look for only one kind of error at a time. For example, proofread once for capitalization and once for spelling.)

Step 2: Check for errors in grammar, usage, and mechanics. Then correct any errors in your paper. Refer to the proofreading checklist on page 10.

Step 3: Make a clean copy of your revised and proofread paper.

Step 4: Now publish your writing by sharing it with an audience. Use one of the three following methods, or you can think up your own idea for sharing.

a. You could become a storyteller and share your experience by telling it aloud. Be sure to practice before a mirror or with a friend. Use facial expressions and gestures to make your telling more interesting.

b. Work with the class to create a class collection of childhood memories.

c. Send the narrative of your experience to your school newspaper or local paper.

FOR YOUR PORTFOLIO

If you have a writing portfolio, write down your answers to these questions on a separate sheet of paper. Then put these answers and your narrative in your portfolio.

1. Why did you write about this topic?
2. What do you think are the strengths of this paper?
3. Describe an insight you gained or a lesson that you learned from writing about a childhood memory.
4. Look in magazines and newspapers for examples of other people's memories. Make copies of your favorite stories.

A TALL TALE

Have you ever heard the story of Pecos Bill, the make-believe cowboy who dug the Rio Grande? That story is an example of a ***tall tale,*** a highly unlikely, humorous story. A tall tale stretches the facts so far that no one could possibly believe them. For example, Paul Bunyan's cook had a griddle that was two city blocks wide. Another tall tale hero, Pecos Bill, straddled a cyclone and squeezed it to create rain.

Tall tales were very popular in the Old West, but the following story is a modern, nonwestern tall tale. It's a humorous, colorful, unbelievable story about a math wizard.

Miriam the Math Wizard

Five minutes after Miriam was born, she picked up a pencil and wrote "2 + 2 = 4" on the hospital wall. The first words she spoke were "5,784 divided by 8 equals 723." On her fourth birthday, she counted all the grains of rice in the pantry. When she was seven, she sat by the busiest freeway in New Hampshire for six months and counted all the cars that went by.

But no one thought much about what Miriam could do until her eighth birthday. That's when her parents gave her a computer and a computer math game. Before long, her fingers flew over the keyboard so fast that they were just blurs. The clacking of the keys was so loud that her parents couldn't hear each other talk. They couldn't even hear the TV. They took to wearing earmuffs, big furry ones, to block out the sound.

Then Miriam's fingers began to fly even faster. They went so fast they created a whirlwind that sucked all the furniture out of the house. Miriam, her computer, and her father landed out on the street. But that didn't stop Miriam.

"Miriam, what's 37,924 times 65, divided by 32, multiplied by 15?" asked her father, taking off his earmuffs for a minute.

"1,155,496.875," Miriam answered, quick as a flash.

Miriam soon began to give her parents advice. It took her only five seconds to tell them they could save .0006 cents per bowl of cereal by buying seven 20-ounce boxes of Crunchoes instead of four 22-ounce boxes. Then word of Miriam's genius got around the neighborhood. Hundreds of people started mobbing the grocery store when Miriam's family went shopping.

Next thing they knew, Miriam was featured on the national news. People from all over the country—Montana, Texas, Florida—showed up on Miriam's street. They kept coming until they caused a traffic jam from New Mexico to New Hampshire.

Miriam's fame spread and spread. Millions of people were calling her and asking her for advice. In fact, they tied up all the telephone lines in the country, and the President had to declare a national emergency.

The Prime Minister of Great Britain called Miriam. He wanted to find out how much it would cost to build a wall around the country. The President moved Miriam to Washington, D.C., so she could help him figure out how much to raise taxes. He wanted to get rid of the national debt.

In two months' time, Miriam had worked out all the world's economic problems. Her whirring fingers created four hurricanes and dozens of tornadoes. But everyone thought Miriam's economic advice was worth the price.

Miriam finally got tired of math, though. She turned off her computer and took up cross-country running. They say she ran across the country so fast that she got to the West Coast before she left the East Coast. Last I heard, she ran up Mount Everest so fast she blew all the snow off. It landed in the middle of the Sahara and created an oasis.

Thinking About the Model

Now that you've read the tall tale on pages 39–40, think about how the writer created it. Then answer the following questions.

1. Tall tales are humorous because writers exaggerate, or stretch, the truth. Miriam's ability to add numbers five minutes after she was born is just an exaggeration. What else in the tale is an exaggeration?

2. Unlikely events also make tall tales humorous. In the model tale, Miriam causes a traffic jam from New Mexico to New Hampshire. What other unlikely events happen in the tale?

3. In some ways, tall tales are like other stories. Characters often have to face problems and try to solve them. What problems does Miriam create? What problems does she solve?

4. The language of a tall tale is often informal and colorful. For example, Miriam's parents "took to" wearing earmuffs rather than "began" wearing them. What other casual and colorful words and expressions can you find in the model?

5. The ending of a tall tale is usually memorable. What image in the last paragraph stands out the most?

ASSIGNMENT: WRITING A TALL TALE

Write a tall tale of your own. Make up people and events that are humorous and exaggerated. Your tall tale should be unbelievable.

Prewriting

Step 1: One way to start planning a tall tale is to think about a character. Then ask yourself "What if?" questions to come up with an unlikely situation or problem the character could face. Here are some examples of characters and situations you could use for a tall tale.

CHARACTER: A teenage girl who wants to make the high school football team

SITUATION: *What if* the girl shows up at tryouts and kicks the ball all the way across the state?

CHARACTER: A small terrier whose owner has recently trained it to bring the morning newspaper to the back door

SITUATION: *What if* one morning, the owner finds six newspapers at her back door?

CHARACTER: A robot that has been programmed to clean your room and do your other chores at home

SITUATION: *What if* the robot's wires get crossed one day, and the robot goes haywire?

If you would like to write about one of the ideas above, write your choice on the lines below. Or think of your own character(s) and situation, and describe them below. Remember that you need a character and a situation that you can exaggerate.

Character(s): ____

Situation: ____

____

____

____

____

Step 2: Next, imagine what the main character in your tall tale is like. Name your character. Think of details about appearance and behavior. In the model tall tale, the writer includes no details of Miriam's appearance. However, many tall tales, such as the stories of Paul Bunyan, do emphasize appearance. Remember to exaggerate, or stretch, details. Use the cluster diagram below to record your ideas. Write your character's name in the center circle, and fill in the other circles with details about appearance and behavior. Add more circles to your cluster if necessary.

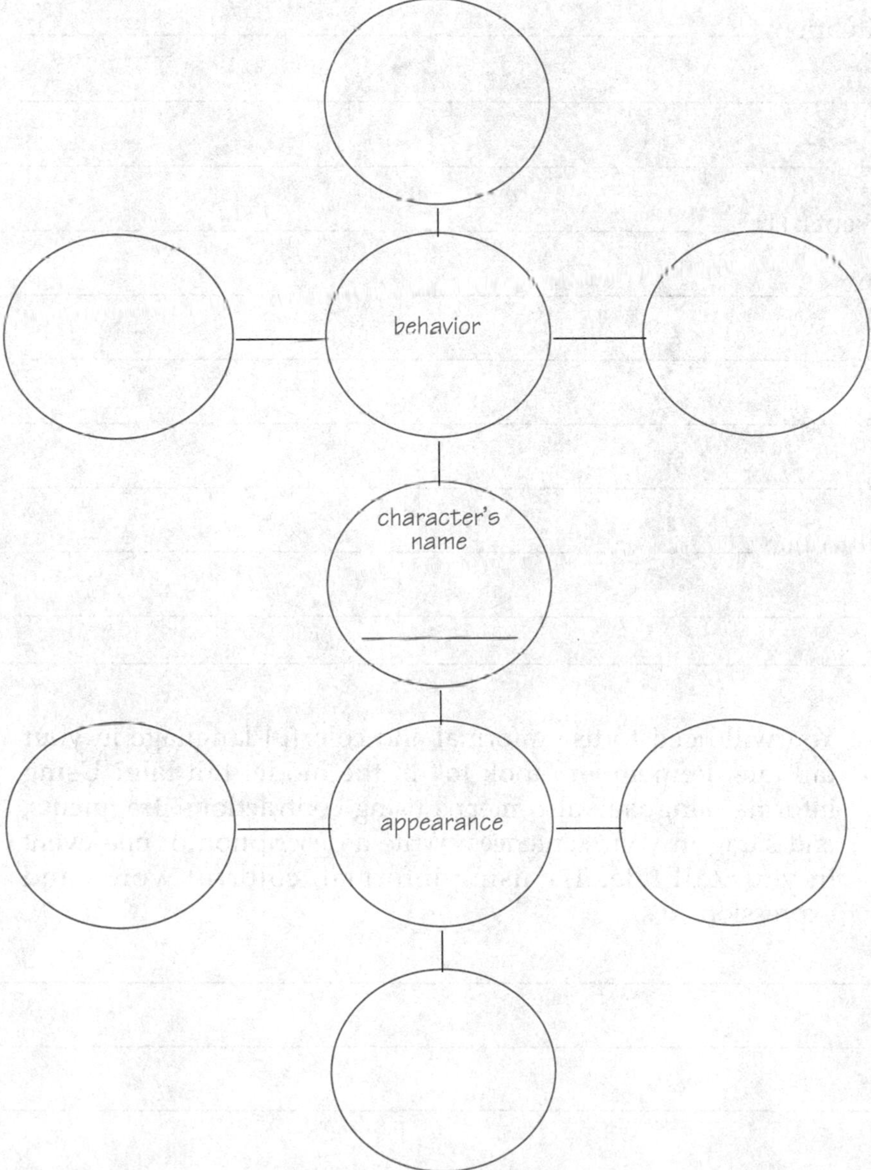

Step 3: What will happen in your tall tale? A tall tale, like other stories, has a plot made up of a series of events. Characters must solve conflicts, or problems. To plan the plot of your tall tale, complete the following map. List the events in the order they would happen. Start with the situation you identified in Step 1, and don't forget to exaggerate the events.

A Plot Map

Situation: ____________________

____

____

Events: (1) ____________________

(2) ____________________

(3) ____________________

(4) ____________________

(5) ____________________

Outcome: ____________________

____

Step 4: You will need to use informal and colorful language in your tall tale. Remember "took to" in the model tall tale? Using informal language also means using contractions, fragments, and slang in your sentences. Write a description of one event in your tall tale. Try using informal, colorful words and expressions.

____

____

____

____

Writing

Use the ideas you generated in prewriting to begin writing your tall tale. Your story map is a plan or outline to guide you as you begin your draft. Here are some suggestions to help you create a tale with a strong beginning, middle, and ending.

Beginning
- Hook your reader right away. Introduce the situation and create humor so that your reader wants to find out what happens next.

Middle
- Exaggerate details to make the story humorous.
- Use language that is informal and colorful. Use short phrases, contractions, and slang.
- Describe events in the order that they happen.

Ending
- Satisfy your reader's curiosity. Tie up any loose ends.

Now, on your own paper, write the first draft of your tall tale. Use your prewriting notes and the suggestions above to help you.

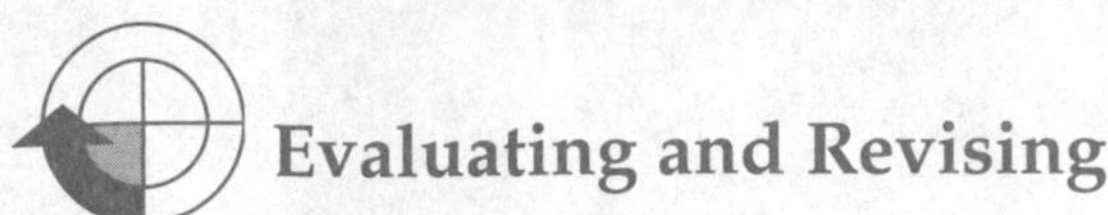

Evaluating and Revising

Use these **Questions for Evaluation** to evaluate your tall tale. Write the answers on your own paper.

Questions for Evaluation

1. Does the beginning of the tale get the reader's attention quickly? If not, what could be added or replaced?
2. Is the tale humorous? Does it include exaggeration and unlikely events? If not, what might be added?
3. Does the tale include details of the character's appearance and behavior? If not, what details might be added or changed?
4. Does the tale use informal and colorful language? If not, what words might be added or replaced?
5. Are events in the tale tied together in an order that makes sense? If not, how could the order be changed?
6. Does the tale have a satisfying outcome? If not, what needs to be added or replaced?

Peer Evaluation

Exchange rough drafts with a classmate. Ask your classmate to follow these steps.

Step 1: Read the tall tale for content, not for grammar or punctuation.

Step 2: Complete the **Questions for Evaluation** on this page. Try to give specific suggestions for revision.

Self-Evaluation

Next, make your own evaluation of your rough draft. Follow these steps.

Step 1: Tall tales are usually told aloud. Read your rough draft aloud and think about changes that might make it flow better. Think also about the suggestions you made about your classmate's rough draft. How might these ideas improve your own work?

Step 2: Read your classmate's evaluation. Circle any suggestions you plan to use in your revision.

Step 3: Reread the **Questions for Evaluation** on page 46. On a separate sheet of paper, jot down notes about specific changes you want to make. You might also write ideas in the margins and between the lines of your rough draft.

Revise your draft until you can answer yes to each of the **Questions for Evaluation**.

Proofreading and Publishing

Step 1: Begin by checking your spelling. If you are not absolutely certain that a word is spelled correctly, look it up in your dictionary. Remember that dictionaries also tell you how to spell words when endings such as *–ed* and *–ing* are added.

Step 2: Next, proofread for errors in grammar, usage, capitalization, and punctuation. Use the proofreading checklist on page 10 to help you. If you have used dialogue, double-check your use of quotation marks and commas.

Step 3: Make a clean copy of your revised tall tale.

Step 4: Publish your tall tale by assembling a collection of tales from class members. Donate the collection to your school library, a hospital, or a retirement community center. Or make a copy of the collection and dedicate it to a favorite friend or relative.

FOR YOUR PORTFOLIO

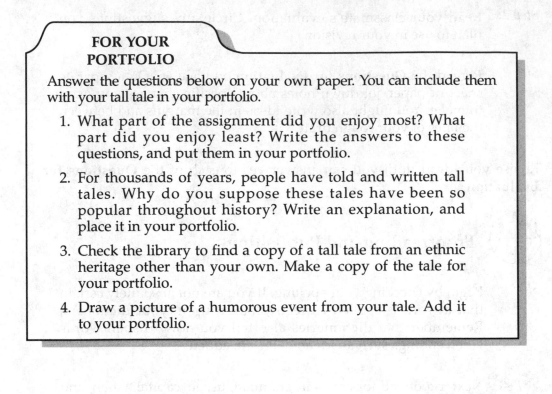

Answer the questions below on your own paper. You can include them with your tall tale in your portfolio.

1. What part of the assignment did you enjoy most? What part did you enjoy least? Write the answers to these questions, and put them in your portfolio.
2. For thousands of years, people have told and written tall tales. Why do you suppose these tales have been so popular throughout history? Write an explanation, and place it in your portfolio.
3. Check the library to find a copy of a tall tale from an ethnic heritage other than your own. Make a copy of the tale for your portfolio.
4. Draw a picture of a humorous event from your tale. Add it to your portfolio.

A SLIDE REPORT

A ***slide report*** is an oral report that uses slides to highlight important information. A police officer may give a slide presentation to teach skateboarding safety. The officer's slides might show proper helmets or kneepads. They could also show safe and unsafe places to practice. Here's the script for a slide report on Native American houses.

Early Native North American Houses

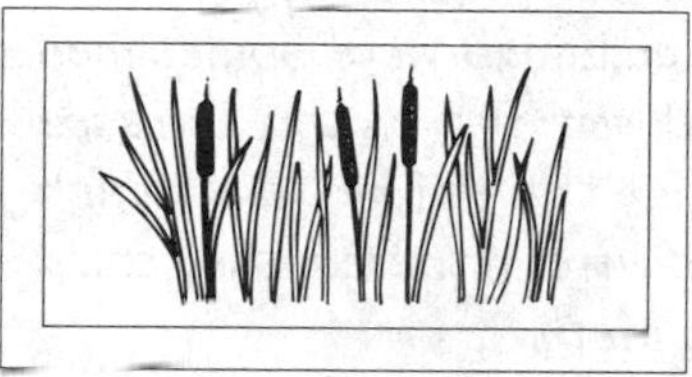

Could you live in a house made of branches tied together at the top? Could you climb a ladder to get in your front door? Hundreds of years ago, many Native North Americans lived in such houses, and some still do today. They built houses that were right for the ways they lived and for the places they lived.

The people of the Chippewa nation first lived in the northeastern part of North America. The weather was often cold and wet. The Chippewas gathered cattails, which grew near the many rivers. The Chippewas used young trees called saplings to build their houses. They put the saplings into the ground and bent them together. At the top, the saplings were arched to make a dome. Then the Chippewas covered this frame with tree bark or with woven cattails. The result was a snug, dry wigwam.

The southern end of the Florida peninsula, where the Seminole people lived, was hot and wet. Therefore, the Seminoles built their houses with open sides. They also built the houses on poles to protect the houses from the wet ground. Plants such as the palmetto were used to make thatched roofs. These special ways of building homes kept the Seminoles cool and dry.

Most Native North Americans of the Great Plains, such as the Blackfoot, the Crow, and the Comanche, hunted buffalo. The Plains peoples were always traveling, looking for new hunting grounds, so they needed houses that were light and could be easily taken apart. The answer was the tipi.

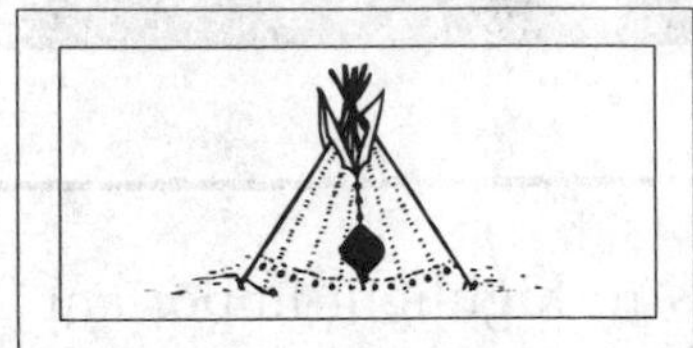

First, the Plains peoples built a frame of pine wood. Then they covered it with buffalo skins that had been tanned, stretched, and sewn together. Smoke from a fire inside the tipi escaped through a flap at the top. The tipis were warm even during the icy, windy Plains winters.

Pueblo peoples, such as the Zuni and the Hopi, lived in the Southwest. Their home was a dry, hot desert without forests for wood. However, they made a brick called adobe from clay. With their adobe bricks, the Pueblos made buildings also called pueblos. These buildings were sometimes several stories high and were flat on top. Terraces and ladders connected the buildings to each other. When the Pueblos were attacked, they could pull up the ladders for safety.

The western areas of North America were home to other nations, such as the Paiute and the Nez Perce. The climate of the West was cold but still dry. Much of the land was desert, so the people were always moving to find food. However, they were not like the people of the Plains nations. They did not have the buffalo to rely on for food and materials for shelter. Instead, they built houses such as the wickiup. The wickiup was usually built around an oval frame made from branches. The frame was covered with brush, leaves, or tree limbs.

Today, many Native North Americans and their descendents live in wooden or brick houses, while others continue to live in traditional houses. Either way, their homes are an important part of the heritage of North America.

Thinking About the Model

You've read the model slide report on pages 49–50. Now think about how the writer created it. Answer the following questions on the lines provided.

1. A slide report has a ***broad subject***. It also has a ***narrow topic*** that can be presented in fifteen or twenty minutes. The general subject in the model report is "houses." What is the narrow topic?

   ____

   ____

2. An informative slide report includes many facts. You can check facts in books and other sources. The model report has many facts. In the second paragraph of the report, for example, one fact is that the Chippewa people are from the Northeast. What are three other facts in the second paragraph?

   A. ____

   B. ____

   C. ____

3. The ***main idea*** of a report is its most important idea. What is the main idea of the model report?

   ____

   ____

4. Each slide in the presentation shows something about the topic and the main idea. In the model report the first slide shows the cattails that grew near the rivers where the Chippewas lived. The Chippewas used the cattails to build their houses. Look at the descriptions of each of the following slides from the model report on pages 49–50. Then tell what each slide shows about the main idea.

   Slide 3: ____

   Slide 5: ____

   Slide 7: ____

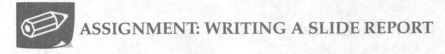

ASSIGNMENT: WRITING A SLIDE REPORT

Write the script for a brief slide report to present to your classmates and teacher. Sketch the slides that go with your written script.

Prewriting

Step 1: Begin by choosing a subject that you think is interesting. List three or four general subjects, such as music, sports, games, or food.

____

____

Step 2: Think about the subjects that you listed in Step 1. Which one seems most interesting? Which one do you know the most about? Circle a subject you listed in Step 1 that you wish to use for your report.

Step 3: Narrow the subject you have selected to a topic you can discuss in ten to fifteen minutes (for example, from the subject "snakes" to the topic "poisonous snakes in the United States"). How would you identify or describe your topic? In the following space, write a sentence or two about your narrowed topic. (For example, "Poisonous snakes in the United States include the rattlesnake, the water moccasin, and the coral snake.")

____

____

____

Step 4: What can you tell your audience about your topic? The *5W-How?* questions, or the reporter's questions, are *Who? What? Why? When? Where?* and *How?* You can use these questions to gather facts and other details. For example: *Who* were some Native American peoples? *What* kinds of homes did they build? *How* did they build their homes? Try to write two questions of each kind about your own topic.

Who A. ______________________________?

B. ______________________________?

What A. ______________________________?

B. ______________________________?

Why A. ______________________________?

B. ______________________________?

When A. ______________________________?

B. ______________________________?

Where A. ______________________________?

B. ______________________________?

How A. ______________________________?

B. ______________________________?

Step 5: How can you answer your questions in Step 4? Begin by thinking about what you already know about your topic. Then learn what you can by reading or by watching television programs or videos. You can also learn information by talking to experts.

When you use an outside source, write down its title (for example, "American Indian," *The New Encyclopaedia Britannica,* 1992 ed.).

Step 6: Decide on a main idea for your report. Answer this question: *What is the most important thing I have to say about my topic?*

____

____

Step 7: Decide how you will arrange your ideas. Three common ways to arrange ideas are ***chronological*** (time), ***spatial*** (location), and ***logical*** (related ideas). The model report on pages 49–50, for example, uses spatial order. The writer tells about Native American houses from the eastern to the western United States. Identify the order you will use. Then list the facts and details you plan to use in your report in the order that you will use them.

Kind of Order: ______________________________

First: ______________________________

Second: ______________________________

Third: ______________________________

Fourth: ______________________________

____

Writing

Your slide report has two parts: the visual part (the slides you show) and oral part (what you say). To prepare the visual part of your report, use boxes on the left to draw a sketch of each slide. Your sketches don't have be great art. For example, you can use stick figures for people. On the li to the right, make notes about what you plan to say about each slide. U the information from your prewriting notes to help you. Then use your o paper to write a draft of the oral script for your report. Follow yo prewriting plans.

Slide 1

____

____

____

Slide 2

Slide 3

Slide 4

Slide 5

Slide 6

Evaluating and Revising

When you *evaluate* writing, you decide on the strengths and weaknesses of your writing. To evaluate your slide report, you will use the following **Questions for Evaluation**.

Questions for Evaluation

1. Is the report based on a narrowed topic? What is the topic?

   ____

2. Are enough facts included to make the topic clear and interesting? If not, what facts might be added?

   A. ______________________________

   B. ______________________________

   C. ______________________________

3. Is the main idea of the report clear? What is the main idea?

   ____

4. Does each slide show something about the topic and main idea? If not, which slides should be dropped or added? On your own paper, sketch the slides you want to add.

   ____

5. Does the order of facts and details make sense? If not, what order would make sense?

   First: ______________________________

   Second: ______________________________

   Third: ______________________________

   Fourth: ______________________________

   Etc.: ______________________________

COMBINING BY USING CONNECTING WORDS

8f Another way to combine short sentences is to use the conjunctions *and, but,* and *or.*

ORIGINAL Elena enjoys bowling. Theo likes to bowl, too.
COMBINED **Elena and Theo** enjoy bowling. [compound subject]

ORIGINAL Kevin swung at the ball. He missed it.
COMBINED Kevin **swung** at the ball **but missed** it. [compound verb]

ORIGINAL Rudy threw the ball to Mike. Mike dropped it.
COMBINED Rudy threw the ball to Mike**, but** Mike dropped it. [compound sentences]

When you combine two sentences with closely related ideas, you form a compound sentence. As the third example above shows, a comma is inserted before the connecting word *and, or,* or *but* in a compound sentence.

EXERCISE 7 Combining Sentences with Connecting Words

On your own paper, combine the pairs of sentences below by using the connecting word *and, but,* or *or.* Remember to punctuate compound sentences correctly.

EX. 1. Emilio grows tomatoes. He makes tomato sauce. (compound verb with *and*)
1. Emilio grows tomatoes and makes tomato sauce.

1. Juan is absent today. Susanna is absent today. (compound subject with *and*)
2. I enjoy mountain hikes. This mountain is too steep. (compound sentence with *but*)
3. George Winston writes songs. He plays the piano. (compound verb with *and*)
4. Could you leave my book on the table? Could you put it on my desk? (compound verb with *or*)
5. Did you go to the game alone? Were you with a group? (compound sentence with *or*)

8g If two sentences are closely related, combine them by using a subordinate clause.

A *clause* is a group of words that contains a subject and a verb. A clause that cannot stand alone because it doesn't express a complete thought is *subordinate*. A clause that expresses a complete thought can stand alone, so it is called *independent.*

To combine short sentences, you can turn one sentence into a subordinate clause. Then attach it to the other sentence (the independent clause). There are two ways to turn a simple sentence into a subordinate clause.

(1) Insert *who, which,* or *that* in place of the subject.

ORIGINAL Nantucket is an island. It lies off the coast of Massachusetts.
COMBINED Nantucket is an island **that** lies off the coast of Massachusetts.

(2) Add to the beginning of a clause a word that tells time or place.

Such words include *before, after, when, where, whenever,* and *while.*

ORIGINAL Rufus was walking to the library. He found a stray dog.
COMBINED **While** Rufus was walking to the library, he found a stray dog.

If you put a subordinate clause at the beginning of the sentence, use a comma after the clause.

EXERCISE 8 Combining Sentences with Connecting Words

On your own paper, combine each pair of sentences below by making one sentence a subordinate clause. Follow the hints in parentheses.

EX. 1. The woodchuck is a burrowing animal. It often digs tunnels under fields. (Use *that.*)
1. The woodchuck is a burrowing animal that often digs tunnels under fields.

1. The woodchuck is a mammal. It belongs to the squirrel family. (Use *that.*)
2. Some people call woodchucks by their other name, "groundhogs." The people live in Canada and the United States. (Use *who.*)
3. Woodchucks enjoy alfalfa and clover. Alfalfa and clover are wild plants. (Use *which.*)
4. Woodchucks eat large amounts of food. They hibernate in the winter. (Use *before.*)
5. Robert Frost wrote an interesting poem. The poem is called "A Drumlin Woodchuck." (Use *that.*)

IMPROVING SENTENCE STYLE

8h A *stringy sentence* is made up of several independent clauses strung together with words such as *and* or *but*.

Stringy sentences ramble on and on. They don't give the reader a chance to pause before each new idea. You can fix a stringy sentence in two ways.

(1) Break the sentence into two or more shorter sentences.
(2) Turn some independent clauses into phrases or subordinate clauses.

STRINGY Elena's best friend, Valerie, was coming for dinner, and Elena wanted to make something special, but she couldn't decide what to make, and so she got out all her cookbooks, and she read several recipes, and she decided to make trout with almonds.

REVISED Elena's best friend, Valerie, was coming for dinner, and Elena wanted to make something special. Because she couldn't decide what to make, she got out all her cookbooks. After she read several recipes, she decided to make trout with almonds.

When you revise a stringy sentence, you may decide to keep *and* or *but* between two independent clauses. If you do, be sure you have a comma before the *and* or *but.*

8i *Wordy sentences* use more words than are needed.

You can revise a wordy sentence in three ways.

(1) Replace a phrase with one word.

WORDY We talked in a brief manner about the movie.
REVISED We talked **briefly** about the movie.

(2) Take out *who is* or *which is*.

WORDY I gave the gift to Ms. Renaldo, who is my flute teacher.
REVISED I gave the gift to Ms. Renaldo, **my flute teacher.**

(3) Take out a whole group of unnecessary words.

WORDY I'd like to begin my performance tonight by singing a song that is called "Evergreen."
REVISED My first song tonight will be "Evergreen."

EXERCISE 9 Revising Stringy Sentences

On your own paper, revise each of the stringy sentences below.

EX. 1. Phillis Wheatley was born around 1754, probably in West Africa, but in 1761 she was captured by slave traders, and they put her on a slave ship, and they took her to Boston.

1. Phillis Wheatly was born around 1754, probably in West Africa. In 1761, she was captured by slave traders, who put her on a slave ship and took her to Boston.

1. Susannah Wheatley lived in Boston, and she was the wife of a wealthy merchant, and Susannah bought the young African woman as a slave, and Susannah gave the new slave the name Phillis Wheatley.
2. Phillis worked in the Wheatley household, but she also learned how to speak, read, and write English, and she studied Latin, and she began to write poetry.
3. She read her poems to Susannah Wheatley and Susannah enjoyed them and Susannah took Phillis to friends' homes to read them.
4. There was trouble in the colonies and British soldiers arrived in Boston in 1768, and Phillis wrote a poem called "On the Arrival of the Ships of War, and Landing of the Troops."
5. In 1772, Susannah Wheatley asked a London publisher to print a book of Phillis's poems and Phillis went to England and many people hailed her as a great poet.

EXERCISE 10 Revising Wordy Sentences

On your own paper, revise each of the wordy sentences below.

EX. 1. At the time that the bus came, I met Al, who is my neighbor.

1. When the bus came, I met my neighbor Al.

1. We spent days and days rehearsing the play, which is *Our Town*.
2. Many of the men and women and boy and girls who live near me in my neighborhood work hard to keep the sidewalks free of litter.
3. I am very happy and pleased to be a player on our soccer team due to the fact that it is a winning team.
4. In the event that it rains, the graduation ceremony will be inside in the gym.
5. The two animals that I keep as pets are the following ones: Chips, who is a dog, and Mimi, who is a cat.

CHAPTER REVIEW

A. Revising a Paragraph to Eliminate Fragments and Run-ons

On your own paper, rewrite the paragraph below, correcting the fragments and run-on sentences.

EX. Toronto is in the province of Ontario, it is on the northwest shore of Lake Ontario.
Toronto, which is on the northwest shore of Lake Ontario, is in the province of Ontario.

Toronto is the second largest city. In Canada after Montreal. Toronto is one of Canada's major ports ships arrive there from all over the world. Also a bustling commercial center. Manufactured goods include machinery, electrical appliances, and clothing many are exported to foreign countries. Twice in Canada's history Toronto was the nation's capital. From 1849 to 1851 and from 1855 to 1859.

B. Revising Choppy Sentences

Revise the paragraph below on your own paper. Combine some of the short sentences in different ways. Use the examples on page 73 as a guide.

EX. My town has an arboretum. It is filled with many rare plants. It also has many rare trees.
My town has an arboretum filled with many rare plants and trees.

I know the manager of the arboretum. His name is Frank Alonzo. He is a friendly man. He likes to take people through the arboretum. He enjoys taking them on tours. I have hiked through the arboretum many times with him. I always stop at my favorite tree. It is a pink dogwood tree. It is not really rare. But it is beautiful. It is especially beautiful in late spring. Then it is covered with blossoms. They are pink. This spring the dogwood surprised me. It had something new. It had a fragile nest. The nest was on one of its lower branches. I stood on tiptoe. I could see a baby bird in the nest. The baby bird will leave the nest by late summer. Mr. Alonzo will take the nest down in the fall. He said he will give it to me.

C. Revising a Paragraph to Eliminate Stringy and Wordy Sentences

On your own paper, revise the sentences in the following paragraph that are stringy or wordy.

EX. What I want to tell you about is a really, really special bowl that my mother owns and my great-great-grandfather once made.
Let me tell you about my mother's very special bowl that my great-great-grandfather made.

At the time that my grandmother was a young woman of twenty-one years, her grandfather gave her a special present, which is the subject of the paragraph that I am writing. Her grandfather, who would be my great-great-grandfather, was a carpenter. One morning in 1914, he was building a fence for someone, and a sudden storm came up suddenly, and lightning hit a tree, and a huge branch fell to the ground. He hurried into a shed to get out of the rain, and he saw something strange in the huge branch, and after the storm was over he went over to the branch to examine it, and what he found was that the branch had a beautiful knot in it. He took his saw, and he cut the big knot right out of the branch, and he took the knot home to his house. He carved out the wood all around the knot, and he made a beautiful bowl. He gave that bowl to my grandmother for her birthday, and many years later, my grandmother gave it to my mother. Someday in the future my mother will give that bowl to me. Every time I examine the beautiful, smooth wood, I think of my great-great-grandfather, and I think that he was a great artist, and I wish that I had known him.

CHAPTER 9: LANGUAGE WORKSHOPS

CHOOSING YOUR WORDS I

FORMAL AND INFORMAL ENGLISH

Because the English language is flexible, it allows you to say one thing many different ways. One choice you must make is whether to use formal or informal language.

FORMAL ENGLISH I worked for an hour and then rested briefly.
INFORMAL ENGLISH I worked an hour, then chilled a while.

Each level of formality has its uses. Formal English is appropriate for written work and for talking to most adults. You would use it for essays, tests, reports, and formal speeches. Informal English is appropriate for talking to your friends or writing personal letters, notes, or journal entries.

EXERCISE 1 **Identifying and Revising Informal English**

Each sentence below contains two words or phrases in italics. Choose the one that is more informal and replace it with a more formal word or phrase. On your own paper, write your revised sentences.

EX. 1. Their band is the *worst* and ours is the *coolest.*
1. Their band is the worst and ours is the best.

1. The children decided to *bury the hatchet* and *apologize to each other.*
2. Ariel feared we *would be late* and asked us to *get a move on.*
3. Our group *met* during study hall and *kicked around* a few ideas.
4. Each day after school, *I must complete my homework* before *I'm okayed to watch the tube.*
5. Their soccer team *was much stronger* than ours, and they *really put us down.*
6. The first story is *crummy,* but the next one is *worth reading.*
7. Saturday is an *active day,* but on Sundays I usually *hang at* home all afternoon.
8. The investigator followed Jules *for an hour,* but later Jules *gave him the slip* and vanished.
9. Mrs. Wong *changed her tune* after she had heard *the reason for* the noise.
10. That driver *likes* sports sedans but is *totally gaga over* roadsters.

DENOTATION AND CONNOTATION

A word's ***denotation*** is its actual meaning. A word's ***connotation*** is the emotional association that the word has. Words often have both a denotation and a connotation. For example, the words *warm* and *stuffy* have similar meanings. However, the words have different emotional associations.

POSITIVE CONNOTATION	That woman is **determined**.
NEGATIVE CONNOTATION	That woman is **stubborn**.
POSITIVE CONNOTATION	My new hat was **inexpensive**.
NEGATIVE CONNOTATION	My new hat was **cheap**.

EXERCISE 2 Responding to Connotations

For each sentence below, underline the word in parentheses that seems more negative. On the line after the sentence, write the reason for your answer.

EX. 1. Let's (*snoop, investigate*) to find more clues.
Snoop creates a sneakier image than investigate.

1. The meat had a strong (*odor, aroma*). ______

______

2. The chief heard a (*rumor, report*) about one officer. ______

______

3. Why did they (*disagree, fight*) about the schedule? ______

______

4. On holidays, my family has a (*tradition, habit*) of eating lasagna. ______

______

5. That movie star looks (*slim, skinny*). ______

______

CHOOSING YOUR WORDS II

TIRED WORDS AND EXPRESSIONS

A ***tired word*** is a dull, worn-out word. It has been used so often and carelessly that it has become almost meaningless. Tired words, such as *very, fine, great,* and *wonderful,* are often too vague and overused to be effective in writing.

TIRED WORD	We enjoyed the *great* party.	The room was *dark.*
REVISED	We enjoyed the *lively* party.	The room was *shadowy.*

Tired expressions are often called ***clichés.*** Many expressions are striking and vivid the first time they are used. But after a while, they lose their originality, as with the examples below.

clear as a bell	easier said than done	eat like a horse
sadder but wiser	the crack of dawn	busy as a bee

Many writers have favorite words and expressions that they tend to overuse. If a word appears too often in your writing, try to replace it with a *synonym*—a word with a similar meaning. A thesaurus or a dictionary can help you find synonyms. Because no two words have exactly the same meaning, make sure a synonym has the meaning that you intend.

EXERCISE 3 Revising Sentences to Eliminate Tired Words and Clichés

For each of the following sentences, find other words to use in place of the italicized tired word or expression. On the line following the sentence, revise the sentence by using the words you have found.

EX. 1. Mrs. Kibbe certainly is a *nice* woman.
Mrs. Kibbe certainly is a friendly woman.
____

1. That dog of yours is *big!* ____________________________

____

2. Baseball practice made me *very* hungry. ____________________

____

3. When Elise heard the noise, she turned *as white as a sheet.* ____________

____

4. I want you to *run like the wind* when you hear the starting gun. ________

____

5. The hero was a *man of few words.* ____________________

____

JARGON

Jargon is special language that is used by a particular group of people, such as people who share the same occupation, sport, or hobby. For example, the word *crown* means one thing to a checker player and something entirely different to a dentist. *Crown* can mean one playing piece stacked on top of another. It can also mean dental material that is added to a tooth.

Jargon can be practical and effective if your readers understand it. It can reduce the number of words that you use to explain something. However, don't use jargon when you are writing or speaking to a general audience who might not be familiar with the terms.

EXERCISE 4 Translating Jargon

Each sentence below contains jargon that is shown in italics. On your own paper, revise each sentence by rewriting the jargon in plain English. Use a dictionary to check the meaning of any unfamiliar jargon.

EX. 1. The plumber was able to fix the sink with her *snake.*
1. The plumber was able to fix the sink with her long, flexible metal tool.

1. The photo had to be *cropped* so it wouldn't *bleed* into the *gutter.*
2. The banker *rolled over* the funds before the *note matured.*
3. Enter the *bow* of the boat from the *port* side.
4. The *sweeper headed* the ball up the field.
5. Should I play this *phrase allegro*?

CHAPTER REVIEW

A. Rewriting Informal English

The following passage is written using informal language. On the lines below, rewrite the passage so that it is appropriate for a written report. Use your own paper if you need more room for your sentences.

EX. [1] It's really neat the way the elephant uses its trunk.

1. The way an elephant uses its trunk is amazing.

[1] An elephant is pretty weird in some ways. [2] For one thing, it is humongous! [3] An elephant can weigh tons and tons. [4] Secondly, it has this awesome trunk. [5] An elephant uses its trunk in bunches of ways. [6] It smells with it; it grabs food with it; and it squirts water into its mouth with it. [7] And does it ever drink! [8] An elephant can guzzle twenty gallons of water every day. [9] Baby elephants are way cool. [10] I definitely thought it was a wild idea to go to the circus today.

B. Responding to Connotations

For each of the following sentences, underline the word in parentheses that seems more negative.

EX. 1. Angelo bought a less expensive radio because he is (*thrifty, stingy*).

1. Under these lights, your hair looks (*chalky, silvery*).
2. The sun was shining brightly outside, but inside, the room was (*dim, gloomy*).
3. The cabin was built near a small town, which was (*quiet, dull*) during the summer.
4. This juice tastes quite (*sour, tart*) because it has lemon in it.
5. In one photograph, Olga seems to be wearing a slight (*smirk, smile*).

C. Revising Sentences to Eliminate Tired Words and Clichés

For each sentence below, replace the italicized word or expression with a word or expression that is not overused and worn out. On your own paper, write your revision.

EX. 1. The family lived in a *wonderful* house.
1. The family lived in a clean, roomy house.

1. When the music stopped, Ed stood there *like a lost soul.*
2. You'll like Donna because she *is full of fun.*
3. The mattress that I slept on last night was *as hard as a rock.*
4. When I stood up to speak, I felt *awful.*

D. Using Jargon

Choose any activity that you know or like, such as a sport, game, or hobby. On your own paper, write the name of the activity at the top of the page. Then write five examples of jargon that are related to that activity. Use each example in a sentence. Be prepared to explain each example.

EX. Bicycle Riding
1. wheelie
Jay did a wheelie down the street. (Riding a bicycle on only the back wheel is called "doing a wheelie.")

SENTENCE SENSE

10a A *sentence* is a group of words that expresses a complete thought. A sentence begins with a capital letter and ends with a period, a question mark, or an exclamation point.

EXAMPLES The writing lab has several new computers.
Please be on time for play rehearsal.
Have you read the chapter on the Civil War?
Stop the car now!

10b A *declarative sentence* makes a statement. It is always followed by a period.

EXAMPLES Shanti was elected class president two years in a row.
Here are two more suggestions.

10c An *imperative sentence* gives a command or makes a request. It is usually followed by a period. A strong command is followed by an exclamation point.

The subject of a command or a request is always *you,* but *you* doesn't usually appear in the sentence. When *you* doesn't appear, it is called the ***understood subject.*** *You* is the understood subject even when the person is addressed by name.

EXAMPLES [You] Please shut the window.
[You] Watch out!
Rosaria, [you] please read the first two sentences aloud.

10d An interrogative sentence asks a question. It is followed by a question mark.

EXAMPLES How did you know my name?
Do you live in Canada?

10e An exclamatory sentence shows excitement or expresses strong feeling. It is followed by an exclamation point.

EXAMPLES What an exciting soccer game that was!
I can't believe we are finally at the cabin!

EXERCISE 1 Identifying Sentences

On the line before each sentence, write *s.* if the group of words is a sentence or *n.s.* if the group of words is not a sentence. Add correct punctuation if the group of words is a sentence.

EX. ___n.s.___ 1. Whenever she rides her mountain bike

___s.___ 2. Alana wears her helmet whenever she rides her mountain bike.

_____ 1. Before the music began to play

_____ 2. Did Brad send Danielle a bouquet of yellow roses

_____ 3. Listening to the distant sound of thunder and seeing lightning crack across the nighttime sky

_____ 4. There is a way out of the tunnel

_____ 5. There wasn't much left to eat by the time Malcolm arrived

_____ 6. Dr. García uses all the latest equipment in her dental practice

_____ 7. Walking to the party

_____ 8. Tyrone sat on the beach because he had broken his ankle

_____ 9. Imagine what could happen in the future

_____ 10. Where did I put my library card

EXERCISE 2 Classifying and Punctuating Sentences

Classify each of the following sentences by writing *dec.* for declarative, *imp.* for imperative, *int.* for interrogative, or *exc.* for exclamatory on the line before the sentence. Then add the correct punctuation.

EX. ___exc.___ 1. How loud that music is!

_____ 1. Every year, the island loses sand to the shifting tides and shrinks an inch or two

_____ 2. What a frightening experience that was

_____ 3. Hang up your coat in the front closet

_____ 4. I can't believe how close to us that dolphin swam

_____ 5. Were you able to answer all the questions on that test

THE SUBJECT

10f The *subject* tells whom or what the sentence is about.

To find the subject of a sentence, ask *who* or *what* is doing something or *whom* or *what* is being talked about. The subject may come at the beginning, the middle, or the end of a sentence.

EXAMPLES On his trip to the Amazon rain forest, **Mr. Bergeron** took hundreds of photographs. [*Who* took photographs? *Mr. Bergeron* did.]

Hanging from the thick tree branch was a **hairy sloth**. [*What* was hanging from the tree branch? *A hairy sloth* was.]

The **rain forest** is the habitat of many interesting animals. [*What* is being talked about? *The rain forest* is.]

10g The *complete subject* consists of all the words needed to tell *whom* or *what* a sentence is about. The *simple subject* is the main word or words in the complete subject.

EXAMPLE **That spiny little creature** is a hedgehog.
COMPLETE SUBJECT **That spiny little creature**
SIMPLE SUBJECT **creature**

EXAMPLE Does **Groundhog Day in the United States** fall on February 2?
COMPLETE SUBJECT **Groundhog Day in the United States**
SIMPLE SUBJECT **Groundhog Day**

In this book, the term *subject* means the simple subject unless it is defined otherwise.

EXERCISE 3 Identifying Subjects

Underline the subject in each of the following sentences.

EX. 1. The rain forest supports a tremendous diversity of life.

1. Many scientists are now studying rain forest plants.
2. The United States National Cancer Institute knows of over two thousand rain forest plants with cancer-fighting properties.

3. In her report, Jenna explained the effect of the rain forest on the weather.
4. The rain forest in the Amazon region influences the rainfall there.
5. "El Yunque" is the name of a rain forest in Puerto Rico.
6. With its fierce winds, Hurricane Hugo practically eliminated the Puerto Rican parrot from El Yunque.
7. Roaming the rain forests of New Guinea are huge, ferocious birds called cassowaries.
8. Standing almost as tall as a man, cassowaries have wings but can't fly.
9. The female cassowary lays four to eight green eggs on the forest floor.
10. Do people know enough about ways to preserve the world's rain forests?

EXERCISE 4 Identifying Complete Subjects and Simple Subjects

Underline the complete subject in each of the following sentences. Then draw a second line under the simple subject.

EX. 1. Our history teacher told us about the Shona culture.

1. The people of this culture lived in southern Africa many years ago.
2. The buildings of their capital city still stand today.
3. The capital, called Great Zimbabwe, lies near the Sabi River.
4. More than ten thousand people may have lived in the capital city.
5. Every year, fascinated tourists come to this home of one of the great cultures of the ancient world.

THE PREDICATE

10h The *predicate* of a sentence is the part that says something about the subject.

Like the subject, the predicate may be found anywhere in a sentence.

EXAMPLES The Lincoln Memorial **is a national monument.**
High above all the other buildings in Washington, D.C., stands the Washington Monument.
Throughout the city we **saw historic sites.**

10i The *simple predicate, or verb,* is the main word or group of words in the complete predicate. The *complete predicate* consists of all the words that say something about the subject.

EXAMPLE The author **autographed copies of his latest book.**
COMPLETE PREDICATE **autographed copies of his latest book**
SIMPLE PREDICATE (VERB) **autographed**

A *verb phrase* has a main verb and one or more helping verbs. Helping verbs include *will, can, do, should, would, could,* and forms of the verbs *be* and *have*. [See the list of helping verbs on page 111.]

The words *not* and *never* are adverbs, not verbs. They are never part of a verb or verb phrase.

EXERCISE 5 Identifying Predicates

Underline the complete predicate in each of the following sentences.

EX. 1. On July 4, 1986, Americans celebrated the birthday of the Statue of Liberty.

1. Two million people gathered along the shore of New York Harbor.
2. The occasion was the hundredth birthday of Lady Liberty.
3. For the big event, workers repaired the statue.
4. The repairs cost more than sixty-nine million dollars.
5. The Statue of Liberty was ready for her birthday party.
6. She had new elevators, a new torch, and a repaired crown.

7. At the celebration, spectators saw a dazzling display of fireworks.

8. Forty thousand fireworks soared into the sky over the harbor.

9. From the enormous crowd of people came a loud chorus of cheers and applause.

10. This was one of the largest displays of fireworks in the history of the United States.

EXERCISE 6 Identifying Complete Predicates and Verbs

Underline the complete predicate in the sentences below. Then write the verb or verb phrase on the line following the sentence.

EX. 1. You should have brought pictures of your vacation.
should have brought

1. Actor and comedian Bill Cosby writes funny stories about his childhood.

____

2. The library will be closed on Fridays during the summer.

____

3. The boys want pizza and salad for supper.

____

4. I can never remember our new telephone number.

____

5. Put the dirty dishes in the sink.

____

COMPOUND SUBJECTS AND COMPOUND VERBS

10j A *compound subject* consists of two or more connected subjects that have the same verb. The usual connecting word is *and* or *or*.

EXAMPLES The **bear** and the **badger** hibernate in the winter. [*Bear* and *badger* are both subjects of the verb *hibernate*. The two parts of the subject are connected by *and*.]

Freda, Thomas, or his **sister** will baby-sit for the Grants. [*Freda, Thomas,* and *sister* are all subjects of the verb phrase *will baby-sit*. The three parts of the subject are connected by *or*.]

10k A *compound verb* consists of two or more connected verbs that have the same subject. A connecting word—usually *and, or,* or *but*—is used to join the verbs.

EXAMPLE Kim **trained** hard and then **worked** as a camp counselor. [Both verbs, *trained* and *worked*, have the same subject, *Kim*.]

Namir **may set** the table, **serve** the meal, or **wash** the dishes. [*Namir* is the subject of the verbs *may set, serve,* and *wash*.]

Sometimes the subject of a sentence is difficult to locate. In such cases, find the verb first and then ask yourself *whom* or *what* the verb is referring to.

EXAMPLES In English class, we are reading poetry. [The verb phrase is *are reading*. *Who* are reading? *We* are reading. *We* is the subject of the sentence.]

In the bowl were ripe fruit and cheese sticks. [*Were* is the verb. *What* were in the bowl? The answer is *fruit* and *sticks*. *Fruit* and *sticks* are the subjects.]

E RCISE 7 Identifying Compound Subjects

Ci the verb and underline the compound subject in each of the foll ng sentences.

EX. Nutrition and health (are) interesting topics.

1. es and oranges are healthful choices for a snack.
2. V n C and dietary fiber are found in apples.

3. However, oranges and the juice of oranges contain five times as much vitamin C.
4. Iron and vitamins are plentiful in whole wheat bread.
5. White eggs and brown eggs are equally nutritious.

EXERCISE 8 Identifying Compound Verbs

In the following sentences, circle the verbs or verb phrases that make up the compound verb and underline the subjects.

EX. 1. Some people can operate huge machines but will not touch a computer.

1. The sun gives light and provides warmth.
2. Baby penguins stand on their parents' feet and cuddle.
3. John bought tickets but never arrived for the play.
4. Dodo birds and dinosaurs once existed but now are extinct.
5. In late autumn the leaves on the oak tree turn bright red and fall to the ground.
6. Staple or clip the pages of your report together.
7. The *Titanic* hit an iceberg and sank.
8. The math problems looked hard but were really very simple.
9. Will Father drive us to the movie and take us home later?
10. Magda read the book and then wrote a review of it for the school newspaper.

CHAPTER REVIEW

A. Identifying Sentences by Purpose

On the line before the sentence, identify each sentence by writing *dec.* for declarative, *imp.* for imperative, *int.* for interrogative, or *exc.* for exclamatory. Then add the correct punctuation mark.

EX. ___int.___ 1. Would you rather see a movie about baseball or watch a baseball game?

_____ 1. Mom, please get the movie *Field of Dreams* while you are out

_____ 2. What a great baseball movie that was

_____ 3. How long will it take for your mother to return

_____ 4. We can make some popcorn while we wait

_____ 5. Don't touch that hot pan

B. Identifying Complete Subjects and Complete Predicates

Underline the complete subjects once and the complete predicates twice in the following sentences.

EX. 1. The entire population of the city welcomed the winning team back home.

1. The baseball team had never won a championship in the history of our school.
2. During the season, the players and coaches worked hard.
3. Their dedication to the game was obvious.
4. Among their greatest achievements was perfect attendance by each player.
5. People in this town may never again feel such pride and joy.

C. Identifying Simple Subjects and Verbs

Underline the simple subjects and circle the verbs or verb phrases in the following sentences.

EX. 1. Dorothea Dix (became) a schoolteacher at the age of fourteen.

1. This amazing woman also wrote children's books.
2. In 1841, she visited a jail in Massachusetts.

3. The jail housed not only criminals but also people with mental disorders.
4. The Massachusetts schoolteacher was horrified.
5. Because of Dorothea's work, states built proper hospitals for people with mental health problems.

D. Using Compound Subjects and Compound Verbs in Writing

You live in the year 2300. You have been on a long journey into space. On the lines below, write notes for a log that tells about your experience. Write your notes in sentence form. Include and label at least five compound subjects and five compound verbs in your notes. Use your own paper if you need more space. These are some of the questions you might answer in your notes.

1. What did you see on your journey?
2. Did you make any stops? If so, where?
3. What was the most unusual experience you had on your journey?
4. What was the most amusing thing that occurred on the journey?
5. What was the most frightening thing that happened on your journey?

comp. verb

EX. *June 14, 2300—After twenty-five days in space, we saw and photographed an amazing meteor collision.*

CHAPTER 11: PARTS OF SPEECH

NOUNS

The words in our language are classified into groups according to the jobs they perform in sentences. These groups are called ***the eight parts of speech***: *nouns, pronouns, adjectives, verbs, adverbs, prepositions, conjunctions, and interjections.*

11a A *noun* is a word that names a person, place, thing, or idea.

Persons	Placido Domingo, children, choir
Places	Utah, desert, restaurant, island
Things	llama, money, plants, Nobel Prize
Ideas	truth, justice, love, freedom

11b A *proper noun* is a specific name for a particular person, place, thing, or idea. It always begins with a capital letter. A *common noun* is a general name for a group of persons, places, things, or ideas. It is not capitalized.

Proper Nouns	Common Nouns
Michelangelo	painter
South America	continent
USA Today	newspaper
Emilio Estevez	actor

Notice that some nouns are made up of more than one word. Such nouns are called ***compound nouns.*** As the following examples show, the parts of a compound noun may be joined or written separately.

EXAMPLES tablecloth Hollywood Abraham Lincoln
brother-in-law high school Labor Day

11c A *concrete noun* names a person, place, or thing that can be perceived by one or more of the senses (sight, hearing, taste, touch, and smell). An *abstract noun* names an idea, a feeling, a quality, or a characteristic.

Concrete Nouns	sea, drumbeat, yogurt, deer, roses
Abstract Nouns	loyalty, curiosity, health, grace, sweetness

EXERCISE 1 Identifying and Classifying Nouns

Underline each of the nouns in the sentences below. Then on the line before each sentence, write *con.* if the noun is concrete or *abs.* if it is abstract. If there is more than one noun in a sentence, separate your answers with a semicolon.

EX. con.; con. 1. The jellyfish is an unusual animal.

_____ 1. I feel joy each time I walk on the beach.

_____ 2. The Milky Way contains several hundred billion stars.

_____ 3. Harriet thought an eternity had passed.

_____ 4. Thomas Edison was among the pioneers in making movies.

_____ 5. In ancient Greece, winning athletes were awarded a leafy crown.

EXERCISE 2 Revising Sentences by Using Proper Nouns

On the lines after each sentence below, revise the sentence by substituting a proper noun for each common noun. You may need to change some of the other words in the sentences. You may also make up proper names.

EX. 1. My parrot sounds just like my uncle. ________
Paco sounds just like Uncle Mort.

1. The president traveled to his hometown. ________

____

2. That novel was written by my best friend. ________

____

3. A story about a large building was in the newspaper. ________

____

4. This popular actress stars in a newly released movie. ________

____

5. My cousin moved to a city in a faraway country. ________

____

PRONOUNS

11d A *pronoun* is a word used in place of a noun or more than one noun.

EXAMPLE Gather the chickens and put the chickens in the henhouse.
Gather the chickens and put **them** in the henhouse.

Following are examples of pronouns:

Singular	I, me, my, mine, you, your, yours, he, him, his, she, her, hers, it, its, myself, yourself, himself, herself, itself, this, that, everybody, someone
Plural	we, us, our, ours, you, your, yours, they, them, their, theirs, ourselves, yourselves, themselves, these, those

REFERENCE NOTE: In addition to the pronouns listed above, there are many other kinds of pronouns. See the lists on pages 103, 173–175, and 213–216.

An ***antecedent*** is the word that a pronoun stands for (or refers to).

EXAMPLE Because the **senator** thought the crowd looked bored, **she** finished **her** speech early. [*Senator* is the noun that *she* and *her* refer to.]

Sometimes an antecedent is not stated.

EXAMPLES **I** hoped Kameron would enjoy our party.
Francis wondered **who** was at the door.

EXERCISE 3 Identifying Pronouns and Antecedents

Underline all pronouns in the following sentences. Circle the antecedent of each pronoun. Write *none* if a pronoun has no antecedent.

EX. 1. (Leo) said that he would run the business.

1. Startled by its own shadow, the pony slipped out of its halter.

2. Mr. Chisholm spent most of his vacation on the island of Hawaii.

3. Please buy the red flowers, for they are the most colorful.

4. Because he was so tired from chopping wood, the lumberjack took his lunch break early.
5. Rafael said, "I am ready to go home now."
6. "For some reason, I thought New Hampshire was in the other direction," said Jaime.
7. Grandfather won the race in his age group.
8. "Adam, you should clean your room thoroughly before you go out," said Mother.
9. Jason said, "Alejandro, do you want to ride with me?"
10. I asked Andrés if he had done his homework.

EXERCISE 4 Identifying Nouns and Pronouns

Rewrite each sentence, replacing the underlined words or phrases with pronouns. [Note: If necessary, rearrange some of the words.]

EX. 1. Leonardo da Vinci was a great painter, but Leonardo da Vinci was also an inventor.
Leonardo da Vinci was a great painter, but he was also an inventor.

1. Leonardo da Vinci painted Leonardo da Vinci's masterpiece the *Mona Lisa* in the early 1500s. ____________________

____

2. Some people disagree about the real name of the painting *Mona Lisa*—the real name of the painting could be *La Gioconda*. ____________

____

3. Lisa del Giocondo was the model for the painting, and Lisa del Giocondo had no eyebrows. ____________________

____

4. Because Mona Lisa's smile is unusual, Mona Lisa's smile has caused many arguments. ____________________

____

5. Because many painters wanted to paint like da Vinci, many painters copied da Vinci's masterpiece. ____________________

____

ADJECTIVES

11e An *adjective* is a word that modifies a noun or a pronoun.

To ***modify*** a word means to describe the word or to make its meaning more definite. An adjective modifies a noun or a pronoun by telling *what kind, which one, how much,* or *how many.*

What Kind?	Which One *or* Ones?	How Many *or* How Much?
long weekend	*last* year	*thirty* days
fast skates	*his* toys	*no* wheels
cheerful nurse	*our* friend	*ninety* people

Some teachers prefer to call possessive forms of pronouns (such as *our, your, his,* and *their*) adjectives. Follow your teacher's instructions regarding possessive forms.

Sometimes an adjective comes after the word that it modifies.

EXAMPLE The play was **funny**. [The adjective *funny* modifies *play*.]

The most commonly used adjectives are *a, an,* and *the.* These adjectives are called ***articles.*** *A* and *an* are called ***indefinite articles*** because they refer to someone or something in general. *The* is called a ***definite article*** because it refers to someone or something in particular.

When a noun modifies another noun or a pronoun, it is considered an adjective.

Nouns	Nouns Used as Adjectives
compact	*compact* car
summer	*summer* storm
city	*city* lights
turkey	*turkey* dinner

EXERCISE 5 Identifying Adjectives

Underline the adjectives in the sentences below, and draw two lines under the noun or pronoun each adjective modifies. Do not include the articles *a*, *an*, and *the*.

EX. 1. Many students rode on the purple bus.

1. Most tornadoes occur on hot, humid days.
2. When we toured the city, we saw shiny, new skyscrapers next to old, historical buildings.
3. Summer temperatures lasted for only two months.
4. She saw many stars in the clear sky.
5. The moon weighs eighty-one billion tons.

EXERCISE 6 Using Nouns as Adjectives

Pick four words from the group below. For each word, write two sentences on the lines provided. Use each word first as a noun, then as an adjective.

EX. annual 1. The annuals in our garden are daisies.
The annual picnic always attracts a large crowd.

dress	wood	committee	boat	Lincoln	scratch
black	Texas	seafood	speech	cat	flower

1. ______________________________
____
2. ______________________________
____
3. ______________________________
____
4. ______________________________

DEMONSTRATIVE AND PROPER ADJECTIVES

11f ***This, that, these,* and *those* can be used both as adjectives and as pronouns. When they modify a noun, they are called *demonstrative adjectives.* When they are used alone, they are called *demonstrative pronouns.***

Demonstrative Adjectives	How long did it take you to come to **this** conclusion about **that** subject? **These** pearls are superior to **those** pearls.
Demonstrative Pronouns	**This** came from Tanzania, and **that** came from Zambia. **These** belong with **those**.

11g A proper adjective is formed from a proper noun.

Proper Nouns	Proper Adjectives
Poland	*Polish* hat
Fourth of July	*Fourth of July* cookout
Congress	*Congressional* hearing
Asia	*Asian* countries

EXERCISE 7 Identifying Demonstrative Adjectives and Pronouns

In each of the following sentences, underline the demonstrative adjectives, and circle the demonstrative pronouns.

EX. (This) is a story about <u>those</u> bears.

1. The weather has been very hot in this part of the state.
2. That chair beside the table was made by my grandfather.
3. Fruit is my favorite food during this time of year.

4. Those who wish to go to the beach should follow this path.
5. These basketball sneakers were made in Korea.

EXERCISE 8 Identifying Common and Proper Adjectives
In the following paragraph underline the common adjectives, and circle the proper adjectives. Do not include the articles *a, an,* and *the.*

EX. [1] Denim jeans originated in an (Italian) town.

[1] There, a cotton cloth similar to denim was used to make work clothes. [2] The town, Genoa, was known to French weavers as Genes. [3] An immigrant tailor, Levi Strauss, came to San Francisco during the 1850s. [4] He sold heavy canvas for making tents. He realized that the gold miners quickly wore out their trousers from the hard work. [5] Strauss made many overalls for the miners from his heavy-duty fabric. [6] After a few years, he replaced this canvas material with a softer fabric, denim. [7] Strauss borrowed an idea from a Russian Jewish tailor to strengthen the pockets by adding copper rivets at the pocket seams. [8] He used blue fabric so that stains would not show. [9] The San Francisco denim became quite famous. [10] In 1935, these practical trousers became very popular when a fashion magazine ran an advertisement for them.

CHAPTER REVIEW

A. Identifying Nouns, Pronouns, and Adjectives

Identify each italicized word in the sentences below by writing *n.* for a noun, *pron.* for a pronoun, or *adj.* for an adjective on the lines before the sentences. Separate your answers with a semicolon.

EX. n.; pron. 1. *Laverne* spent many hours practicing *her* speech.

________ 1. The construction *workers* stopped for a *lunch* break.

________ 2. If history repeats *itself, we* are in for one big surprise.

________ 3. When *you* are thirsty, *heat* becomes less bearable.

________ 4. After the celebration, *Jiro* walked to the *train* station.

________ 5. In swimming, the *front* crawl used to be called the *Australian* crawl.

________ 6. *Tasmania* is *part* of Australia.

________ 7. The Tasmanian devil has *black* fur with white *patches.*

________ 8. Did *Picasso* paint *this* picture or sculpt that monument?

________ 9. Did *you* buy a *British* novel?

________ 10. Even though *she* is reading that speech, the ideas in it are from *John.*

B. Identifying Pronouns and Antecedents

In the sentences below, underline each pronoun, and circle its antecedent. [Note: A sentence may have more than one pronoun.]

EX. 1. The (director) said that <u>she</u> would promote the play by placing ads in the local paper.

1. Mr. Mayor, are you going fishing?
2. Louis Armstrong, known to his fans as "Satchmo," had a friendly smile.
3. We, the people, have decided to override the director's decision.
4. Ask Wenona if she brought her sandwiches for the picnic.
5. "I am my own best friend," said the small boy.

C. Identifying Adjectives

In the following paragraph, underline the adjectives and circle the words that they modify. Do not include *a, an,* and *the.*

EX. 1. The popular author James Herriot has written several books.

[1] One excellent book was made into a popular television series. [2] The setting for Herriot's powerful stories is beautiful Yorkshire, England, where the grassy hills make a rich background for several memorable characters. [3] All the major characters are not humans, though. [4] Because Herriot is a real-life veterinarian, most of these outstanding stories feature animals. [5] In many ways, Herriot's books are unforgettable tours through the small, rural towns of the northern part of England.

D. Using Nouns, Pronouns, and Adjectives

You are a copywriter for a radio station. You have been asked to write a brief advertisement for a new amusement park. This park will open in your hometown this summer. Remember that good advertising is brief and clear. Use your five senses: sight, hearing, taste, smell, and touch. On your own paper, write a short radio spot of at least five sentences. Then underline the nouns, draw two lines under the pronouns, and circle each adjective. Do not circle *a, an,* and *the.*

EX. Leave the twentieth century behind! Journey back to prehistoric times! You can hear the powerful roar of the Allosaurus. You can see the Stegosaurs as they munch on leaves. Yes, all these sights can be seen at exciting, new Dinosaur Park on Highway 49. Get your tickets and join us today.

CHAPTER 12: PARTS OF SPEECH

VERBS

12a A *verb* is a word that expresses an action or a state of being.

EXAMPLES The rabbit **scampered** into the bushes.
Lionel **is** in the seventh grade.

12b An *action verb* is a verb that expresses physical or mental action.

EXAMPLES Cara **built** a model airplane.
Remember your books!

12c A *transitive verb* is an action verb that expresses an action directed toward a person or thing.

EXAMPLES The grocer **helped** the customers.
Only the hardiest plants **survived** the frost.

With transitive verbs, the action passes from the doer—the subject—to the receiver of the action. Words that receive the action of transitive verbs are called ***objects***.

☞ **REFERENCE NOTE:** For more information about objects and their uses in sentences, see pages 123–125.

12d An *intransitive verb* expresses action (or tells something about the subject) without passing the action to a receiver.

EXAMPLES The audience **clapped**.
His eyeglasses **shattered** on the pavement.

A verb may be transitive in one sentence and intransitive in another.

EXAMPLES Leta **sang** a song. [transitive]
Leta **sang** softly. [intransitive]

EXERCISE 1 Identifying Action Verbs

Underline the action verb in each of the following sentences.

EX. 1. Dolphins remember sounds.

1. In San Francisco we visited an aircraft carrier.
2. Throw the ball to the pitcher.
3. Yoshi saw the notice on the bulletin board.

4. Who waters the plants every day?
5. First, melt the butter in the skillet.

EXERCISE 2 Identifying Transitive and Intransitive Verbs

Identify the italicized action verbs by writing *trans.* for transitive or *intr.* for intransitive on the line before each sentence.

EX. trans. 1. Look carefully through the early morning mist.

________ 1. The Statue of Liberty *stands* in New York Harbor.

________ 2. The people of France *gave* the statue to the United States.

________ 3. The French people *raised* most of the money themselves.

________ 4. Frédéric Auguste Bartholdi *designed* the statue.

________ 5. The statue *rises* above star-shaped Fort Wood.

EXERCISE 3 Writing Sentences with Transitive and Intransitive Verbs

Choose five verbs from the group below. Use each verb to write two sentences on your own paper. In one sentence, use the verb as a transitive verb and underline its object. In the other, use the verb as an intransitive verb. You may use different tenses of the verb. Identify each verb by writing *transitive* or *intransitive*.

EX. 1. draw Monet drew sketches of the waterlilies. (transitive)
Monet drew quickly. (intransitive)

bake forget join play stop turn watch

LINKING VERBS

12e A *linking verb* is a verb that links, or connects, the subject of a sentence with a noun, a pronoun, or an adjective in the predicate.

EXAMPLES Nancy Lopez **is** a golfer. [The verb *is* connects *golfer* with the subject *Nancy Lopez*.]

Most of the runners **seemed** tired after the race. [The verb *seemed* links *tired* with the subject *runners*.]

Linking Verbs Formed from the Verb *Be*		
am	has been	may be
is	have been	might be
are	had been	can be
was	will be	should be
were	shall be	would have been

Other Linking Verbs					
appear	become	feel	grow	look	remain
seem	smell	sound	stay	taste	turn

Some words may be either action verbs or linking verbs, depending on how they are used.

ACTION Farmers **grow** a variety of crops.

LINKING Children **grow** taller each year. [The verb links *taller* with the subject *children*.]

ACTION **Look** at the seeds through the microscope.

LINKING **Look** happy! [The verb links *happy* with the understood subject *you*.]

 **REFERENCE NOTE:** For more information about understood subjects in imperative sentences, see page 87.

EXERCISE 4 Identifying Linking Verbs

Underline the linking verb in each of the following sentences.

EX. 1. Her name sounded unfamiliar to me.

1. Is Kimiko a new student in our school?
2. At first, she appeared shy and nervous.
3. Like many immigrants, she often felt homesick.
4. After a few weeks at school, she became more confident.
5. With the support of the teacher and students, she grew comfortable in her new surroundings.
6. The English language now seems easier for her.
7. After having studied it for several years, Kimiko is fluent in Chinese.
8. In Japan she had been a member of a gymnastics team.
9. The sport of gymnastics looks very difficult to me.
10. Maybe someday I can be a gymnast like Kimiko.

EXERCISE 5 Identifying Linking Verbs

Underline the linking verb in each of the following sentences. Circle the two words connected by each linking verb.

EX. 1. Mars was the Roman god of war.

1. The planet Mars appears red in the nighttime sky.
2. It is smaller than the earth.
3. Throughout the ages, Mars has been a source of mystery.
4. An icecap at the south pole remains frozen during the entire Martian year.
5. During autumn and winter, the icecap grows larger.

HELPING VERBS

12f A *verb phrase* contains a main verb and one or more helping verbs.

EXAMPLES Theo **did remember** his overdue books.
I **might have seen** your jacket in the lunch room.
The painting **may have been painted** by Winslow Homer.

12g A *helping verb* helps the main verb to express action or a state of being.

EXAMPLES Soon the judges ***will be*** **announcing** the winner.
The meat ***should have been*** **cooked** more thoroughly.

Helping Verbs					
am	is	are	was	were	be
being	been	have	has	had	do
does	did	may	might	must	can
could	shall	should	will	would	

Sometimes a verb phrase is interrupted by another part of speech, such as a pronoun or an adverb.

EXAMPLES **Am** *I* **singing** only in the second act?
He **does** *not* **have** a new car.

EXERCISE 6 Identifying Verb Phrases and Helping Verbs
Underline each verb phrase in the following paragraph. Draw a second line under the helping verb.

EX. 1. Have you ever played tennis?

[1] Tennis can be traced back to an old French game. [2] Over the years, the rules of the game have remained largely the same. [3] However, the players' equipment has changed greatly. [4] During the twelfth and thirteenth centuries, players would hit the ball with the palms of their

hands. [5] The sheepskin ball was filled with sawdust. [6] Later, pieces of wood and gloves were used instead of hands. [7] By the middle of the fifteenth century, strung rackets had been invented. [8] Today, many professional players do not use wooden rackets. [9] Modern racket frames are made from a combination of materials, such as fiberglass, graphite, and metal. [10] Different kinds of stringing have also been tried.

EXERCISE 7 Identifying Verb Phrases and Helping Verbs

Underline the verb phrases in the sentences below. Draw a second line under the helping verbs.

EX. 1. Abraham Lincoln was born in Kentucky.

1. By his eighth birthday, Lincoln had moved twice.
2. As a young man he had become a lawyer.
3. By 1848, he had been elected to the United States Congress.
4. He was elected to the office of President of the United States in 1860.
5. He is regarded for his honesty.
6. George Washington was born in 1732 in Westmoreland County, Virginia.
7. Although smart, he never did receive much formal education.
8. In 1759, he was married to Martha Custis.
9. Congress had chosen him as commander of the Continental Army by 1776.
10. He would become the first United States president in 1789.

Peer Evaluation

Exchange rough drafts with a classmate. Ask your classmate to follow these steps.

Step 1: Read the report, stopping to examine the slides along the way.

Step 2: On a separate sheet of paper, complete the **Questions for Evaluation** on page 56. Make specific, positive suggestions.

Self-Evaluation

Next, evaluate your rough draft yourself. Follow these steps.

Step 1: Reread the rough draft of your slide report. Remember that a slide report is an oral presentation. As you read your report, think of how it will sound aloud. Think about the comments you made about your classmate's rough draft. Which of these comments apply to your own draft?

Step 2: Read your classmate's evaluation of your rough draft. Circle any comments that you plan to use as you are revising.

Step 3: Answer the **Questions for Evaluation** as they apply to your own rough draft.

Using your classmate's suggestions and your own answers to the **Questions for Evaluation**, revise your rough draft.

Proofreading and Publishing

Step 1: First, check for errors in spelling. Look at each word separately to judge its correctness. If you can't give each word an A+ for correctness, look it up in a dictionary. Be especially careful with foreign words and phrases, as well as with scientific terms.

Step 2: Next, proofread your report for errors in grammar, usage, punctuation, and capitalization. Refer to the proofreading checklist on page 10. Double-check your use of capital letters for proper nouns and adjectives. Use the rules in Chapter 22 to correct capitalization errors in your paper.

Step 3: Publish your slide report by presenting it aloud to your classmates and teacher or to another audience. These suggestions will help you with the oral part of your report.

A. Begin with an interesting introduction that hooks your audience. The introduction may be an interesting fact, a little story, or even some questions.
B. Prepare a separate note card to go with each slide.
C. Number the cards in the order that you plan to use them.

Here are four ways you can handle the visual part of your report.

A. Draw sketches on 8 1/2- by 11-inch sheets of paper. Hold the sketches up for the class to see as you give your report.
B. Make slides from photographs, and show the slides on a slide projector.
C. Make transparencies from photographs or sketches, and show the transparencies on an overhead projector.
D. Look in books or magazines for photographs or artwork that you can display.

FOR YOUR PORTFOLIO

Write your responses to the following suggestions. Keep the answers with your slide report.

1. Someone once said, "A picture is worth a thousand words." What have you learned from this assignment that makes you agree or disagree with that statement?
2. Check your school or local newspaper for ideas for a slide presentation on an important issue. For example, perhaps you have read an article opposing shipping elephants and gorillas to wildlife amusement parks. Make a list of slides you would use for your presentation.
3. Draw a sketch of a slide that could introduce the model slide report on pages 49–50. Draw a sketch of a slide that could illustrate the conclusion of the report.

A LETTER TO THE EDITOR

What do you feel strongly about? Should the whale in your local sea park be freed? Perhaps your school-bus stop should be moved closer to your house. One way to express your opinion is to write a *letter to the editor*. A ***letter to the editor*** is a public letter to the editor of a newspaper or a magazine. The following letter is to the editor of a school newspaper.

1475 Broadway
Chicago, IL 60605
November 21, 1994

The Editor
The Courier
120 Union Avenue
Chicago, IL 60605

Dear Editor:

Our school's parent-teacher organization has just finished its yearly fund drive. Now its members are about to vote on how to spend the money. I think the money should be spent on repairing our outdoor basketball court.

Today, the court is full of large piles of smelly trash. Ugly weeds have grown up between cracks, and big holes in the pavement make the court unsafe. Last month the principal closed the court. Now students can't play there any more.

Basketball is a very popular sport in our school. Last year, more than one hundred students tried out for the basketball team. Without this outdoor court, however, many students won't be able to practice and then might not make the team. Many students now attend our games, but without good players, we might not win as much. Then students would quit coming to the games. Thus, a better court would help our school spirit.

The court should be repaired because a better court would also give students a safe place to play after school. Our school does not have a playground. Without this basketball court, students sometimes play on nearby crowded sidewalks or in the streets.

A better outdoor basketball court would help the school and the students. The money should be spent to repair the court.

Maribeth Williams

Thinking About the Model

The writer of the model letter on page 59 expresses a strong opinion. Now that you've read the letter, think about how the writer persuades others. Answer the following questions about the model letter.

1. An ***opinion*** is a writer's personal belief. It cannot be proved true or false, and people have different feelings about it. What opinion does the writer of the model letter feel strongly about?

 ____

2. Reasons are one way to convince others about your opinion. A ***reason*** tells *why* something should be done. The writer of the model letter gives two reasons for repairing the outdoor basketball court. The first reason is that a better court will improve school spirit. What is the second reason?

 ____

3. A letter to the editor also supports the writer's opinion with facts. A ***fact*** can be checked and proved true. You can check facts through observation or in a source such as an encyclopedia. One fact in the model letter on page 59 is that the basketball court has piles of trash on it. What are three other facts in the model letter?

 ____

 ____

 ____

4. Words that affect people's feelings can also persuade others. In the model letter, the writer uses the words *ugly* and *smelly* to convince readers that the courts need attention. What are two other such words the writer uses to do this?

 ____

5. Ideas in a letter to the editor are usually arranged in order of importance. What is the most important reason in the model letter? Where does the writer place it in the letter?

 ____

6. Letters to the editor sometimes end with a restatement of the opinion. What sentence is the author's restatement?

 ____

ASSIGNMENT: WRITING A LETTER TO THE EDITOR

Write a letter to the editor of your school or local newspaper. In your letter, identify and support your opinion. As you write, think about your audience. What supporting reasons and facts will be most convincing to them?

Prewriting

Step 1: Start with a subject or idea that's important to you. What's going on in your school, neighborhood, or city that you would like to change? Do you think your community should put aside areas for skateboarders and in-line skaters as it does for bicyclists? Should your school have both male and female cheerleaders? Complete the following sentences to help you explore possible ideas.

A. I think that ______________________________

____

should ______________________________

____

B. I'm concerned about ______________________________

____

because ______________________________

____

C. We should change ______________________________

____

because ______________________________

____

D. ______________________________ is unnecessary

____

because ______________________________

____

Step 2: Choose a topic from Step 1 that you care about and that your readers will also care about. Or think of a new topic. Then, in the chart on page 63, write a statement of your opinion about the topic. For example, you might write "The school board should reduce class size."

Step 3: Once you've chosen a topic and identified your opinion, you are ready to gather supporting ideas. People won't automatically agree with your opinion: To change their minds, you will need to give them convincing facts and reasons. You may also need to use some persuasive words, words that will affect your readers' feelings. Here are some examples of support for the opinion statement "The school board should reduce the number of students in our classes."

Type of Support	Example
Fact	Our school has 700 students this year. 25 more than last year.
Reason	Students are more successful in smaller classes.
Persuasive Words	*Cramped, stuffy* rooms; *helpless* students

What reasons, facts, or persuasive words can you use to support your opinion? Brainstorm for ideas; talk to other people; check the library. The more support you find, the better your chance of convincing your readers.

Step 4: List your support in the chart on page 63. Begin by listing reasons. Then add any facts that you have identified. Finally, list some persuasive words and phrases you might use to appeal to your readers' feelings.

Opinion Statement:

____

____

Support:

Reasons

____

____

____

Facts

____

____

____

Persuasive Words

____

____

Step 5: Not all support is equal. Some reasons and facts will be more important, or persuasive, than others. Since people usually remember the last thing they read, you'll want to put the most important support at the end of your letter.

Study your list of support, and decide which is most important. Put an *L* for *last* beside that piece of support. Then decide which support is least important. Put an *F* for *first* beside it.

Writing

Use your prewriting notes to write a draft of your letter to the editor. Write your letter on the lines given on the next page. Follow the proper form for a business letter given below.

The Parts of a Business Letter	
Heading	Divide the letter in half by drawing an imaginary line vertically down the middle. Begin the heading to the right of the line. Write these parts of the heading on separate lines. • writer's street address • city, state, and ZIP Code (A comma follows the name of the city.) • date of letter (A comma separates the day of the month from the year.)
Inside Address	Leave a margin at the left of the letter. Begin the inside address at the margin. Include these parts on separate lines. • the name or the title of the person you are writing to (*The Editor*) • the name of the publication (*Pensacola News Journal*) • street address of the publication • city, state, and ZIP Code of the publication
Salutation	Begin the salutation, or greeting, at the left margin. Begin the first word and all nouns in the salutation with a capital letter. Follow the salutation with a colon. (*Dear Editor:*)
Body	The body of the letter is made up of what you have to say to the receiver. Indent the first line of each paragraph.
Closing and Signature	The closing lines up under the heading. You might write *Sincerely* or *Yours truly*. Only the first word should be capitalized. Follow the closing with a comma. Skip four lines and type or print your full, legal name. Sign your letter in the space just below your closing. In signing your letter, you should use your legal name also.

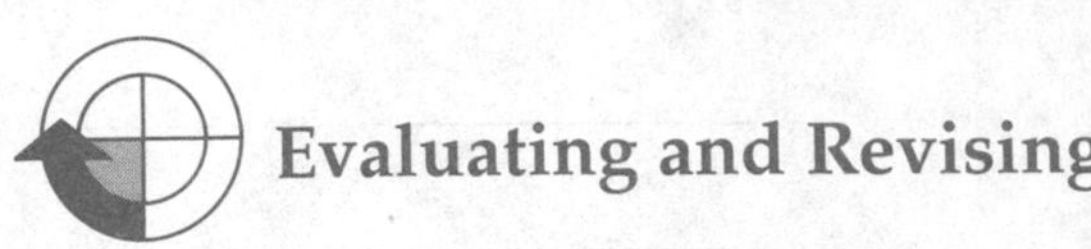

Evaluating and Revising

Now that you've drafted your letter to the editor, you have a chance to improve it. First you have to evaluate it. That means looking for its strengths and its weaknesses. Then you are ready to revise it, turning those weaknesses into strengths.

You can use the following **Questions for Evaluation** when you evaluate your paper or a classmate's paper.

Questions for Evaluation

1. Does the letter clearly state an opinion? What is it?
2. Is enough support given for the opinion? Will the support convince readers? If not, what reasons might be added? What facts might be added? What words and phrases that affect readers' feelings might be added?
3. Are ideas arranged in order of importance? Does the most important idea appear last? If not, how might ideas be rearranged?
4. Does the letter end with a restatement of the opinion statement? If not, what sentence or sentences might be added?

Peer Evaluation

Exchange rough drafts with a classmate. Ask your classmate to follow these steps.

Step 1: Read the rough draft carefully. Look at content, not grammar or mechanics.

Step 2: Complete the **Questions for Evaluation** on a separate sheet of paper. Be specific when you suggest a change.

Self-Evaluation

Next, evaluate your own rough draft. Follow these steps.

Step 1: Reread your own rough draft carefully.

Step 2: Think about the suggestions you made about your classmate's draft. Which ones apply to your own draft?

Step 3: On your own paper, answer the **Questions for Evaluation** on page 66.

Step 4: Think about your classmate's suggestions and about your answers to the **Questions for Evaluation**. On your own paper, revise your rough draft until you can answer *yes* to each of the questions.

Proofreading and Publishing

A letter to the editor is a public letter. Because it will be read by others, prepare it carefully. Follow these steps.

Step 1: Use the **Guidelines for Proofreading** on page 10 to help you. Begin by checking each word separately for correct spelling. Check carefully the spelling of words that have added endings such as *–ed* or *–ing*. Use a good dictionary to look up words that give you trouble.

Hint: One way to find misspelled words is to read your paper from right to left, instead of from left to right.

Step 2: Check your letter for errors in grammar, usage, capitalization, and punctuation.

Step 3: Make a clean copy of your revised and proofread letter.

Hint: If possible, wait a day or two before you proofread. You are more likely then to catch mistakes.

Step 4: Use one of the following suggestions to publish your letter.

A. Send your letter to the editor of your school or local newspaper. Be sure your letter follows the proper business letter form given on page 64.

B. Work with the class to prepare a bulletin board display of letters to the editor.

C. Post your letter on the refrigerator door or in another spot at home for family members to read.

FOR YOUR PORTFOLIO

Along with your letter to the editor, you might add all these pieces of writing to your portfolio.

1. Suppose you were writing your letter to a friend instead of a newspaper. How might your letter be different? Write an explanation of the differences. Or write the letter to your friend, making the changes you think are needed.
2. Newspaper editors sometimes give titles to letters to the editor, such as REPAIR BASKETBALL COURT. Write a title for your letter.
3. Look through the letters to the editor in your school or local newspaper. Choose one or two letters that you think are very convincing. Cut out the letters, and keep them with your own letter.

SENTENCE FRAGMENTS

8a A *sentence fragment* is a part of a sentence that has been punctuated as if it were a complete sentence.

FRAGMENT Visited the Air and Space Museum. [The subject is missing. *Who* visited the Air and Space Museum?]

SENTENCE Miriam visited the Air and Space Museum.

FRAGMENT Charles Lindbergh's plane, the *Spirit of St. Louis*. [The verb is missing. *What* about the plane?]

SENTENCE Charles Lindbergh's plane, the *Spirit of St. Louis*, hung from the ceiling of the museum.

FRAGMENT When he made his first solo flight across the Atlantic. [This word group has a subject and a verb, but it doesn't express a complete thought. *What happened* when he made his flight?]

SENTENCE When he made his first solo flight across the Atlantic, he became a national hero.

As you can see from the first two examples, you can correct some sentence fragments by adding a subject or a verb. Other times a sentence fragment just needs to be attached to the sentence next to it.

NOTE A word that ends in *–ing* cannot stand alone as a verb unless it has a helping verb (such as *is*, *are*, or *were*) with it.

FRAGMENT The class **studying** the history of air travel. [Without a helping verb, this word group isn't a complete thought.]

SENTENCE The class **was studying** the history of air travel.

EXERCISE 1 Identifying Sentences and Sentence Fragments

On the line before each group of words, write *sent.* if the group is a sentence or *frag.* if the group is a sentence fragment.

EX. frag. 1. Feeding the pandas at the National Zoological Park.

_____ 1. The National Zoological Park is in Washington, D.C.

_____ 2. Pandas sitting in the shade, eating leaves.

_____ 3. Their black and white fur and beautiful eyes make the bears look like giant stuffed toys.

_____ 4. They attract many visitors.

_____ 5. Giraffes, elephants, hippopotamuses, and rhinoceroses.

_____ 6. Wandering around in large, open areas are a variety of birds.

_____ 7. In one section, exotic birds such as the scarlet ibis.

_____ 8. Showing visitors its bright red feathers.

_____ 9. The howler monkeys are quite noisy.

_____ 10. The monkeys swinging through trees and chattering loudly.

EXERCISE 2 Correcting Sentence Fragments

On the lines after each sentence fragment, rewrite the fragment to make it a complete sentence.

EX. 1. The lighthouse at Stevens' Point.
The lighthouse at Stevens' Point is fifty-three feet tall.

1. the students working all night long on the decorations for the dance

____

____

2. while we were visiting the state of Texas

____

____

3. loves the musical group known as 10,000 Maniacs

____

____

4. in the distance, the tall pine trees

____

____

5. a palette knife, an easel, some paints, brushes, and a canvas

____

____

RUN-ON SENTENCES

8b A *run-on sentence* is two complete sentences punctuated as one sentence.

In a run-on, the thoughts run into each other. The reader cannot tell where one idea ends and another one begins.

RUN-ON Laverne is a finalist in the tennis tournament, let's watch the match tomorrow.

CORRECT Laverne is a finalist in the tennis tournament**.** **L**et's watch the match tomorrow.

RUN-ON Laverne plays basketball she's also on the tennis team.

CORRECT Laverne plays basketball**, and** she's also on the tennis team.

To spot run-ons, read your writing aloud. A natural, distinct pause in your voice usually marks the end of one thought and the beginning of another. If you pause at a place where you don't have any end punctuation, you may have found a run-on sentence.

To revise run-on sentences, use one of the following methods.

(1) Make two sentences.

RUN-ON Charles Drew was a doctor and a teacher he taught at Howard University.

CORRECT Charles Drew was a doctor and a teacher**.** **H**e taught at Howard University.

(2) Use a comma and a coordinating conjunction.

RUN-ON Drew taught classes, he performed operations.

CORRECT Drew taught classes**, and** he performed operations.

A comma marks a brief pause in a sentence, but it does not show the end of a sentence. If you use just a comma between two complete sentences, you create a run-on sentence.

RUN-ON Drew was a pioneer in blood research, he experimented with plasma.

CORRECT Drew was a pioneer in blood research**, and** he experimented with plasma.

EXERCISE 3 Identifying and Revising Run-ons

On the lines after each run-on sentence below, rewrite the sentence correctly. You can make it two sentences or use a comma and a coordinating conjunction.

EX. 1. Tony Garulo has a farm he raises miniature horses there.
Tony Garulo has a farm. He raises miniature horses there.

1. The farm is in Pennsylvania it is near the city of Gettysburg.

2. Garulo went to Argentina he learned about Falabella horses there.

3. They look just like full-sized horses they are the size of dogs.

4. They are very tame they seem to enjoy performing.

5. Visitors can watch the miniature horses jump, these animals also dance and pull tiny wagons.

EXERCISE 4 Revising to Correct Run-ons

On your own paper, rewrite the paragraph below to correct the run-on sentences.

Our class went on a spring trip to Baltimore, Maryland, it was really fun. In the morning, we strolled along the Inner Harbor and looked at all the sailboats, we saw a tropical rain forest and a coral reef at the National Aquarium in Baltimore. Later we visited Fort McHenry, the flag waving over this fort gave Francis Scott Key the idea to write "The Star-Spangled Banner." Finally, we toured the USS *Constellation*, it was one of the first U.S. warships, and it was built in 1797.

COMBINING BY INSERTING WORDS AND PHRASES

Short sentences can sometimes express your ideas well. But if you use only short sentences, your writing will sound choppy and dull. Combining short sentences to form longer sentences will make your writing clearer and more interesting to read.

8c One way to combine short sentences is to take a key word from one sentence and insert it into another sentence.

ORIGINAL The grizzly is a type of bear. It is a brown bear.
COMBINED The grizzly is a type of **brown** bear.

8d A second way to combine short sentences is to change the form of a key word by adding an ending such as *–ed, –ing, –ful,* or *–ly.* In its new form, the key word can be used to describe another word in a sentence.

ORIGINAL Our neighbor raises giant daisies. The giant daisies interest me.
COMBINED Our neighbor raises **interesting** giant daisies.

EXERCISE 5 Combining Sentences by Inserting Words

On your own paper, rewrite each pair of sentences below as one sentence. Insert the italicized key word into the first sentence. The directions in parentheses tell you how to change the form of the key word.

EX. 1. Lavinia sings. She has a *beautiful* voice. (Add *–ly.*)
1. Lavinia sings beautifully.

1. The spider has long legs. It has *eight* legs. (insert word)
2. The painting shows boats on the sea. They *sail* on the sea. (Add *–ing.*)
3. Pat the dog. Use a *gentle* touch. (Add *–ly.*)
4. May I have some fish? Will you *broil* it? (Add *–ed.*)
5. Poison ivy grows with clusters of leaves. Each cluster has *three* leaves. (insert word)

8e A *phrase* is a group of words that does not have a subject and a verb. You can combine sentences by taking a phrase from one sentence and inserting it into another sentence.

ORIGINAL Many tourists visit the Liberty Bell. It is in Philadelphia.
COMBINED Many tourists visit the Liberty Bell **in Philadelphia.**

Some phrases need to be set off by commas when they rename or explain nouns or pronouns. If you use a phrase in this way, set it off with a comma (or two commas, if the phrase is in the middle of the sentence).

ORIGINAL I sent Rafael a gift. Rafael is my cousin in Tucson.
COMBINED I sent Rafael**, my cousin in Tucson,** a gift.

EXERCISE 6 Combining Sentences by Inserting Phrases

On your own paper, combine each pair of sentences below by inserting the italicized words into the first sentence.

EX. 1. Conrad Weiser immigrated to the New York colony. He came *from Germany.*
1. Conrad Weiser immigrated to the New York colony from Germany.

1. As he grew up in the colony of New York, he became friendly with the Iroquois. They were *a Native American group living nearby.*
2. During the winter, he lived as the adopted son of Quayhant, an Iroquois leader. It was the winter *of 1712–1713.*
3. Over the years, Weiser became a close friend of Shikellamy. Shikellamy was *one of the Iroquois.*
4. Weiser moved to Pennsylvania in 1729. *His wife and children* moved, too.
5. They settled at the foot of Eagle Peak. They settled *with other German immigrants.*
6. Weiser owned eight hundred acres of land. He worked as *a farmer and a tanner.*
7. He and his family lived in a one-room house with an attic. The house was *German-style.*
8. Weiser added a room to the house. He added the room *in 1751.*
9. Weiser later worked with James Logan. Logan was *the Provincial Secretary of Pennsylvania.*
10. Both Shikellamy and Weiser were helpful to Logan. They were helpful to Logan *in keeping peace with the Iroquois.*

CHAPTER 12: PARTS OF SPEECH

ADVERBS

12h An adverb is a word that modifies a verb, an adjective, or another adverb.

An adverb answers the following questions:

Where?	How often?	To what extent?
When?	*or*	*or*
How?	How long?	How much?

EXAMPLES Greta moved **quietly**. [*Quietly* is an adverb modifying the verb *moved;* it tells *how.*]

The meeting ended **rather suddenly**. [*Rather* is an adverb modifying the adverb *suddenly;* it tells *to what extent. Suddenly* is an adverb modifying the verb *ended;* it tells *how.*]

I **often** write **very** long letters to my friends. [*Often* is an adverb modifying the verb *write;* it tells *how often. Very* is an adverb modifying the adjective *long;* it tells *to what extent.*]

Later, we went **inside**. [*Later* is an adverb modifying the verb *went;* it tells *when. Inside* is an adverb modifying the verb *went,* it tells *where.*]

Words Often Used as Adverbs	
Where?	away, here, inside, near, there, up
When?	ago, later, next, now, soon, then
How?	clearly, easily, quietly, slowly
How often? or *How long?*	always, briefly, continuously, endlessly, forever, never, usually
To what extent? or *How much?*	almost, extremely, least, more, not, quite, so, too, very

Many adverbs end in *–ly*. These adverbs are formed by adding *–ly* to adjectives. However, some words ending in *–ly* are used as adjectives.

Adverbs Ending in *–ly*
loud + –ly = loudly
slow + –ly = slowly

Adjectives Ending in *–ly*		
daily	friendly	lively
early	kindly	lonely

EXERCISE 8 Identifying Adverbs

Underline the adverbs in the following sentences. Draw an arrow to the word that each adverb modifies. [Note: A sentence may contain more than one adverb.]

EX. 1. A rather large boat sailed past.

1. The denim skirt was too long and too expensive.
2. Was the sun shining then?
3. Emilio will soon call his relatives in Costa Rica.
4. Suddenly, giant hailstones pounded the area, and extremely high winds uprooted many trees.
5. Yesterday, the seventh-grade class visited the Smithsonian Institution in Washington, D.C.
6. The huge tiger growled fiercely and angrily.
7. Later, the traffic in the city seemed unusually heavy.
8. My cat seldom goes outside.
9. Kamaria always does her homework before supper.
10. Our old clock works amazingly well.

Nancy reprinted by permission of UFS, Inc.

EXERCISE 9 Choosing Adverbs to Modify Adjectives

The adverb *very* is used far too often to modify adjectives. Write five sentences that each use an adverb other than *very* to modify one of the adjectives below. Use a different adverb with each adjective. Write your answers on your own paper.

EX. 1. strong 1. This elephant is incredibly strong.

1. clever 3. happy 5. neat 7. sweet 9. tired

2. dishonest 4. narrow 6. nervous 8. taller 10. valuable

CHAPTER 12: PARTS OF SPEECH

REVIEW EXERCISE

A. Identifying Action Verbs and Linking Verbs

Underline the verb in each of the following sentences. Then on the lines before the sentences, identify the verb by writing *a.v.* for action verb or *l.v.* for linking verb. If the verb is a linking verb, circle the two words that it connects.

EX. l.v. 1. Not all (dinosaurs) looked (fierce).

_____ 1. Can you picture a dinosaur in your mind?

_____ 2. These creatures ruled the planet for millions of years.

_____ 3. Dinosaurs had skeletons like those of birds.

_____ 4. Some of these skeletons have been preserved as fossils.

_____ 5. Like the skins of reptiles, dinosaur skins might have felt scaly.

_____ 6. Some meat-eating dinosaurs were huge.

_____ 7. The largest dinosaurs might have been warmblooded.

_____ 8. Some plant-eaters were the size of chickens.

_____ 9. Scientists do not know the color of dinosaurs.

_____ 10. The true appearance of dinosaurs will probably remain a mystery.

B. Writing Adverbs

Rewrite the following sentences on your own paper. Make them more precise by adding to each a different adverb that answers the question in parentheses.

EX. 1. The teacher gave the instructions. (how?)
1. The teacher gave the instructions slowly.

1. The team had gone to the stadium. (when?)
2. It was an enjoyable trip. (to what extent?)
3. The deer ran across the meadow. (how?)
4. During the storm the girls went. (where?)
5. Did Carlos buy the tickets? (when?)

C. Writing Notes with Action and Linking Verbs

You are an athlete on a physical-fitness show on television. Your job is to tell the producer what exercises you think should be demonstrated on the show. Using the drawings below, make some notes about each exercise to explain how the exercises will be performed. On your own paper, write at least five sentences containing action verbs and five sentences containing linking verbs. Underline each action verb and circle each linking verb.

EX. 1. Bend the upper body to the right.

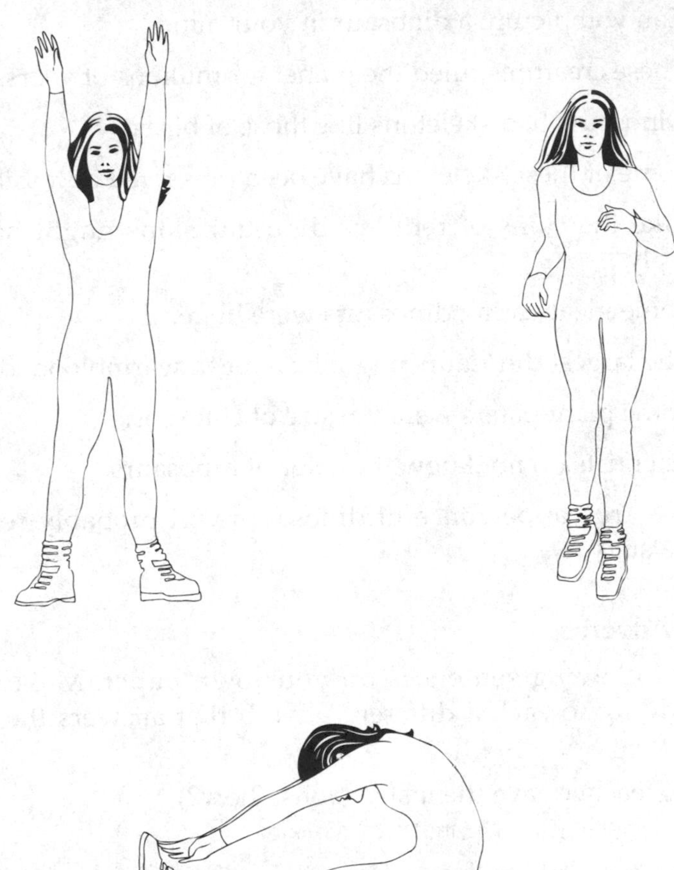

PREPOSITIONS

12i A preposition is a word that shows the relationship between a noun or a pronoun and another word in the sentence.

Notice how changing the prepositions in the following sentences changes the relationship of *Martha* to *lake* and of *bushes* to *house*.

EXAMPLES Martha walked **beside** the lake.
Martha walked **to** the lake.
Martha walked **toward** the lake.

The bushes **around** the house need trimming.
The bushes **behind** the house need trimming.
The bushes **in front of** the house need trimming.

Commonly Used Prepositions				
aboard	before	for	off	toward
about	behind	from	on	under
above	below	in	out	underneath
across	beneath	in front of	out of	unlike
after	beside	inside	over	until
against	between	instead of	past	up
along	beyond	into	since	up to
among	by	like	through	upon
around	down	near	throughout	with
as	during	next to	till	within
at	except	of	to	without

Some words may be used as prepositions or as adverbs. Remember that a preposition always has an object. An adverb never does. If you can't tell whether a word is used as an adverb or a preposition, look for an object.

PREPOSITION I climbed **aboard** the ship. [*Ship* is the object of the preposition *aboard*.]

ADVERB I climbed **aboard**. [*Aboard* is an adverb modifying the verb *climbed*; it tells *where*.]

EXERCISE 10 Writing Prepositions

Write a different preposition on the line in each of the sentences below.

EX. 1. My poodle lay ___on___ the sofa.

1. The person __________ the counter is the owner.
2. Several sheep were grazing __________ the fence.
3. The helicopter flew __________ the clouds.
4. The woman who lives __________ us plays the oboe.
5. Your napkin is lying __________ the table.
6. The books __________ my desk are overdue at the library.
7. The flowers __________ the house bloomed early.
8. I looked __________ my brother when I came home.
9. Please meet me __________ the science museum.
10. The painting __________ the mantel was created by a famous artist.

EXERCISE 11 Identifying Adverbs and Prepositions

Identify the italicized word in each of the sentences below as either an adverb or a preposition. On the line before each sentence, write *adv.* for adverb or *prep.* for preposition.

EX. ___prep.___ 1. Is the story of John Henry based *on* an actual event?

_____ 1. *In* American folklore, John Henry is a legendary character.

_____ 2. This African American became the Paul Bunyan *of* railroad construction.

_____ 3. Using a hammer, he pounded steel spikes *down* into rocks.

_____ 4. Other steel drivers were amazed *by* his strength.

_____ 5. Spectators came from miles *around* to watch him compete against a machine.

CONJUNCTIONS AND INTERJECTIONS

12j A conjunction is a word that joins words or groups of words.

(1) ***Coordinating conjunctions*** **connect words or groups of words used in the same way.**

Coordinating Conjunctions						
and	but	for	nor	or	so	yet

EXAMPLES bridges **or** tunnels [two nouns]
powerful **yet** gentle [two adjectives]
before recess **and** after lunch [two prepositional phrases]
The alarm didn't go off, **so** I was late for school. [two complete ideas]

The word *for* may be used either as a conjunction or as a preposition. When *for* joins groups of words that are independent clauses or sentences, it is used as a conjunction. In most cases, it is used as a preposition.

CONJUNCTION Guido is studying, **for** he has a test tomorrow.
PREPOSITION Guido is studying **for** his test.

NOTE When *for* is used as a conjunction, a comma should always come before it.

(2) ***Correlative conjunctions*** **are pairs of conjunctions that connect words or groups of words used in the same way.**

Correlative Conjunctions		
both . . . and	neither . . . nor	whether . . . or
either . . . or	not only . . . but also	

EXAMPLES **Both** Jupiter **and** Saturn have rings. [two nouns]
We will go **either** to the movies **or** to the ball game. [two prepositional phrases]
Not only did Wilma play the piano, **but** she **also** sang two songs. [two complete ideas]

EXERCISE 12 Identifying Conjunctions

Underline the conjunction in each of the following sentences. [Note: A sentence may contain more than one conjunction.]

EX. 1. That animal is <u>either</u> an alligator <u>or</u> a crocodile.

1. Both the alligator and the crocodile are reptiles.
2. A crocodile has fewer but sharper teeth than the alligator.
3. Not only are crocodiles more vicious, but they are also more active than alligators.
4. These reptiles look alike, yet it is easy to tell them apart.
5. Neither alligators nor crocodiles are found in many areas, for they have been widely hunted.

INTERJECTIONS

12k An *interjection* is a word that expresses strong emotion.

An interjection has no grammatical relationship to the rest of the sentence. Usually an interjection is followed by an exclamation point.

EXAMPLES **Wow!** That sounds exciting.
Ugh! These books are heavy.
Whew! I'm exhausted.

Sometimes an interjection is set off by a comma or commas.

EXAMPLES **Oh,** I just stubbed my toe.
That should take, **oh**, one hour to complete.

EXERCISE 13 Writing Interjections

You have just seen an exciting mystery movie. Write five sentences about the movie. In each sentence, use a different interjection from the list below. Underline the interjections that you use. Write your answers on your own paper. [Remember that an interjection may be set off either by an exclamation point or by a comma.]

EX. 1. <u>Aha!</u> I know who the villain is.

oh oops ouch ugh well wow yes

CHAPTER 12: PARTS OF SPEECH

CHAPTER REVIEW

A. Identifying Verbs, Adverbs, Prepositions, Conjunctions, and Interjections

Identify the part of speech of each italicized word in the sentences below. On the line before each sentence, write *v.* for verbs, *adv.* for adverbs, *prep.* for prepositions, *conj.* for conjunctions, and *intj.* for interjections.

EX. adv. 1. Have you *ever* seen the strong man at the circus?

_____ 1. Circus strong men can *bend* steel with their bare hands.

_____ 2. *Well,* a blacksmith can bend steel also.

_____ 3. Many years ago, blacksmiths supplied people *with* a variety of everyday items.

_____ 4. They made cooking utensils, tools, plows, and *sometimes* even metal toys.

_____ 5. Today, factories make most of the metal products on the market, *but* not all of them.

_____ 6. *Surprise!* Blacksmiths are still at work in some places.

_____ 7. Their *most* important piece of equipment is a forge.

_____ 8. The blacksmith *heats* metal in the forge.

_____ 9. Then the softened metal is shaped by being hammered *or* pressed.

_____ 10. Plunging the hot metal *into* water cools the metal so that it keeps its new form.

B. Identifying Action Verbs and Linking Verbs

In the following sentences, underline each action verb and circle each linking verb.

EX. 1. Sonya brought her bike to a local shop for repairs.

1. Wenona carried her books to school.
2. Annie and Lily gave Roscoe their calculator.
3. Jesse helped me with the problem.
4. A pigeon is building its nest on the platform.

5. The twins are moving to Oregon in the fall.
6. Chicken soup tastes wonderful.
7. Marini has become a leader in her class.
8. Derrick showed his rock collection to the class on Thursday.
9. Vince, are you ready for the contest?
10. The bike is not new, but it is in excellent condition.

C. Identifying Adverbs and Prepositions

In the sentences below, identify each italicized word as either an adverb or a preposition. On the line before each sentence, write *adv.* for adverb or *prep.* for preposition.

EX. adv.; prep. 1. He watched *uneasily* as the deer walked *in* the garden.

_________ 1. Three people fell *off* the boat *suddenly.*

_________ 2. *Fortunately*, another boat was passing *by* when the accident happened.

_________ 3. The people who fell were *among* the many treated *for* injuries.

_________ 4. *At* the end of the trip, we were *repeatedly* asked to report what we had seen.

_________ 5. I had *never* been in a storm like that *before.*

D. Writing Sentences

On your own paper, write ten sentences that meet the following requirements. Underline the word that you are asked to use in each sentence, and identify how it is used.

EX. 1. Use *up* as an adverb and as a preposition.
1. All the graduates stood up.—adverb
The firefighter climbed up the ladder.—preposition

1. Use *hard* as an adjective and as an adverb.
2. Use *before* as an adverb and as a preposition.
3. Use *so* as an adverb and as a conjunction.
4. Use *yet* as a conjunction and as an adverb.
5. Use *well* as an interjection and as an adjective.

DIRECT OBJECTS

13a A *complement* is a word or a group of words that completes the meaning of a verb.

Every sentence has a subject and a verb. In addition, the verb often needs a complement to complete its meaning.

INCOMPLETE Jared (S) enjoys (V) [*what?*]

COMPLETE Jared (S) enjoys (V) **tennis** (C).

INCOMPLETE Jared (S) is (V) [*what?*]

COMPLETE Jared (S) is (V) **an athlete** (C).

The *direct object* is one type of complement. It completes the meaning of a transitive verb. [For more on transitive verbs, see page 107.]

13b A *direct object* is a noun or a pronoun that receives the action of a verb or shows the result of that action. A direct object answers the question *Whom?* or *What?* after a transitive verb.

EXAMPLES The coach called **Lana**. [*Lana* receives the action of the verb *called* and tells *whom* the coach called.]
That company makes **equipment** for the sports team. [*Equipment* tells *what* the company makes.]

A direct object can never follow a linking verb because a linking verb does not express action. Also, a direct object is never in a prepositional phrase.

LINKING VERB Ms. Castillo **is** our tennis coach. [The verb *is* does not express action. Therefore, it has no direct object.]

PREPOSITIONAL PHRASE She teaches **at our school**. [*School* is not the direct object of the verb *teaches*. It is the object in the prepositional phrase *at our school*.]

A direct object may be a compound of two or more objects.

EXAMPLE I enjoy **tennis, baseball,** and **soccer**. [The compound direct object of the verb *enjoy* is *tennis, baseball*, and *soccer*.]

REFERENCE NOTE: For more information about linking verbs, see page 109. For more about prepositional phrases, see pages 133–137.

EXERCISE 1 Identifying Direct Objects

Underline the direct object in each of the following sentences. [Remember: A direct object may be compound.]

EX. 1. We watched a video about the migration of birds.

1. Jeremy walked the Henderson's dog each day for a week.
2. Henry lost his wallet and his jacket.
3. After the party, Joni saw your brother at the swimming pool.
4. The school principal posted the rules on the bulletin board.
5. Last night, we rented a movie.
6. As we listened, he answered our questions carefully.
7. I need directions to your house.
8. Ms. Martínez teaches Spanish and French at the high school.
9. Someone left a message on the table for you.
10. The cars and buses on the freeway pollute the air.

EXERCISE 2 Writing Sentences with Direct Objects

Complete each sentence by adding a direct object.

EX. 1. Georgio plays basketball.

1. Beatrice caught the ______.
2. I saw a ______ yesterday.
3. At the game, we met ______.
4. Jim kicked a ______.
5. The pitcher threw a ______.
6. Mimi won the ______.
7. At the end of the season, our team had a ______.
8. All of the players received ______.
9. At the banquet, the coach praised the ______.
10. Of all sports, I particularly like ______.

INDIRECT OBJECTS

The *indirect object* is another type of complement. Like a direct object, an indirect object helps to complete the meaning of a transitive verb. A sentence with an indirect object always has a direct object.

13c An *indirect object* is a noun or pronoun that comes between a verb and a direct object. It tells *to whom* or *to what* or *for whom* or *for what* the action of the verb is done.

EXAMPLES Mario gave **me** a gift. [The pronoun *me* is the indirect object of the verb *gave*. It answers the question *"To whom did Mario give a gift?"* The noun *gift* is the direct object.]

Juanita left **Tom** a note. [The noun *Tom* is the indirect object of the verb *left*. It answers the question *"For whom did Juanita leave a note?"* The noun *note* is the direct object.]

Like a direct object, an indirect object may be a compound of two or more objects.

EXAMPLE He made his **mother** and **father** an anniversary card. [The nouns *mother* and *father* are the indirect objects of the verb *made*. They answer the question *"For whom did he make an anniversary card?"* The noun *card* is the direct object.]

Linking verbs do not have indirect objects because they do not show action. Also, an indirect object is never in a prepositional phrase.

INDIRECT OBJECT Mr. Chávez offered me a job.
PREPOSITIONAL PHRASE Mr. Chávez offered a job to me.

EXERCISE 3 Identifying Direct Objects and Indirect Objects

In each of the following sentences, underline the direct object once. Underline the indirect object twice. [Remember: Objects may be compound.]

EX. 1. I loaned Babette my brown boots.

1. Hillary taught her dog a new trick.
2. I drew them a map of the town center.

3. Yesterday my mother gave me a ride to school.
4. Helen read the class a poem by Langston Hughes.
5. Please tell us your new address.
6. During her vacation, my aunt sent me a postcard from Puerto Rico.
7. Harold told Kim and Filbert a story before their nap.
8. Sometimes Dr. Milano offers his neighbors vegetables from his garden.
9. Fortunately, the park ranger gave the hikers a warning about the mud slide.
10. I might give my little sister or my little brother this old jacket.

EXERCISE 4 Revising Sentences by Using Indirect Objects

Rewrite each of the following sentences on your own paper. Use the italicized information to write an indirect object. Underline the indirect objects in your revised sentences.

EX. 1. Mr. Desiderato gave an award to *Minnie.*
1. Mr. Desiderato gave Minnie an award.

1. Minnie told the whole story *to us.*
2. Last month, she wrote a letter *to the city council.*
3. She gave *to them* several ideas about summer programs for kids.
4. They offered summer jobs *to Minnie and her classmates.*
5. Together, the class taught many games *to the neighborhood children.*
6. They also offered swimming lessons *for the children.*
7. The city owed many thanks *to Minnie* for her ideas and her organizational skills.
8. The neighborhood parents bought a trophy *for Minnie.*
9. *For Minnie and the swimming coaches,* all the children brought cards and banners.
10. Minnie had given *to the city* a summer of fun.

PREDICATE NOMINATIVES

13d A *subject complement* completes the meaning of a linking verb and identifies or describes the subject.

There are two kinds of subject complements—the *predicate nominative* and the *predicate adjective.*

EXAMPLES Julio is the **leader** of the school jazz band. [*Leader* is the predicate nominative following the linking verb *is*. It identifies the subject *Julio.*]
The sun was **bright** this morning. [*Bright* is the predicate adjective following the linking verb *was*. It describes the subject *sun.*]

REFERENCE NOTE: For more information about linking verbs, see page 109.

13e A *predicate nominative* is a noun or pronoun that follows a linking verb and explains or identifies the subject of the sentence.

Like other subject complements, a predicate nominative may be compound.

EXAMPLES A guanaco is a wild **animal** from South America. [*Animal* is a predicate nominative following the linking verb *is*. It explains the subject *guanaco.*]
Hiroshi became **treasurer** of our club. [*Treasurer* is the predicate nominative following the linking verb *became.* It identifies and explains the subject *Hiroshi.*]
The stars of the show might be **Greg** and **she**. [*Greg* and *she* are compound predicate nominatives following the linking verb *might be*. They identify the subject *stars.*]

Be careful not to confuse a predicate nominative with a direct object. A predicate nominative always follows a linking verb. A direct object always follows an action verb. Also, remember that a predicate nominative is never part of a prepositional phrase.

PREDICATE NOMINATIVE	Felicia is an artist.
DIRECT OBJECT	Felicia paints pictures.
PREPOSITIONAL PHRASE	Felicia may become famous as an artist.

EXERCISE 5 Identifying Predicate Nominatives and Linking Verbs

In each sentence, underline the linking verb once. Underline the predicate nominative twice.

EX. 1. Movies are great entertainment.

1. Al Pacino was the leading actor in that movie.
2. Another great actor is Robert De Niro.
3. Once famous as the star of action movies, Clint Eastwood has become a director.
4. The winner of the 1993 Academy Award for Best Director was he.
5. Rita Moreno is a talented actress, singer, and dancer.
6. Her best movie might be *West Side Story*.
7. Other stars in that movie were Natalie Wood, George Chakiris, and Richard Beymer.
8. *West Side Story* is a modern version of the Shakespearean tragedy *Romeo and Juliet*.
9. Of the many songs in that movie, my favorites were "Tonight" and "Maria."
10. The composer of the music for *West Side Story* was Leonard Bernstein.

EXERCISE 6 Writing Sentences with Predicate Nominatives

Each of the following items is written as an equation. On your own paper, rewrite each one as a sentence with a linking verb and a predicate nominative.

EX. 1. Maria Tallchief = ballerina
1. Maria Tallchief became a famous ballerina.

1. encyclopedia = reference book
2. my best friends = Lisette and Jobelle
3. some industrial gases = argon, nitrogen, helium, neon
4. this rock = granite
5. winners of the award = Mina and I

PREDICATE ADJECTIVES

13f A *predicate adjective* is an adjective that follows a linking verb and describes the subject of the sentence.

Like other complements, a predicate adjective may be compound.

EXAMPLES I felt **proud** about my report. [*Proud* is the predicate adjective that follows the linking verb *felt*. It describes the subject *I*.]
The apple was **red** and **shiny**. [*Red* and *shiny* are the predicate adjectives that follow the linking verb *was*. They describe the subject *apple*.]

EXERCISE 7 Identifying Predicate Adjectives and Linking Verbs

In each sentence below, underline the linking verb once. Underline the predicate adjective twice.

EX. 1. That music seems too loud.

1. The vegetable soup smells good.
2. The sky is cloudy and dark today.
3. Your brother Reza is really funny!
4. During the drought, the lettuce in Sabrina's garden became limp and wilted.
5. The hikers remained brave during the storm.

EXERCISE 8 Writing Sentences with Predicate Adjectives

Use five of the following nouns to write sentences on your own paper. Use each noun as the subject of a sentence. Complete each sentence with a linking verb and a predicate adjective that describes the subject. Underline the predicate adjective in each of your sentences.

EX. 1. traffic
1. The traffic was heavy on the freeway this morning.

1. oranges
2. dog
3. doctor
4. computers
5. Julio
6. soccer
7. dinosaurs
8. English

REVIEW EXERCISE

A. Identifying Direct Objects, Predicate Nominatives, and Predicate Adjectives

On the lines before each sentence, identify the word in italics by writing *d.o.* for *direct object*, *p.n.* for *predicate nominative*, and *p.a.* for *predicate adjective.*

EX. d.o. 1. The Aztec Indians spoke a *language* called "Nahuatl."

_____ 1. They inhabited a *city* called Tenochtitlan, which is now the site of present day Mexico City.

_____ 2. The jewelry and pottery that the Aztecs made were *important* to their trade with other peoples.

_____ 3. Recently, I became the *president* of the Spanish Club at school, and we took a trip to Mexico.

_____ 4. Our plane would have been *late* arriving in Mexico City, but our pilot skillfully avoided the storm.

_____ 5. We bought many *souvenirs* on our trip.

B. Writing Sentences with Complements

On your own paper, write 10 sentences that might be clues for a crossword puzzle about volcanoes. In your sentences, draw a line to show where the complements belong. You may use your science book and other resource books to gather facts. On a second sheet of paper, list the complements that you left out of your sentences. After the complements, write what kinds of complements they are. Trade sentences with a classmate. Use clues in your classmate's sentences to identify complements that will complete the sentences. Write your answers on the lines in the sentences. Above each answer, write what kind of complement it is. When you are finished, exchange papers again with your classmate so that you have your own sentences back.

EX.

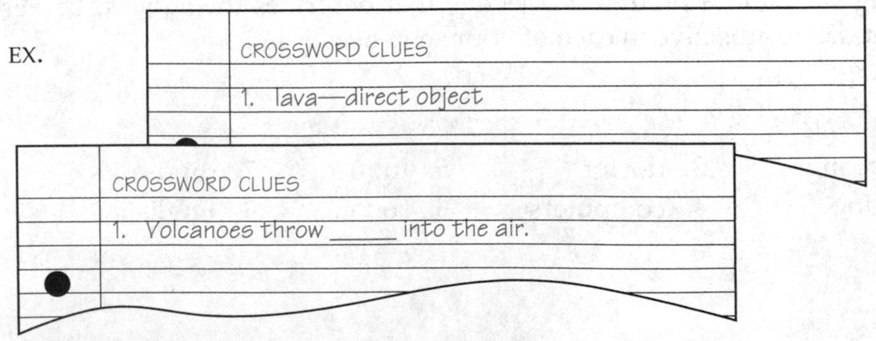

CROSSWORD CLUES
1. lava—direct object
CROSSWORD CLUES
1. Volcanoes throw _____ into the air.

CHAPTER REVIEW

A. Identifying and Classifying Complements

Underline each complement in the sentences below. On the line before each sentence, identify the complement by writing *d.o.* for *direct object, i.o.* for *indirect object, p.n.* for *predicate nominative,* or *p.a.* for *predicate adjective.* Separate your answers with a semicolon. [Remember: Complements may be compound.]

EX. i.o.; d.o. 1. Jack gave me an article about Rachel Davis DuBois.

_______ 1. Rachel Davis DuBois was an important American teacher.

_______ 2. As a Quaker, Dr. DuBois had strong feelings about equality and human rights.

_______ 3. She developed a worldwide program for education and communication.

_______ 4. The basic idea behind her program seemed simple and wise.

_______ 5. She gathered people of different ethnic backgrounds for conversation and sharing.

_______ 6. Through her sessions, people became more knowledgeable about each other.

_______ 7. Knowledge and understanding gave them a better chance for living and working together peacefully.

_______ 8. The name of the program was "Group Conversation."

_______ 9. Some of the people she talked with were Martin Luther King, Jr.; Eleanor Roosevelt; and George Washington Carver.

_______ 10. The NAACP and the State Department have used Dr. DuBois' program both in the United States and throughout the world.

B. Writing Sentences with Complements

Each of the following items is an unfinished sentence. On your own paper, write a complete version of the sentence. Add words to form the type of complement shown in parentheses. Underline the complements in your completed sentences. [Note: Some sentences will require the addition of two complements.]

EX. 1. Ralph gave (indirect object) a (direct object).

1. Ralph gave Julio a ticket to the concert.

1. My favorite singer is (predicate nominative).
2. The river is (compound predicate adjective).
3. Ms. Robinson made (compound indirect object) some (direct object).
4. Two important historical figures are (compound predicate nominative).
5. The weather today is (predicate adjective).

C. Writing a Class Prophecy

You are writing a prophecy for the school yearbook. Your job is to look into the future and tell what careers four of your friends and classmates might have as adults or what activities they might be doing. On your own paper, write brief profiles of four classmates or friends. Use complements in at least three of your sentences. When you have finished each profile, underline and label the complements you have used.

EX. 1. Profile: Saleo is a reporter for the nightly news. She has won two awards for her newscasts.
Complements used: reporter—p.n.; awards—d.o.

PREPOSITIONAL PHRASES

14a A *phrase* is a group of related words that is used as a single part of speech and does not contain both a subject and a verb.

EXAMPLES will be studying [phrase, no subject]
from that country [phrase, no subject or verb]

14b A *prepositional phrase* is a group of words consisting of a preposition, a noun or pronoun that serves as the object of the preposition, and any modifiers of that object.

EXAMPLES The boat **on the water** was swaying.
For this reason, I am trying to finish the race.
Will the wagons go **into the wilderness**?

A preposition is used to show the relationship between a noun or a pronoun and another word in a sentence.

☞ **REFERENCE NOTE:** Prepositions are words like *across, after, by, over,* and *to*. For a list of prepositions, see page 117.

The object of a preposition may be compound.

EXAMPLES Are you going to the concert **with Atul and Mady**?
The judges divided the prize money **between them and us.**

EXERCISE 1 Identifying Prepositions and Prepositional Phrases

Underline the prepositional phrases in the following sentences. Circle the preposition in each phrase.

EX. 1. Children often like shoes with colorful designs.

1. Some people think about comfort when they buy shoes.
2. Others are more interested in a shoe's style and color.
3. Over the years, fashion has influenced shoe styles.
4. Ancient Romans wore high boots with open toes.
5. Only the emperor of Rome could wear purple boots.
6. Did you know that during the Middle Ages soft leather shoes were popular?

7. Lords and ladies walked in wide, floppy shoes.
8. Knights had long toe pieces on their armor.
9. Hip boots gave protection from rough weather.
10. In recent years, sneakers with fancy designs and bright colors have become popular.

EXERCISE 2 Identifying Prepositional Phrases and Objects of Prepositions

Underline the prepositional phrases in the sentences below. Circle the object of the preposition in each phrase.

EX. 1. Jonas and I often go to the park.

1. No one except Rosa completed the assignment.
2. Prizes will be awarded to them tomorrow.
3. The first African American governor of a state was Louisiana's P.B.S. Pinchback.
4. The largest animal in the world is the blue whale.
5. We met many immigrants from Southeast Asia.

EXERCISE 3 Writing Sentences with Prepositional Phrases

On your own paper, write five sentences. Include one of the prepositional phrases below in each sentence. Use each prepositional phrase only once. Underline each phrase.

EX. 1. by the wind
1. The red-and-blue fishing boat was tossed by the wind.

1. under his hat
2. at that moment
3. with brown eyes
4. of the city
5. to the mall

ADJECTIVE PHRASES

14c An adjective phrase modifies a noun or a pronoun.

A prepositional phrase used as an adjective is called an ***adjective phrase.***

ADJECTIVE The **concerned** children participated in a program to help the homeless.

ADJECTIVE PHRASE The children **of Washington Middle School** participated in a program to help the homeless.

Adjective phrases answer the same questions that single-word adjectives answer.

What kind? Which one?
How many? How much?

EXAMPLES I took a photograph **of my aunt**. [The prepositional phrase *of my aunt* is used as an adjective to modify the noun *photograph.* The phrase answers the question *What kind?*]

His sailboat is the one **with the red hull.** [*With the red hull* is used as an adjective to modify the pronoun *one.* The phrase answers the question *Which one?*]

That box **of tapes on the table** is yours. [The two adjective phrases *of tapes* and *on the table* modify the noun *box.* Both phrases answer the question *Which one?*]

The picture **of the girl with the black hair** was sold. [The adjective phrase *of the girl* modifies the noun *picture,* and answers the question *Which one.* The adjective phrase *with the black hair* modifies the noun *girl,* the object of the preposition in the first phrase, and answers the question *Which one?*]

EXERCISE 4 Identifying Adjective Phrases

Underline the adjective phrase in each of the following sentences, and draw an arrow from the phrase to the word it modifies. [Note: A sentence may contain more than one phrase.]

EX. 1. Cesar Chavez was the subject of the news story.

1. The man in the photograph was Cesar Chavez.
2. His contributions to society are well known.

3. A series of migrant labor camps was the scene of his youth.
4. He always wanted better working conditions for migrant farm workers.
5. He believed that dedication to them was important.
6. The grape pickers held a long strike against the California growers.
7. Chavez was one of the strike leaders.
8. Chavez was the organizer of the United Farm Workers.
9. Stories about Chavez's early struggles make interesting reading.
10. Have you read any articles about him?

EXERCISE 5 Identifying Adjective Phrases

Underline the adjective phrases in the paragraph below, and draw an arrow from each phrase to the word that it modifies. [Note: A sentence may contain more than one phrase.]

EX. [1] The waves on the ocean were foamy.

[1] I'll never forget the view of the seaside town. [2] Houses of whitewashed stone lined the winding road to the pier. [3] Children played loudly and bought paper kites with long tails. [4] Later, a boat from one of the islands docked early. [5] Its arrival meant our visit to the island had ended.

EXERCISE 6 Using Adjective Phrases

On your own paper, write four sentences. In each sentence, use one of the phrases below as an adjective phrase. Underline each adjective phrase.

EX. 1. of the supermarket
1. The owner of the supermarket opened the store early.

1. with long legs
2. on the green carpet
3. of South America
4. about sports and medicine
5. between the four students

ADVERB PHRASES

14d An adverb phrase modifies a verb, an adjective, or another adverb.

A prepositional phrase used as an adverb is called an ***adverb phrase.***

ADVERB The shoppers hurried **home.**
ADVERB PHRASE The shoppers hurried **toward the exit.**

Adverb phrases answer the same questions that single-word adverbs answer.

When?	*How?*	*To what extent?*
Where?	*How often?*	*How much?*

EXAMPLES Paris is famous **for its restaurants.** [The adverb phrase *for its restaurants* modifies the adjective *famous,* telling *how.*]
The meeting ran late **into the night.** [The adverb phrase *into the night* modifies the adverb *late,* telling *when* or *how.*]
We planted roses **beside the house.**[The adverb phrase *beside the house* modifies the verb *planted,* telling *where.*]

Notice that, unlike most adjective phrases, adverb phrases can appear at various places in sentences.

EXAMPLE **Beside the house** we planted roses.

EXERCISE 7 Identifying Adverb Phrases

Underline the adverb phrase in each of the following sentences, and draw an arrow to the word it modifies. [Note: A sentence may contain more than one phrase.]

EX. 1. Some birds fly south for the winter.

1. Animal migrations are common in nature.
2. Some animals can travel for long periods.
3. Across northern Canada, caribou migrate often.
4. These large deer live in herds.
5. Each spring, the animals move into open areas and look for food.

6. As winter approaches, the caribou head for the woods.
7. They feed on small plants called lichens.
8. The monarch butterfly looks fragile, but it can fly for great distances.
9. In a single year, some monarchs travel four thousand miles.
10. However, the insects die soon after the long trip.
11. Arctic terns nest near the Arctic Circle.
12. The terns leave for Antarctica in the autumn.
13. With small radios, scientists have mapped the terns' routes.
14. During its lifetime, a tern may travel a million miles or more.
15. A tern's pointed wings carry it over long distances.
16. Canadian geese return to the North when they nest.
17. The geese make their trip in stages.
18. Geese frequently stop at small ponds for food and water.
19. In the air the older birds lead the flock.
20. Young geese usually fly in protected positions.

EXERCISE 8 Using Adverb Phrases

Select five phrases from the group below. On your own paper, use each phrase in a sentence. Underline each adverb phrase once, and underline the word or words each phrase modifies twice.

EX. 1. with great force

1. The hurricane hit the city with great force.

1. in the rain forest
2. with her savings
3. under the old bed
4. at four o'clock
5. by the team
6. after the long movie

REVIEW EXERCISE 1

A. Identifying Prepositional Phrases, Prepositions, and Objects

In the paragraph below, underline the prepositional phrases. In each phrase, draw a second line under the preposition, and circle the object of the preposition. [Note: A sentence may contain more than one prepositional phrase.]

EX. [1] Working with planes can be interesting.

[1] Monday was an important day in Mei-Ling's life. [2] She enlisted in the Air Force. [3] Mei-Ling will soon be stationed near Los Angeles. [4] During the first weeks, she will go through basic training. [5] After that time, she will take several tests to qualify for certain jobs. [6] Mei-Ling will then transfer to a special school. [7] She would like a job in radar. [8] However, she is also considering the field of space medicine. [9] Within a few months, she will be given her choice of assignments. [10] Mei-Ling can then expect to have a long career in the Air Force.

B. Identifying and Classifying Prepositional Phrases

In the sentences below, underline each prepositional phrase, and classify it as an *adjective phrase* or an *adverb phrase* by writing *adj. phr.* or *adv. phr.* on the line before the sentence. Then circle the word or words the phrase modifies.

EX. adj. phr. 1. Do you know anything about space travel?

________ 1. Life in a spacecraft requires much planning.

________ 2. An air conditioner removes carbon dioxide from the air.

________ 3. It also keeps the temperature of the air constant.

________ 4. Weightlessness is a difficult problem for astronauts.

________ 5. On long space missions, astronauts must exercise regularly.

C. Writing Instructions Using Adjective Phrases and Adverb Phrases

You are moving into the house shown on the following floor plan. The moving company will arrive with your furniture while you are away. Even though a friend will unlock the door for the movers, you feel that you need to sketch pictures of the furniture on the floor plan. You also need to leave instructions about where to place the furniture that is listed below.

1. On your own paper, write detailed instructions for the movers.
2. Use at least three adjective phrases and four adverb phrases to describe where you want the movers to place your furniture.
3. Underline and label your phrases *adj.* for adjective phrases and *adv.* for adverb phrases.

EX. Place the dining table in the middle [adv.] of the dining room [adj.]. Put the four dining chairs around the table [adv.]. Center the hutch on the north wall [adv.] of the dining room [adj.].

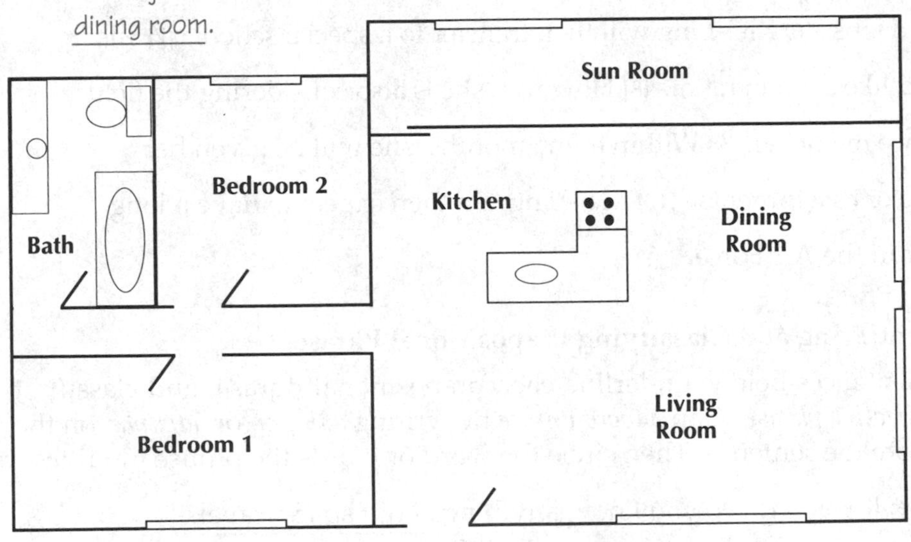

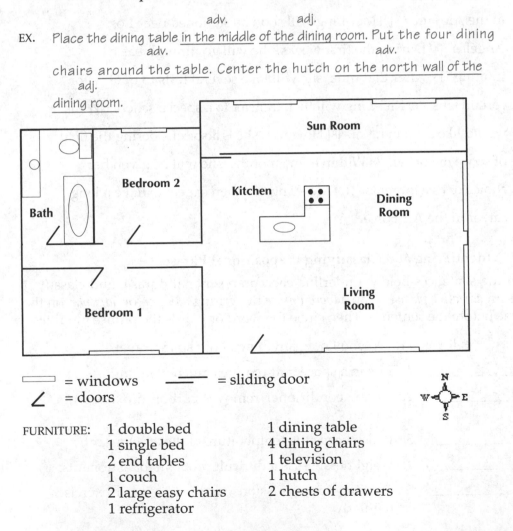

= windows = sliding door

= doors

N W E S

FURNITURE:

1 double bed
1 single bed
2 end tables
1 couch
2 large easy chairs
1 refrigerator
1 dining table
4 dining chairs
1 television
1 hutch
2 chests of drawers

VERB PHRASES AND VERBALS

14e A *verb phrase* combines an action verb or a linking verb with one or more auxiliary, or helping, verbs.

EXAMPLES He **has been swimming** for an hour. [The action verb is *swimming,* and the helping verbs are *has* and *been*.]
I **will buy** a cookbook for my brother. [The action verb is *buy,* and the helping verb is *will*.]
Bernice **should be** the team's captain. [The linking verb is *be,* and the helping verb is *should*.]

The parts of a verb phrase may be separated by other words.

EXAMPLES **Have** you **changed** your mind?
He **did** not **know** the answer.

14f A *verbal* is a verb form used as a noun, an adjective, or an adverb. Do not confuse verbals with verbs.

EXAMPLES **Swimming** is good exercise. [*Swimming* is a verbal used as a noun.]
The **waxed** floors were slippery. [*Waxed* is a verbal used as an adjective to describe *floors*.]
To arrive at daybreak, the emergency supplies must be flown out before ten o'clock. [*To arrive* is a verbal used as an adverb to modify the verb phrase *must be flown*.]

EXERCISE 9 Identifying Verb Phrases and Verbals

Identify the italicized verb phrases and verbals in the following sentences by writing *v.* for verbal or *v. phr.* for verb phrase on the line before the sentence.

EX. __v.__ 1. a. *Eating* watermelon is fun.
__v. phr.__ b. The man *is eating* watermelon for breakfast.

________ 1. a. *Replacing* the food was expensive for the shopkeeper.

________ b. The shopkeepers *were replacing* the food in their stores.

_____________ 2. a. Ethan wants *to shop* at the mall on Saturday.

_____________ b. Ethan *will shop* at the mall on Saturday.

_____________ 3. a. Brook *was giving* the closing speech.

_____________ b. Brook likes *giving* the closing speech.

_____________ 4. a. She *will take* your orders.

_____________ b. By *taking* our orders, she helped the hostess.

_____________ 5. a. *Losing* the dogs' leashes caused many problems for the trainers.

_____________ b. The trainers *have lost* the dogs' leashes.

EXERCISE 10 Using Verb Phrases and Verbals

Use the verb given before each pair of sentences to create a verb phrase and a verbal that will complete the meaning of the sentences. Remember to add helping verbs to create verb phrases.

EX. rest 1. a. The resting dog stretched its back feet.

b. The team is resting before the last match.

drive 1. a. Mr. Torres _________________ his new car last night.

b. The _________________ rain caused floods in the valley.

hide 2. a. The boys looked for hours for the _________________ toy.

b. For this game, Miriam _________________ under the bed.

lose 3. a. The _________________ earring was found by Maria.

b. We _________________ money on this project.

cook 4. a. Aunt Salema _________________ the dinner this year.

b. We all enjoyed the juicy, _________________ meat.

worry 5. a. _________________ is simply a waste of time.

b. The students _________________ about their tests.

PARTICIPLES AND PARTICIPIAL PHRASES

THE PARTICIPLE

14g A *participle* is a verb form that can be used as an adjective.

There are two kinds of participles: *present participles* and *past participles.*

(1) ***Present participles* end in *–ing.***

EXAMPLES The detective searched for the **missing** necklace. [*Missing* is the present participle of the verb *miss.* The participle modifies the noun *necklace.*]

The **barking** dogs chased the truck. [*Barking* is the present participle of the verb *bark.*] The participle acts as an adjective modifying the noun *dogs.*]

(2) ***Past participles* usually end in *–d* or *–ed.***

EXAMPLES When he saw the **broken** bat, Spiro cried. [The irregular past participle *broken* modifies the noun *bat.*]

Disliked by the public, the television show was canceled. [The past participle *Disliked* modifies the noun *show.*]

 **REFERENCE NOTE:** Some past participles are irregularly formed. See the list of irregular verbs on pages 193–194.

EXERCISE 11 Identifying Participles and the Words They Modify

Underline the participles used as adjectives in the following sentences. Then circle the noun or pronoun each participle modifies.

EX. 1. The (children) didn't hear their friends <u>calling</u> them.

1. A fallen tree blocked our path.
2. The tourist next to us took a photograph of the setting sun.
3. The men searched the ruins for the buried treasure of the Pharaohs.
4. Deep in the jungle the explorers found a deserted village.
5. Mr. Ling held the winning ticket in his hand.

PARTICIPIAL PHRASES

14h A *participial phrase* consists of a participle together with its modifiers and complements. The entire phrase is used as an adjective.

A participial phrase should be placed close to the word it modifies. Otherwise, the phrase may appear to modify another word, and the sentence may not make sense.

EXAMPLES **Humming softly**, she swept the sidewalk. [The participle *humming* is modified by the adverb *softly*. *Humming softly* is used as an adjective to modify the subject *she*.]

The directions, **written in Spanish**, were difficult for me to read. [The participle *written* is modified by the prepositional phrase *in Spanish*. *Written in Spanish* is used as an adjective to modify the subject *directions*.]

EXERCISE 12 Identifying Participial Phrases

Underline the participial phrase in each of the sentences below. Then draw an arrow from the phrase to the word or words that each phrase modifies.

EX. 1. Two cowboys, riding on a snowy day, discovered Mesa Verde.

1. The ruins, lining the canyons, seemed to rise out of the rock.
2. Dating from the thirteenth century, they remain a wonderful sight.
3. The ruins, known as pueblos, were home to the Anasazi, ancestors of today's Pueblo Indians.
4. Developing their skills, the people became expert stoneworkers.
5. The people, working hard, built their homes in rocky terrain.
6. Chaco Canyon's Pueblo Bonita, started in A.D. 920, had several hundred rooms.
7. Pueblo Bonita was five stories high with ladders connecting each level.
8. The Anasazi, using dry-land farming, raised beans and squash.
9. A drought lasting for many years may have forced them to move.
10. Abandoning these homes, the Anasazi moved to new villages south and east of their earlier dwellings.

INFINITIVES AND INFINITIVE PHRASES

THE INFINITIVE

14i An *infinitive* is a verb form, usually preceded by *to*, that can be used as a noun, an adjective, or an adverb.

EXAMPLES I want **to try.** [*To try* is an infinitive used as a noun. It is the direct object of the verb *want*.]

Anna is the one **to ask.** [*To ask* is an infinitive used as an adjective. It modifies the pronoun *one*.]

Are you well enough **to run?** [*To run* is an infinitive used as an adverb. It modifies the adverb *enough*.]

To plus a noun or a pronoun (*to Jaime, to me*) is a prepositional phrase, not an infinitive.

EXERCISE 13 Identifying Infinitives

Underline the infinitive in the sentences below.

EX. 1. Is this game easy to play?

1. Would you like to travel on a boat, far away across the sea?
2. Having large brains, dolphins are quick to learn.
3. To leave so early during the performance would be rude.
4. Those are the poems to memorize for speech class.
5. To prepare for the test, Hala studied for two hours.
6. How expensive is this bicycle tire to repair?
7. To escape the snarling lion was Nora's only thought.
8. Wong needs to practice his part for the play.
9. To succeed, you must study every day.
10. It was exciting to read the novel by Margaret Craven.

INFINITIVE PHRASES

14j An *infinitive phrase* consists of an infinitive together with its modifiers and complements. The entire phrase may be used as a noun, an adjective, or an adverb.

EXAMPLE **To design a computer program** takes skill. [The infinitive phrase is used as a noun. The infinitive *to design* has a complement, *a computer program*.]

Which is the best stroller **to buy for a baby**? [The infinitive phrase is used as an adjective to modify the noun *stroller*. The infinitive *to buy* is modified by the prepositional phrase *for a baby*.]

It was exciting **to win at chess yesterday**. [The infinitive phrase is used as an adverb to modify the adjective *exciting*. The infinitive *to win* is modified by the prepositional phrase *at chess* and by the adverb *yesterday*.]

EXERCISE 14 Identifying Infinitive Phrases

Underline the infinitive phrase in each of the sentences below.

EX. [1] Lizards are interesting to study in school.

[1] Lizards are able to protect themselves in many ways. [2] Some lizards seem to match their surroundings. [3] The chameleon, for instance, likes to change its color for protection. [4] Other lizards like to play tricks on their enemies. [5] For example, some lizards will break off their tails to escape their enemies. [6] To replace their old tails, these lizards grow new ones. [7] A third way lizards defend themselves is to fly short distances. [8] The so-called flying dragon seems to sail from tree limb to tree limb. [9] Several lizards will fight to defend themselves. [10] One of these fighters, the monitor, thrashes its tail to whip its enemy.

REVIEW EXERCISE 2

A. Identifying and Classifying Participles and Infinitives

Underline the verbal in each sentence. Then label it participle or infinitive by writing *part.* or *inf.* on the line before the sentence.

EX. __inf.__ 1. Are you ready to go?

______ 1. Exhausted, the hikers walked slowly into the camp.

______ 2. Do you know the name of the person to interview?

______ 3. The relay racers need time to rest.

______ 4. Gloria put the frozen dinner into the oven.

______ 5. The laughing children enjoyed the playfulness of the harp seals.

______ 6. To succeed requires determination.

______ 7. Most of the questions were easy to answer.

______ 8. Broken glass was all over the cellar floor.

______ 9. The librarian will help you to find a book about turtles.

______ 10. Soccer can be a challenging sport.

B. Identifying and Classifying Participial and Infinitive Phrases

In each of the following sentences, underline the participial phrase or the infinitive phrase. On the line before the sentence, label each phrase by writing *part. phr.* for a participial phrase or *inf. phr.* for an infinitive phrase.

EX. __part. phr.__ 1. Singing the song, the children marched in the parade.

__________ 1. Jupiter takes almost twelve Earth years to circle the sun once.

__________ 2. It is hard to imagine a world like Jupiter.

__________ 3. Covered by thick clouds, its atmosphere is almost entirely liquid hydrogen.

__________ 4. The clouds, swirling constantly, form colorful belts or zones.

__________ 5. The Great Red Spot, discovered three hundred years ago, lies near its equator.

__________ 6. According to astronomers, the red spot seems to vary in color.

__________ 7. From Earth it is impossible to photograph the surface of Jupiter.

__________ 8. The Pioneer and Voyager series spacecrafts were launched to get a close-up view of the planet.

__________ 9. Moving at great speeds, the spaceships traveled for more than a year.

__________ 10. To reach the distant planet was an incredible accomplishment.

C. Writing a Paragraph Using Participial Phrases and Infinitive Phrases

As part of a social studies project, your classmates are compiling a photo album of your community. You want to include a photograph and a description of your favorite place in the community. On your own paper, make a chart such as the one that you see here. Answer the following questions about this place for prewriting. Include either infinitive phrases or participial phrases in some of your answers. Underline and label each phrase. Then use your prewriting notes to write a first draft of a paragraph describing the place.

QUESTIONS	RESPONSES
Where is this place?	beside the river; across the city bridge
Why is it special to you?	It's where I used to fish with my friends (inf.: to fish with my friends)
What sounds do you hear?	loudly chirping birds; cars honking at people (part.: loudly chirping birds; part.: honking at people)
What do you see?	tall oak trees bending over; clear blue water (part.: bending over)

CHAPTER 14: THE PHRASE

CHAPTER REVIEW

A. Identifying Prepositions, Objects, and the Words Modified

In each of the sentences below, find all of the prepositional phrases. Underline the preposition, and circle the object of the preposition. Then, on the line before each sentence, write the word or words the phrase modifies. [Note: A sentence may contain more than one phrase.]

EX. liked 1. On the farm Mr. Orizini liked milking the cows.

_______ 1. Pioneer women made colorful quilts from fabric scraps.

_______ 2. A huge bowl of fruits decorated the table.

_______ 3. We often climb the hill behind our house.

_______ 4. During World War I, armies dug long trenches.

_______ 5. Some cacti can live for years without any water.

_______ 6. Early in the morning, we see Pedro jogging.

_______ 7. The difference between a toad and a frog is obvious.

_______ 8. A triangle is a polygon with three sides.

_______ 9. Instead of paste, please buy paper.

_______ 10. Holland is famous for its tulips.

B. Identifying Phrases

In the sentences below, underline all verbal phrases, and circle all prepositional phrases. [Note: A sentence may contain more than one phrase.]

EX. 1. Tourists love to visit Switzerland in the winter.

1. The Swiss mountains are popular spots for hot-air balloon trips.
2. Balloonists travel together on an adventurous trip.
3. Guided by wind currents, the balloon glides over the mountain.
4. To float over the snow-clad Alps is a marvelous experience.
5. Never miss the opportunity to make a hot-air balloon flight.

C. Identifying Phrases

Underline the prepositional, participial, and infinitive phrases in the paragraph below. Label these phrases *prep. phr.* for prepositional, *part. phr.* for participial, or *inf. phr.* for infinitive. [Note: In this exercise, "writing" is used as a noun, not a participle.]

prep. phr. inf. phr.

EX. [1] Early civilizations used types of symbols to represent words.

[1] To record language was a major step in civilization's development. [2] The Sumerians used the earliest system of true writing about five thousand years ago. [3] Living in Mesopotamia, the Sumerians carefully pressed tools into wet clay tablets to make impressions. [4] This type of writing, known as cuneiform, was later refined by the Babylonians. [5] Today, scholars study cuneiform to learn the history of the Sumerians.

INDEPENDENT AND SUBORDINATE CLAUSES

15a A *clause* is a group of words that contains a verb and its subject and is used as a part of a sentence.

Every clause contains a subject and a verb. However, not all clauses express complete thoughts.

15b An *independent* (or *main*) *clause* expresses a complete thought and can stand by itself as a sentence.

EXAMPLES Gloria tied her sneakers.
She wore a red jersey.

When an independent clause stands alone, it is called a sentence. Usually, the term *independent clause* is used only when such a clause is joined with another clause.

SENTENCE She leaped over the hurdle.
INDEPENDENT CLAUSE When she reached the turn, **she leaped over the hurdle.**

15c A *subordinate* (or *dependent*) *clause* does not express a complete thought and cannot stand alone.

A subordinate clause must be joined with at least one independent clause to express a complete thought. Notice that words such as *since, that,* and *if* signal the beginning of a subordinate clause.

SUBORDINATE CLAUSES since we moved here
that you will like
if the night is clear

SENTENCES **Since we moved here,** I have learned to ski.
Ralph rented a movie **that you will like.**
If the night is clear, you will see shooting stars.

EXERCISE 1 Identifying Independent and Subordinate Clauses

For each of the following sentences, identify the italicized clause by writing *indep.* for independent or *sub.* for subordinate on the line before the sentence.

EX. sub. 1. Please bring your camera *when you visit.*

_____ 1. The tomatoes, *which we grew ourselves,* taste wonderful.

_____ 2. *Jennifer bought that dog* when it was just a puppy.

_____ 3. This is Diego, *whose sister you met yesterday.*

_____ 4. *If you need more paper,* I can loan you some.

_____ 5. *Rain has fallen every weekend* since I bought my skates.

_____ 6. When the plane lands, *please stay in your seats.*

_____ 7. The door opened *as we walked up the stairs.*

_____ 8. *You can talk to Mr. Shankar* before class starts.

_____ 9. *The instrument* that you heard *is an oboe.*

_____ 10. Because you read quickly, *you can finish this story in an evening.*

EXERCISE 2 Writing Sentences with Subordinate Clauses

Add independent clauses to the following subordinate clauses to create sentences. Write your sentences on the lines after each clause. Underline the independent clause in each sentence.

EX. 1. because it is gold ______________________________

The statue will never rust because it is gold.

1. who wrote this report ______________________________

____

2. when you're ready ______________________________

____

3. as the winners were announced ______________________________

____

4. if you want tickets to the concert ______________________________

____

THE ADJECTIVE CLAUSE

15d An *adjective clause* is a subordinate clause that modifies a noun or a pronoun.

Like an adjective or an adjective phrase, an adjective clause may modify a noun or a pronoun. Unlike an adjective phrase, an adjective clause contains a verb and its subject.

ADJECTIVE a **big** computer

ADJECTIVE PHRASE a computer **with a big screen** [does not have a verb and its subject]

ADJECTIVE CLAUSE a computer **that has a big screen** [does have a verb and its subject]

An adjective clause usually follows the noun or pronoun it modifies and tells *which one* or *what kind*.

EXAMPLES The girl **who reported to the teacher** is my cousin. [The adjective clause modifies the noun *girl,* telling *which one.*]
I want a jacket **that zips up the front**. [The adjective clause modifies the noun *jacket,* telling *what kind.*]

An adjective clause is almost always introduced by a *relative pronoun.*

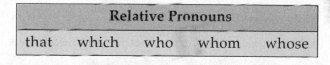

Relative Pronouns				
that	which	who	whom	whose

EXERCISE 3 Identifying Adjective Clauses

Underline the adjective clause in each of the following sentences.

EX. 1. I played baseball, which is my favorite sport.

1. Maria Tallchief is the ballerina whom you saw.
2. The conductor, who looked familiar, was a friend of my sister.
3. This is the store that is having the sale on blank tapes.
4. The photograph, which was taken in 1953, looks faded now.
5. The person whose name you have picked will be your partner.
6. At last, the surgeon, who looked tired, finished the operation.

7. The wok that I'm using belongs to Tanya.
8. I got a stain on this sweater, which belongs to my older sister.
9. Ralph Ellison is the author whom we met.
10. The keyboard that looks different is a new design.

EXERCISE 4 Identifying Adjective Clauses and Relative Pronouns

Underline the adjective clause in each of the following sentences. Draw a second line under the relative pronoun that begins the clause.

EX. 1. The woman whose biography you read was a great singer.

1. This is the first opera that I've seen.
2. The baritone is the man whose voice you hear.
3. The story, which is complicated, is explained in the program.
4. This is the character whom you saw in the first act.
5. All the songs that you heard were written by Scott Joplin.
6. The person who replaced the singer was Martina Arroyo.
7. Mr. Topin gave me a book that tells the plot of this opera.
8. One section of the stage, which moves up and down, creates that special effect.
9. The man who designed the sets is Mr. Virgli.
10. The music that you recognized is the theme song of a movie.

EXERCISE 5 Combining Sentences by Using Adjective Clauses

On your own paper, rewrite each set of sentences below by making the second sentence into an adjective clause and attaching it to the first sentence. Use the relative pronoun given in parentheses to begin the clause.

EX. 1. I have the book. The book belongs to Mei-Ling. (*that*)
1. I have the book that belongs to Mei-Ling.

1. The runner is being interviewed. The runner won the race. (*who*)
2. Aunt Sylvia is a talented woman. I admire her. (*whom*)
3. Here is the soup. The soup is my favorite part of the meal. (*which*)
4. We studied an animal. The animal is extinct. (*that*)

THE ADVERB CLAUSE

15e An *adverb clause* is a subordinate clause that modifies a verb, an adjective or another adverb.

Like an adverb or an adverb phrase, an adverb clause may modify a verb, an adjective, or an adverb. Unlike an adverb phrase, an adverb clause contains a verb and its subject.

ADVERB **Once,** Carl appeared in a movie.

ADVERB PHRASE **As a young boy,** Carl appeared in a movie. [does not have a verb and its subject]

ADVERB CLAUSE **When Carl was younger,** he appeared in a movie. [does have a verb and its subject]

An adverb clause answers one of the following questions: *How? When? Where? Why? To what extent? How much? How long?* or *Under what conditions?*

EXAMPLES This statue looks **as if it were alive.** [The adverb clause tells how the statue looks.]

Before you go, look at this mobile. [The adverb clause tells *when* to look.]

The artist collected shells **wherever she traveled.** [The adverb clause tells *where* she collected shells.]

Because maple is a light wood, it goes well with ebony. [The adverb clause tells *why* maple goes well with ebony.]

We can see the whole exhibit **if we stay until five.** [The adverb clause tells *under what conditions* we can see the whole exhibit.]

Notice in these examples that adverb clauses may be placed in various positions in sentences. When an adverb clause comes at the beginning of a sentence, it is usually followed by a comma.

 **REFERENCE NOTE:** See page 267 for more about punctuating introductory adverb clauses.

Adverb clauses begin with *subordinating conjunctions.*

Common Subordinating Conjunctions			
after	as soon as	in order that	until
although	as though	since	when
as	because	so that	whenever
as if	before	than	where
as long as	how	though	wherever

Some subordinating conjunctions, such as *after, as, before, since,* and *until,* may also be used as prepositions.

EXERCISE 6 Identifying Adverb Clauses

Underline the adverb clause in each of the sentences below.

EX. 1. When I read about astronomy, I get excited.

1. Since I was in the first grade, I have been interested in space.
2. I read as much as I can about the planets.
3. I learned an interesting fact while I was reading about Pluto.
4. Before astronomers discovered Pluto's moon in 1978, they had not known the planet's size.
5. Although Pluto is tiny, it has a moon.
6. Because the planet is small, it has little gravitational pull on its neighbors, Uranus and Neptune.
7. Scientists know little about Pluto's surface because the planet is so far from the earth.
8. However, Neptune and Uranus wobble in orbit as if some other small planet were nearby.
9. Unless scientists develop stronger telescopes, people may never see this planet.
10. When space probes fly near Pluto, astronomers will be able to learn more interesting facts about the planet.

CHAPTER REVIEW

A. Identifying and Classifying Independent and Subordinate Clauses

Decide whether each of the following clauses is independent or subordinate. On the line before each clause, write *indep.* if the clause is independent or *sub.* if it is subordinate.

EX. indep. 1. the mahouts in India know a special language
sub. 2. because they work with elephants

_____ 1. wherever elephants are used to perform work

_____ 2. a mahout rides on the elephant's head

_____ 3. while the mahout gives the animal commands

_____ 4. since an elephant may understand dozens of commands

_____ 5. an elephant can lift heavy lumber

_____ 6. because the mahout's orders are given in a special language

_____ 7. whenever a mahout works with an elephant

_____ 8. these words are used only with elephants

_____ 9. although it may be an ancient Indian language

_____ 10. unless someone records this special language soon

B. Identifying and Classifying Subordinate Clauses

Underline the subordinate clause in each of the following sentences. On the line before each sentence, write *adj.* if the clause is an adjective clause or *adv.* if the clause is an adverb clause.

EX. adv. 1. When you want to communicate with distant relatives, you can use a telephone.

_____ 1. People used other methods of communication before they had telephones.

_____ 2. At one time, people probably used hollow logs that they hit with sticks.

_____ 3. The sound traveled to people who lived far away.

_____ 4. Later, they hit drums that were made from animal skin.

_____ 5. Because the drums were different shapes and sizes, they made different sounds.

______ 6. Although sound was used by some people, other people used smoke signals.

______ 7. This was one method that some Chinese, Egyptians, and Native Americans used.

______ 8. However, smoke signals were hard to see if they were sent at night.

______ 9. After electricity was discovered, many new forms of communication appeared.

______10. Today, many people who work in large companies communicate by computer.

C. Writing Notes for an Oral Report

You have just returned from a trip to Egypt. While there, you explored the pyramids. Now you are preparing to give an oral report called "The Building of the Pyramids at Gîza." You need to prepare good notes to use during your report.

1. Gather information from an encyclopedia or another reference book.
2. On your own paper, write notes on the following topics: where the pyramids are located; what they look like; and how, why, and when they were built. In your notes, use five adjective clauses and five adverb clauses.
3. Underline and label the adjective and adverb clauses that you use.

EX. Gîza—pyramid that I liked best (adjective)
Before we went there, Cairo for the night (adverb)
Called the Great Pyramid
Built to honor King Khufu, who was called Cheops by Greeks (adjective)

SIMPLE SENTENCES

16a A *simple sentence* has one independent clause and no subordinate clauses.

☞ **REFERENCE NOTE:** For more information on independent and subordinate clauses, see page 151.

EXAMPLES **Teresa**[s] **ordered**[v] a new tape recorder from a catalog.

Behind the house **grew**[v] a small oak **tree**[s].

A simple sentence may have a compound subject, a compound verb, or both.

EXAMPLES Both **vitamins**[s] and **minerals**[s] **are**[v] important to your health. [compound subject]

Jorge[s] **studied**[v] all of the facts and then **made**[v] his decision. [compound verb]

The **plumber**[s] and her **helper**[s] **replaced**[v] the faucet and **fixed**[v] the leak. [compound subject and compound verb]

EXERCISE 1 Identifying Subjects and Verbs in Simple Sentences

Underline the subject once and the verb twice in the following sentences. [Note: Some sentences may have a compound subject, a compound verb, or both.]

EX. 1. South America is about twice the size of the United States but has about the same number of people.

1. High mountains and tropical forests provide variety in the continent's climate.
2. The Andes Mountains separate Chile and Argentina.
3. The highest point in South America is Aconcagua.
4. Brazil's coastline stretches more than four thousand miles.
5. In South America, most people speak Spanish or Portuguese and belong to the Roman Catholic Church.

6. Manufacturing and mining in South America have grown rapidly in this century and have become vital to the economy.
7. Plantations, farms, and ranches cover vast areas of the continent and employ about a third of all South Americans.
8. Coffee and bananas are two of the major crops of South America.
9. South America exports minerals and agricultural products and imports many manufactured goods.
10. Silver and copper are among South America's mineral exports.
11. Many different animals and birds live in the Amazon basin.
12. The capybara grows to four feet and is the world's largest rodent.
13. South America's largest snake, the anaconda, lives near water and swims in the rivers.
14. On the Galapagos Islands live giant turtles.
15. The hoglike tapir, about the size of a pony, is South America's largest wild animal.

EXERCISE 2 Writing Simple Sentences

On the lines below, write five simple sentences. In your sentences, use a compound subject, a compound verb, and both a compound subject and a compound verb. Underline all subjects once and all verbs twice.

EX. 1. My friends and I ate lunch and then went to a movie.

1. ______________________________

2. ______________________________

3. ______________________________

4. ______________________________

5. ______________________________

COMPOUND SENTENCES

16b A *compound sentence* has two or more independent clauses and no subordinate clauses.

EXAMPLE Chi Chen plays the trombone, and Mavis plays the saxophone. [*Chi Chen plays the trombone* and *Mavis plays the saxophone* are independent clauses.]

The independent clauses of a compound sentence are usually joined by a comma and a coordinating conjunction (*and, but, or, nor, for, so,* or *yet*).

EXAMPLE My aunt lost her keys**, but** luckily I had an extra set.

The independent clauses of a compound sentence may be joined by a semicolon.

EXAMPLE Rachel Carson was the author of *Silent Spring***;** she also worked for the U.S. Fish and Wildlife Service.

The independent clauses may also be joined by a semicolon and a conjunctive adverb or a transitional expression, which is followed by a comma.

EXAMPLE Gary Soto thought his first poems were awkward**; therefore,** he worked hard to improve his writing.

EXERCISE 3 Identifying Parts of Compound Sentences

Underline the subject once and the verb twice in each of the following independent clauses. Then circle each coordinating conjunction, semicolon, or conjunctive adverb.

EX. 1. Scientists discovered prehistoric cave paintings, (and) they also found stone tools and animal bones in caves.

1. Prehistoric people could not record history, for they had not invented writing.
2. Early people in cold climates made clothing from animal skins, yet the people could not stay warm enough without fires.
3. Ice sheets lowered sea levels; as a result, people traveled between regions on land bridges.

4. A gradual warming trend melted the ice sheets, so the seas began to cover the land bridges.
5. Hunters often built shelters at campsites, for their group would live for several weeks near a large source of food.
6. A campsite would be divided into sections; the group used some areas for preparing food, and other areas were used for sleeping.
7. Some campsites had garbage heaps, and these give scientists clues about tools, clothing, and food.
8. Many tools were made from stone; others were made of bone and wood.
9. Farming was not developed until around 10,000 B.C., so early people hunted animals and collected wild plants for food.
10. The first farmers grew crops, yet they still hunted for food.
11. Prehistoric hunters probably lived in groups of twenty-five to fifty persons, and each group consisted of several families.
12. The families shared the work of the group, but not all of the group's members hunted for food.
13. A hunting group moved from place to place, yet it rarely met another group.
14. Hunters developed new weapons and methods; therefore, larger animals could be captured and killed.
15. Scientists have pieced together a story of early human development, but many questions are still unanswered.

EXERCISE 4 Writing Compound Sentences

On your own paper, write five compound sentences. Use a semicolon to join the independent clauses of your first sentence. Use the conjunctive adverb *therefore* in your second sentence. In your last three sentences, use the coordinating conjunctions *but, for,* and *or*. Underline all subjects once and all verbs twice.

EX. 1. I take the bus to school, but my older sister drives.

A *compound sentence* is different from a simple sentence with a compound subject, or a compound verb, or both.

SIMPLE SENTENCE **Nicholas**(s) **went**(v) to Rome in April and **stayed**(v) at a small hotel near the Forum. [single subject and compound verb]

COMPOUND SENTENCE **Nicholas**(s) **went**(v) to Rome in April, and **he**(s) **stayed**(v) at a small hotel near the Forum. [Both independent clauses have a single subject and a single verb.]

SIMPLE SENTENCE **Hisoka**(s) and **Tamara**(s) **bought**(v) some sandpaper and **refinished**(v) the top of the table. [compound subject and compound verb]

COMPOUND SENTENCE **Hisoka**(s) and **Tamara**(s) **bought**(v) some sandpaper; later **they**(s) **refinished**(v) the top of the table. [The first independent clause has a compound subject and a single verb. The second independent clause has a single subject and a single verb.]

EXERCISE 5 Distinguishing Compound Sentences from Compound Subjects or Compound Verbs

Identify each of the following sentences as either simple or compound. Write *simp.* for simple or *comp.* for compound on the line before the sentence. Then underline each subject once and each verb twice.

EX. comp. 1. The mosque is a place of worship; the Muslim community goes there to recite prayers.

simp. 2. A mosque may be a small tower or may include several buildings.

_____ 1. Male Muslims pray at the mosque on Fridays, and these special Friday mosques are often large buildings.

_____ 2. A courtyard and a prayer hall usually are important features of a Friday mosque.

_____ 3. The prayer hall has no seats; it has carpets instead.

_____ 4. The call to prayer at first was delivered from the roof of a house but now comes from a minaret, or tower.

_____ 5. Every mosque has at least one minaret, and some have as many as six.

_____ 6. Syria and western Islamic countries have square minarets; those in southwest Asia have spiral shapes.

_____ 7. The builders of some mosques imitated Christian churches and often used columns from older buildings.

_____ 8. Many mosques have rich decorations, but none have pictures of humans or animals.

_____ 9. Flowers and geometrical designs are permitted and often ornament the walls.

_____ 10. Some mosques combine domes with several slender minarets; Istanbul has a mosque in that style.

EXERCISE 6 Writing Simple Sentences and Compound Sentences

On the lines below, write simple and compound sentences. Follow the guidelines below. Underline each subject once and each verb twice.

EX. 1. compound sentence with a compound subject in the second independent clause

1. Basketball tryouts are tomorrow, but Mara and Devon will be out of town.

1. simple sentence with a compound subject ______________________

____

2. simple sentence with a compound verb ______________________

____

3. simple sentence with a compound subject and a compound verb

____

____

4. compound sentence with a compound subject in the first independent clause ______________________

____

5. compound sentence with a compound verb in the second independent clause ______________________

____

COMPLEX SENTENCES

16c A *complex sentence* has one independent clause and at least one subordinate clause.

Two kinds of subordinate clauses are adjective clauses and adverb clauses. *Adjective clauses* usually begin with relative pronouns, such as *who, whose, which,* and *that. Adverb clauses* begin with subordinating conjunctions, such as *after, as, because, if, since, so that,* and *when.*

EXAMPLES The student **who designed the stage set** is in my theater class. [complex sentence with an adjective clause]

Although Columbus made four trips to the Americas, he never set foot on the North American mainland. [complex sentence with an adverb clause]

If you want to make a tortilla, you need a very fine grade of cornmeal, **which is called *masa harina* in Mexico.** [complex sentence with an adverb clause and an adjective clause]

REFERENCE NOTE: For more information on adjective clauses, see pages 153. For more information on adverb clauses, see pages 155–156.

EXERCISE 7 Identifying Subordinate Clauses

Underline the subordinate clause in each of the following sentences. Then circle the subordinating conjunction or the relative pronoun that begins the subordinate clause.

EX. 1. The white oak is a valuable tree because its wood is used for floors and furniture.

1. Native Americans who ate the acorns of the tree taught the European settlers about its importance as a food source.
2. The white oak, which can grow to a height of one hundred feet, is the state tree of Connecticut.
3. The people of the state chose the tree because it played an important role in the early history of the Connecticut colony.
4. In 1662, Charles II, who was king of England, granted a charter to the colony.

5. The charter that Charles II gave the colony served as the state's constitution until 1818.

6. Sir Edmund Andros, who was the governor of the Dominion of New England, tried to seize control of Connecticut.

7. When he arrived in Connecticut in 1687, he demanded the charter.

8. Since the colonists valued their freedom, they refused his demands.

9. Settlers hid the charter in the trunk of a white oak, which is now called the Charter Oak.

10. Although historians are not sure of all the facts, the story of the Charter Oak is always included in the history of Connecticut.

EXERCISE 8 Writing Complex Sentences

On the lines below, write five complex sentences. In your sentences, use subordinate clauses that begin with *because, when, though, who,* and *which.* Underline the subordinate clause in each sentence.

EX. 1. When Roscoe finished his report, he returned his reference books to the school library.

1. ______________________________

2. ______________________________

3. ______________________________

4. ______________________________

5. ______________________________

CHAPTER 16: SENTENCE STRUCTURE

CHAPTER REVIEW

A. Identifying and Classifying Independent and Subordinate Clauses

In the following sentences, underline each independent clause once and each subordinate clause twice.

EX. 1. Tet, which is the Vietnamese New Year, is a time of family gatherings and great celebration.

1. Jim Thorpe, who was a Native American, was one of the greatest athletes of all time.
2. Before Isabel gave her story to the editor, she proofread it.
3. As we watched the last few minutes of the game, the quarterback threw the ball down the field for a touchdown.
4. Robert Moses was commissioner of New York parks when the Verrazano-Narrows Bridge was built.
5. Because heavy winds whipped up the water in the bay, we headed for the harbor.
6. My brother pointed the remote control at the television set while he switched from channel to channel.
7. Although the grand piano was invented more than one hundred years ago, its overall shape has not changed.
8. Oases, which are fertile areas in the desert, vary in size.
9. Charlene wants a job this summer so that she can start saving money for college.
10. Jupiter, which is the fifth planet from the sun, is the largest planet in the solar system.

B. Identifying Simple, Compound, and Complex Sentences

Identify each of the following sentences as simple, compound, or complex. On the line before the sentence, write *simp.* for simple, *comp.* for compound, or *cx.* for complex .

EX. __cx.__ 1. While people have used many kinds of clocks, all clocks have been used to tell time.

________ 1. Before clocks were invented, people studied the motions of the stars at night and checked the shadows on their sundials during the day.

_________ 2. Early Egyptians used water clocks, but in another early timepiece, the hourglass, sand was used.

_________ 3. The water clock was a clay bowl or glass jar with a scale of markings on its side.

_________ 4. As the water ran out, the water that was left in the jar marked the time.

_________ 5. The hourglass had two glass bulbs that were joined at a small opening.

_________ 6. The grains of sand flowed from the top bulb to the bottom bulb in about one hour.

_________ 7. The first mechanical clocks in Western civilization, which were invented during the late 1200s, had no hands.

_________ 8. Because the clock had no hands, it told the time with chiming bells.

_________ 9. In the mid-1300s, Western inventors added an hour hand and a dial to the mechanical clock.

_________10. By the 1920s, many homes had electric clocks; digital clocks gained popularity in the 1970s.

C. Writing Simple, Compound, and Complex Sentences

On your own paper, write five sentences. Follow the guidelines below.

EX. 1. a simple sentence with a compound verb
1. Rosa sawed the boards and nailed them in place.

1. a simple sentence
2. a simple sentence with a compound subject and a compound verb
3. a compound sentence with two independent clauses joined by the coordinating conjunction *and*
4. a compound sentence with two independent clauses joined by the coordinating conjunction *but*
5. a complex sentence

AGREEMENT OF SUBJECT AND VERB

Number is the form of a word that indicates whether the word is singular or plural.

17a When a word refers to one person, place, thing, or idea, it is *singular* in number. When a word refers to more than one, it is *plural* in number.

17b A verb agrees with its subject in number.

Two words *agree* when they have the same number. The number of a verb must always agree with the number of its subject.

(1) Singular subjects take singular verbs.

EXAMPLE The **flag flies** on holidays. [The singular verb *flies* agrees with the singular subject *flag*.]

(2) Plural subjects take plural verbs.

EXAMPLE Some **trees change** color in the fall. [The plural verb *change* agrees with the plural subject *trees*.]

When a sentence contains a verb phrase, the first helping verb in the verb phrase agrees with the subject.

EXAMPLES		
	The **turtle is** racing.	The **flight has** been postponed.
	The **turtles are** racing.	The **flights have** been postponed.

 **REFERENCE NOTE:** Most nouns ending in *–s* are plural (*trees, animals*). Most verbs ending in *–s* are singular (*flies, drives*). For more about spelling the plural forms of nouns, see pages 297–299.

EXERCISE 1 Recognizing Words as Singular or Plural

On the line before each of the following sentences, classify each italicized word by writing *sing.* for singular or *pl.* for plural.

EX. __sing.__ 1. Our library *offers* a huge selection of fiction.

_____ 1. Invented by an American minister in 1869, *rickshaws* now are banned in many Asian cities.

_____ 2. In the summer, the sun *rises* too early for me.

______ 3. Inés *spends* her summer vacations on the Greek island of Aegina.

______ 4. The *musicians* brought their own music to the tryouts.

______ 5. The average porcupine *has* more than thirty thousand quills.

EXERCISE 2 Identifying Verbs That Agree in Number with Their Subjects

For each sentence below, underline the subject of the sentence and the form of the verb in parentheses that agrees with the subject.

EX. 1. The clouds (*fill, fills*) the sky.

1. It is amazing that oysters (*create, creates*) beautiful pearls.
2. They (*join, joins*) the choir for the holiday pageant.
3. In the spring, trees (*sprout, sprouts*) leaves quickly when it rains.
4. Entering the West German Parliament in 1983, the Green party (*has, have*) worked to protect the environment.
5. Some canned foods (*contain, contains*) no salt.
6. Every morning my little brother (*ask, asks*) for oatmeal.
7. In India, they (*serve, serves*) chicken biriyani on special occasions.
8. I (*like, likes*) fish for lunch.
9. You (*is, are*) what you eat.
10. Alicia's missing hamster (*run, runs*) out of the closet.
11. Eric (*make, makes*) a delicious salad with spinach and apples.
12. Tomorrow's championship game (*has, have*) been rescheduled.
13. Each volunteer (*promise, promises*) six hours of service.
14. Concerned parents (*is, are*) encouraging their children to wear sunscreen.
15. The candles (*glow, glows*) brightly in the darkened room.

INTERVENING PREPOSITIONAL PHRASES

17c The number of a subject is not changed by a phrase following the subject.

EXAMPLES The **winner** of those ribbons **is** the spaniel. [The verb *is* agrees with the subject *winner.*]

The seventh-grade **teacher,** along with a few of her students, **walks** to school. [The verb *walks* agrees with the subject *teacher.*]

Musicians from Peru and Ecuador **have** played in our auditorium. [The helping verb *have* agrees with the subject *Musicians.*]

REFERENCE NOTE: If the subject is an indefinite pronoun, its number may be determined by a prepositional phrase that follows it. See pages 173–175 for a discussion of indefinite pronouns.

EXERCISE 3 Identifying Verbs That Agree in Number with Their Subjects

In each of the following sentences, draw a line through the prepositional phrase or phrases between the subject and verb. Underline the subject. Then underline the verb in parentheses that agrees with the subject.

EX. 1. The city ~~of Amsterdam~~ (*has, have*) almost ninety islands.

1. Children from all over the neighborhood (*wants, want*) to attend the birthday party.
2. The library near the White House (*contains, contain*) more than twenty million books.
3. Derrick's speech during the lunch period (*was, were*) heard down the hallway.
4. The Statue of Liberty in Paris, like the one in New York City, (*stands, stand*) on an island.
5. Loretta, along with her two friends, (*eats, eat*) tacos for lunch almost every day.
6. Those books next to the window (*needs, need*) dusting.
7. One of the wheels on my in-line skates (*sticks, stick*) when I skate.

8. Sheila, but not her brother, (*is, are*) working tomorrow.
9. The mountains in the distance (*belongs, belong*) to Italy.
10. The gentleman with the red bow tie (*looks, look*) like my father.

EXERCISE 4 Proofreading Sentences for Subject-Verb Agreement

Most of the sentences below contain errors in subject-verb agreement. If a verb does not agree with the subject, write the correct form of the verb on the line before the sentence. Write C if a sentence is correct.

EX. surrounds 1. A large sheet of ice surround the South Pole.

_______ 1. A continent of ancient forests are buried beneath the ice.

_______ 2. Killer whales, along with leopard seals, lives in the Antarctic.

_______ 3. The sea elephant, a good-natured creature, lie in the sun all day.

_______ 4. These giants of the South Pole weighs a couple of tons.

_______ 5. Sources of food are plentiful in the South Pole.

_______ 6. The sea around the icecap is rich in fish and shrimp.

_______ 7. Penguins at the South Pole lives in huge groups.

_______ 8. Penguins, with their black and white feathers, resemble men in tuxedos.

_______ 9. The killer whale, among the largest animals, grow to be as long as twenty-seven feet.

_______ 10. Many mysteries of the South Pole remains unsolved.

EXERCISE 5 Using Correct Subject-Verb Agreement

You are the manager of a toy store. You want to present your boss with a list of improvements that could be made throughout the store. Create a list of comments that you have heard from the customers about the toys, the employees, and the store itself. Then, on your own paper, write five of these comments as complete sentences. Underline each subject once and each verb twice.

EX. 1. music too loud
1. The music in the store is too loud.

SINGULAR AND PLURAL INDEFINITE PRONOUNS

Personal pronouns refer to specific people, places, things, or ideas. A pronoun that does not refer to a definite person, place, thing, or idea is called an ***indefinite pronoun.***

Personal Pronouns	I we you it he she them
Indefinite Pronouns	anyone both somebody each everyone

Singular Indefinite Pronouns

17d The following indefinite pronouns are singular: *each, either, neither, one, everyone, everybody, no one, nobody, anyone, anybody, someone, somebody.*

EXAMPLES **Each** of the players **wears** a different hat.
Does anybody have the correct time?

EXERCISE 6 Choosing Verbs That Agree in Number with Their Subjects

In each of the sentences below, underline the form of the verb in parentheses that agrees with the subject. Remember that the subject is never part of a prepositional phrase.

EX. 1. Nobody in my classes (*looks, look*) like that!

1. One of the firefighters (*have, has*) the frightened dog.
2. Everyone in the front row (*gets, get*) wet on that ride.
3. Don't take these lamps, because neither of them (*works, work*).
4. When I call that number, no one at your house (*answers, answer*).
5. Someone among the crowd of spectators always (*catches, catch*) those foul balls.
6. Each of the soldiers (*guards, guard*) a different door.
7. Somebody with good handwriting (*writes, write*) on the board.
8. Next time, everybody in both families (*gets, get*) a set of pictures.
9. Because those coins are gold, either of them (*is, are*) still valuable.
10. Anyone with scissors (*is, are*) able to learn origami.

Plural Indefinite Pronouns

17e The following indefinite pronouns are plural: *both, few, many, several.*

EXAMPLES **Few** of my friends **read** science fiction.
Many of them **like** science-fiction movies, though.

EXERCISE 7 Choosing Verbs That Agree in Number with Their Subjects

In each of the sentences below, underline the form of the verb in parentheses that agrees with the subject. Remember that the subject is never part of a prepositional phrase.

EX. 1. Both of the countries (*is, are*) in Central America.

1. Very few of the streets (*is, are*) wide enough for automobiles.
2. Many of the boys (*has, have*) been to the science museum.
3. Several of the pictures (*is, are*) by Georgia O'Keeffe.
4. Few of the students in the contest (*has, have*) won a ribbon before.
5. Many of the newer kits (*is, are*) made of polyester film.
6. Several of the candidates (*want, wants*) to speak to you.
7. Both of the oil spills (*was, were*) finally cleaned up.
8. Several in my class (*has, have*) families in Mexico City.
9. Few of the workers (*knows, know*) when we will go to the new building.
10. Many of the blocks in the building (*was, were*) made of granite.
11. Few of these old books (*is, are*) still in print.
12. Many of the chairs (*match, matches*) this sofa.
13. Several of my friends (*attends, attend*) summer school.
14. Both of the notebooks (*belong, belongs*) to me.
15. (*Does, Do*) many of the students go home for lunch?

ALL, ANY, MOST, NONE, *AND* SOME

17f The indefinite pronouns *all, any, most, none,* and *some* may be either singular or plural.

The number of the pronouns *all, any, most, none,* and *some* is determined by the number of the object in a prepositional phrase following the subject. If the pronoun refers to a singular object, it is singular. If the pronoun refers to a plural object, it is plural.

EXAMPLES **Most** of the meal **is** cooked. [*Most* is singular because it refers to one thing—the *meal.* The verb *is* is singular to agree with the subject *Most.*]

Most of the dishes **are** already washed. [*Most* is plural because it refers to more than one thing—*dishes.* The helping verb *are* is plural to agree with the subject *Most.*]

EXERCISE 8 Choosing Verbs That Agree in Number with Their Subjects

In each of the sentences below, underline the form of the verb in parentheses that agrees with the subject.

EX. 1. Some of the parks (*looks, look*) like gardens.

1. Most of the nearby cities (*offers, offer*) space for community gardens.
2. Some of my neighbors (*works, work*) on plots there.
3. All of my plot (*has, have*) sun most of the day.
4. Most of the families (*raises, raise*) food.
5. None of the parkland (*is, are*) wasted.
6. Some of the gardeners (*grows, grow*) flowers.
7. Today, all of the ground (*seems, seem*) to be covered with plants.
8. (*Do, Does*) any of these plants produce tomatoes?
9. Luckily, none of the plants (*needs, need*) extra care.
10. All of our tools (*helps, help*) us work quickly and easily.

EXERCISE 9 Proofreading Sentences for Subject-Verb Agreement

Many of the sentences below have errors in subject-verb agreement. Draw a line through each verb that does not agree with its subject. Write the correct verb form on the line before the sentence. Write *C* if the sentence is correct.

EX. __are__ 1. None of the instruments ~~is~~ brass.

________ 1. Any of the selections sounds better on modern equipment.

________ 2. Most of the hall get too warm in July and August.

________ 3. None of the stage are used during our performance.

________ 4. Some of the piano is painted with black enamel.

________ 5. When it rains, all of the chairs stays dry under the canvas tent.

________ 6. All of the piccolos join in with the other woodwinds.

________ 7. Any of the music played on the flute are beautiful.

________ 8. None of the students wants to leave early.

________ 9. Most of the people likes summer concerts.

________ 10. Some of my friends is here from Germany.

EXERCISE 10 Choosing Verbs That Agree in Number with Their Subjects

For each sentence below, underline the verb form in parentheses that agrees with the subject.

EX. 1. (*Does*, <u>*Do*</u>) any of those chairs seem ready to be painted?

1. All of your help at the church fair (*was, were*) appreciated.
2. Some of the clothes (*is, are*) dirty.
3. All of the actors (*plays, play*) more than one part.
4. Some of the water damage (*appears, appear*) on the ceiling.
5. None of the guests (*writes, write*) poetry.

REVIEW EXERCISE

A. Identifying Verbs That Agree in Number with Their Subjects

For each sentence below, underline the verb form in parentheses that agrees with the subject.

EX. 1. One of Argentina's most popular dance forms (*is, are*) the tango.

1. Most of Argentina (*has, have*) a mild climate.
2. Most of the people in my class (*knows, know*) that the early Spanish explorers gave Argentina its name.
3. The Chaco, the north-central part of Argentina, (*produces, produce*) lumber.
4. One of the Chaco's most important trees (*is, are*) the quebracho tree.
5. Many of the people in Argentina (*vacations, vacation*) at the beach.
6. Several of the beaches (*extends, extend*) for miles.
7. Some of the swimmers (*enjoys, enjoy*) riding the waves in the surf.
8. Because there are lifeguards on the beach, everyone (*worries, worry*) less about safety.
9. Does everybody (*knows, know*) that Buenos Aires is the capital of Argentina?
10. Most of the southern tip of South America (*is, are*) occupied by Argentina.

B. Proofreading a Paragraph for Subject-Verb Agreement

In the following paragraph, draw a line through each verb that does not agree with its subject. In the space above each incorrect verb, write the correct form. If a verb is correct, write C above it.

EX. [1] Mountains ~~covers~~ cover a large part of the earth.

[1] Many people throughout history has been attracted to mountaintops. [2] Some of the world's most famous landmarks is mountains. [3] One of the most beautiful mountains are Fujiyama in Japan. [4] Every summer, many men and women aim for the summit.

[5] My aunt want to climb it next summer. [6] Also, everyone in Ito's family visit the top. [7] Most of the early climbers was men, because women were forbidden to climb the mountain until 1868. [8] The trip in the old days were difficult. [9] Now, however, several of the earlier problems no longer exists. [10] For example, today many of the climbers can buy food along the way instead of having to bring it.

C. Writing Background Information About Past Presidents

You are a television reporter covering the presidential inauguration in the year 1996. Your job is to provide background information about the last four presidents. This information will be used to introduce the program.

1. First, use biographies, reference books, or encyclopedias to learn some details about the past four presidents. You may want to record some of these details on a chart like the one below.

Presidents	J. Carter	R. Reagan	G. Bush	B. Clinton
Term of Office				
Political Party				
Background				
Accomplishments				

2. On your own paper, use the information you have gathered to write five sentences about past presidents. Think of ways to organize the information. For example, one way to organize is to point out similarities and differences. Write complete sentences, and underline the subjects once and the verbs twice.

EX. 1. Two of these presidents, Jimmy Carter and Bill Clinton, were from the South.

CHAPTER 17: AGREEMENT

COMPOUND SUBJECTS

17g Subjects joined by *and* usually take a plural verb.

EXAMPLE **Justine and** her **brother like** to paint. [Two people like to paint.]

17h A compound subject that names only one person or thing takes a singular verb.

EXAMPLE **Macaroni and cheese is** my favorite dish. [One combination is meant.]
Law and order is a major concern for the city. [One topic is a concern.]

EXERCISE 11 Identifying Verbs That Agree in Number with Their Subjects

For each of the sentences below, underline the correct form of the verb in parentheses. If you choose a singular verb with any of these compound subjects, be prepared to explain why.

EX. 1. Photography and birds (*is, are*) two of my interests.

1. Josh and I (*wants, want*) to join the photography club at school.
2. My friend and his neighbor (*is, are*) giving a demonstration next week.
3. Mr. Tchong and his wife (*is, are*) both professional photographers.
4. Using color film, he and she (*takes, take*) beautiful pictures of birds.
5. Most of the time black and white film (*is, are*) what they use for portraits.
6. (*Does, Do*) Mr. Tchong and the students develop their own film?
7. Inside the darkroom, the paper and the film (*is, are*) kept in a special box.
8. Locks and alarms (*is, are*) needed to protect expensive equipment.
9. During field trips, Lien and I (*watches, watch*) birds at the feeders.
10. A robin and her babies (*lives, live*) in a nearby tree.

17i Singular subjects joined by *or* or *nor* take a singular verb. Plural subjects joined by *or* or *nor* take a plural verb.

EXAMPLES **Neither Talasi nor** her **sister is** in my class. [Both subjects are singular.]
Either the **doctor or** the physician's **assistant is** available. [Both subjects are singular.]

Neither storms nor floods are forecast. [Both subjects are plural.]
Either buses or subways take you there. [Both subjects are plural.]

17j When a singular subject and a plural subject are joined by *or* or *nor,* the verb agrees with the subject nearer the verb.

EXAMPLES **Popcorn or** sunflower **seeds make** a good snack. [The verb agrees with the nearer subject, *seeds.*]
Sunflower **seeds or popcorn makes** a good snack. [The verb agrees with the nearer subject, *popcorn.*]

EXERCISE 12 Identifying Verbs That Agree in Number with Their Subjects

For each of the sentences below, underline the correct form of the verb in parentheses.

EX. 1. Either the artist or his assistant (*is, are*) shown in this picture.

1. Neither fruits nor vegetables (*was, were*) on the table.
2. Models or their props (*is, are*) sketched first.
3. Either the dishes or the cook (*was, were*) later added to the picture.
4. Neither Atul nor Cassie (*is, are*) responsible for that pastel.
5. Either a ticket or a pass (*allows, allow*) you to enter the museum.
6. (*Has, Have*) either Diego Rivera or Candido Partinari painted a mural in this city?
7. A camera or a sketchbook (*helps, help*) you remember the artwork.
8. Either the clerks or a guard (*has, have*) the correct time.
9. Neither our museum nor our galleries (*sells, sell*) that print.
10. Neither the catalog nor the bulletin board (*mentions, mention*) the museum.

COLLECTIVE NOUNS AND INVERTED SENTENCES

17k Collective nouns may be either singular or plural. A collective noun takes a singular verb when the noun refers to the group as a unit. A collective noun takes a plural verb when the noun refers to the individual parts or members of the group.

A ***collective noun*** is singular in form but names a group of persons, animals, or things.

Common Collective Nouns			
audience	committee	group	swarm
class	family	herd	team
club	flock	jury	troop

EXAMPLES The **team has** earned the award. [The team as a unit has earned the award.]
The **team have** arrived in separate cars. [Individual team members are in separate cars.]

17l When the subject follows the verb, find the subject and make sure that the verb agrees with it. The subject usually follows the verb in sentences beginning with *here* or *there* and in questions.

EXAMPLES Here **is** my **computer.**
There **are** new **programs** on the local cable channel.
What **were** those **noises**?
Does lightning strike twice?

NOTE When the subject of a sentence follows the verb, the word order is said to be *inverted*. To find the subject of a sentence with inverted order, restate the sentence in normal word order.

INVERTED In the city **live** several famous **authors.**
RESTATED Several famous **authors live** in the city.
INVERTED **Were** the **Bennetts** with you?
RESTATED The **Bennetts were** with you.

EXERCISE 13 Identifying Verbs That Agree in Number with Their Subjects

On your own paper, write the correct form of the verb in parentheses in each of the sentences below.

EX. 1. The committee (*was disagreeing, were disagreeing*) about the first speaker.
1. were disagreeing

1. A flock of Canada geese (*lives, live*) in our city's park.
2. During the trial, the jury (*stays, stay*) at a nearby hotel.
3. Only one herd (*has appeared, have appeared*) at this water hole.
4. Now the majority (*is voting, are voting*) in the election.
5. The audience (*likes, like*) to applaud those actors.
6. The class (*perform, performs*) next weekend.
7. Visitors must be quiet when the Senate (*debates, debate*).
8. The squad (*does, do*) not agree with its captain.
9. That swarm of bees (*lives, live*) across the meadow.
10. The orchestra (*was, were*) magnificent.

EXERCISE 14 Identifying Verbs That Agree in Number with Their Subjects

Underline the subject in each of the sentences below. Then underline the correct form of the verb in parentheses.

EX. 1. There (*is, are*) many summer holidays.

1. There (*is, are*) a special day each June.
2. (*Is, Are*) the summer solstice here yet?
3. There (*is, are*) two solstices each year.
4. (*Was, Were*) the longest day of the year special?
5. Around the world, there (*is, are*) many celebrations on this day.
6. Here on the table (*lies, lie*) the key to the house.
7. Around eight o'clock, here (*comes, come*) my brothers.
8. (*Is, Are*) there any tomatoes left?
9. There (*is, are*) three reasons for doing that.
10. What (*is, are*) your excuse?

AMOUNTS, TITLES, AND DON'T *AND* DOESN'T

Amounts and Titles

17m Words stating amounts are usually singular.

A word or phrase stating a weight, a measurement, or an amount of money or time is usually considered one item. Such a word or phrase takes a singular verb.

EXAMPLES **Ten grams is** a decagram.
Fifty cents is not much money today.

17n The title of a book or the name of an organization or a country, even when plural in form, usually takes a singular verb.

EXAMPLES ***Black Folktales* was written** by Julius Lester. [one book]
American Youth Hostels has headquarters in Washington, D.C. [one organization]
The **Sandwich Islands is** the old name for Hawaii. [one place]

EXERCISE 15 Identifying Verbs That Agree in Number with Their Subjects

In each of the following sentences, underline the correct form of the verb in parentheses.

EX. 1. The Friends of the Library (*has, have*) a book sale Saturday.

1. *Animal Fables from Aesop* (*is, are*) a book for readers of all ages.
2. Two hours sometimes (*seems, seem*) like a very long time.
3. The United States (*is, are*) full of public libraries.
4. (*Is, Are*) *Great Deeds of Superheroes* available in paperback?
5. Six feet (*is, are*) the average length of our tables.
6. One third plus two thirds (*equals, equal*) one.
7. Yes, *The ABC's of Stamp Collecting* (*has, have*) pictures of many colorful stamps.
8. The Canary Islands (*seems, seem*) like a good setting for a mystery.

9. Sixty-one dollars (*does, do*) seem like too much to pay.
10. On Monday, the Austin Volunteers for Neighborhood Libraries (*receives, receive*) donated books.

Don't and *Doesn't*

17o *Don't* and *doesn't* must agree with their subjects.

The word *don't* is a contraction of *do not,* and *doesn't* is a contraction of *does not.* Use *don't* with all plural subjects and with the pronouns *I* and *you.*

EXAMPLES The clouds **don't** look threatening.
I **don't** believe it!
You **don't** need a coat.

Use *doesn't* with all singular subjects except *I* and *you.*

EXAMPLES The skateboard **doesn't** need paint.
She **doesn't** have kneeguards.
It **doesn't** work.

EXERCISE 16 Writing Original Sentences with *Don't* and *Doesn't*

You are taking two young cousins to a country fair. Your cousins are frightened by most animals, including dogs. They have never seen live chickens, cows, horses, pigs, or rabbits before. They are asking you lots of questions. You are trying to explain that they have nothing to fear. On the lines below, write five sentences about some of the animals. Explain why they are not to be feared or to be fed certain foods. Use *don't* and *doesn't* to agree with a different subject in each sentence.

EX. 1. The chickens don't eat bananas, Otis.
2. No, the horse doesn't kick children.

1. ______
2. ______
3. ______
4. ______
5. ______

PRONOUN-ANTECEDENT AGREEMENT

A pronoun usually refers to a noun or another pronoun called its *antecedent*.

17p A pronoun agrees with its antecedent in number and gender.

Some singular personal pronouns have forms that indicate gender. Feminine pronouns refer to females. Masculine pronouns refer to males. Neuter pronouns refer to things (neither masculine nor feminine) and usually to animals.

Feminine	she	her	hers
Masculine	he	him	his
Neuter	it	it	its

EXAMPLES Julie wondered if **she** would need **her** umbrella. [*She* and *her* are both feminine. They agree with the feminine antecedent *Julie.*]

Ruben asked if **his** friend could drop **him** at the corner. [*His* and *him* are both masculine. They agree with the masculine antecedent *Ruben.*]

The pan with the chili in **it** has lost **its** lid. [*It* and *its* are both neuter. They agree with *pan,* which is a thing.]

☞ **REFERENCE NOTE:** For lists of different kinds of pronouns, see pages 99, 103, 173–175, 205, and 213–216.

(1) Use a singular pronoun to refer to *each, either, neither, one, everyone, everybody, no one, nobody, anyone, anybody, someone,* or *somebody.*

EXAMPLES **Everyone** in the class took **her** or **his** project home. [*Her* and *his* are singular. Because *Everyone* may be either masculine or feminine, both forms are used.]

One of the exhibits lost **its** tag.

In conversation, people often use a plural personal pronoun to refer to a singular antecedent that may be either masculine or feminine. This plural form is also becoming more common in writing, and it may someday be considered standard written English.

EXAMPLE **Everybody** brought **their** pets to the pet fair.

(2) Use a singular pronoun to refer to two or more singular antecedents joined by *or.*

EXAMPLES Either my **mother or** my **aunt** will bring **her** map.
Shane or Clay will lend us **his** travel guide.

(3) Use a plural pronoun to refer to two or more antecedents joined by *and.*

EXAMPLES **Lono and Nick** called **their** parents from the theater.
Hanako and her **friend** left early so that **they** could stop at the school.

EXERCISE 17 Identifying Antecedents and Writing Pronouns That Agree with Them

On the line in each sentence below, write a pronoun that will complete the meaning of the sentence. Then underline the antecedent, or antecedents, for that pronoun.

EX. 1. <u>Each</u> of the women in the audience waved ___her___ hand.

1. Kitty and Bruno worked together on __________ scenes.
2. Either Vern or Mr. Park will lend me __________ jacket.
3. One of the curtains is falling off __________ rod.
4. Vern and Kitty laughed at __________ lines in the first scene.
5. Dawn or Sabrena will bring __________ books from home.
6. Each of the actors should say __________ lines slowly and clearly.
7. Mrs. Park and my mother saved __________ programs from last year.
8. Anyone can try out if __________ enjoys acting.
9. Neither script has marks in __________ margins.
10. The actors took __________ bows in front of a cheering crowd.

CHAPTER REVIEW

A. Proofreading Sentences for Subject-Verb Agreement

Most of the sentences below contain agreement errors. For each error, draw a line through the incorrect verb. Write the correct form on the line before the sentence. Write C if the sentence is correct.

EX. __has__ 1. Either the library or your teacher ~~have~~ the book.

________ 1. Here is the photographs of sod houses.

________ 2. The bricks of this house is made from grass-covered ground.

________ 3. First, a man or a woman have to cut the prairie grass short.

________ 4. Each person then dig out a strip of earth.

________ 5. Where was those sod houses built?

________ 6. *Sod House Memories* are about houses in Nebraska.

________ 7. People in the United States don't build with sod much today.

________ 8. Boards and bricks are available in most parts of the country.

________ 9. Gene and Mai is working on a model of a sod house.

________ 10. Paper bags or cloth are being used for windows.

B. Proofreading a Paragraph for Pronoun-Antecedent Agreement

Find the errors in pronoun-antecedent agreement in the following paragraph. Draw a line through each pronoun that does not agree with its antecedent. In the space above the incorrect pronoun, write the correct form or write C if the sentence is correct.

his or her

EX. [1] Everybody gave ~~their~~ suggestions to Mr. Asari.

[1] Everyone was supposed to suggest ideas for how their class dues should be spent. [2] Jodi and Brian wanted his money spent on

a class trip. [3] Neither Isaac nor Theodore felt that their idea was better. [4] Each of the aquariums needs a new hose for their air system. [5] However, no one said that they wanted their money spent to replace the hoses. [6] Either Tom or Mario gave their suggestion next. [7] Both thought that his class should buy something permanent. [8] Jodi and Brian nodded their heads to this suggestion. [9] Each of the students voted for their choice. [10] Tom and Mario were happy to see that their idea pleased most of their classmates.

C. Writing About Animal Camouflage

You have been asked to conduct a class for the Young Rangers Club. Your topic will be how various animals protect themselves with camouflage.

1. First, do some research on animal camouflage. You might check encyclopedias, books about animals, and other reference books.
2. Find information about two kinds of camouflage, color matching and shape matching, and the animals that use them. Take notes on your own paper, and write at least two sentences about each kind of camouflage. Be sure to use subject-verb agreement and pronoun-antecedent agreement.

color matching: ____________________

____

____

____

____

shape matching: ____________________

____

____

____

____

PRINCIPAL PARTS

The four basic forms of a verb are called the ***principal parts*** of a verb.

18a The principal parts of a verb are the *base form*, the *present participle*, the *past*, and the *past participle*.

Base Form	Present Participle	Past	Past Participle
walk	(is) walking	walked	(have) walked
make	(is) making	made	(have) made

Notice that the present participle and the past participle require helping verbs (forms of *be* and *have*).

The principal parts of a verb are used to express whether the action of the verb takes place in present, past, or future time.

PRESENT TIME He **makes** homemade bread.
He **is making** a loaf of bread now.
PAST TIME Yesterday they **made** rye bread.
They **have** often **made** bread together
FUTURE TIME Tomorrow we **will make** more bread.
By next week, we **will have made** many more loaves.

Because *walk* forms its past and past participle by adding *–ed*, it is called a ***regular verb***. *Make* forms its past and past participle differently, so it is called an ***irregular verb***.

THE FAMILY CIRCUS® By Bil Keane

"You don't say 'he taked my chair' . . . it's 'my chair was tooken.' "

EXERCISE 1 Identifying the Time Expressed by Verbs

For each sentence below, study the verb form in italics. Look for other words that give clues about the time the verb expresses. On the line before the sentence, write *pres.* if the action takes place in the present, *past* if the action takes place in the past, or *fut.* if the action takes place in the future.

EX. past 1. We *have visited* our cousins in Puerto Rico many times.

______ 1. You *are talking* too softly for us to understand your words.

______ 2. I *heard* a great joke yesterday.

______ 3. My family *lived* in Philadelphia for three years.

______ 4. Pete *asked* Felicia for a ride to last night's drama club meeting.

______ 5. Ms. Doty *is driving* to her guitar lesson in her new car.

______ 6. I *will make* your lunch in a few minutes.

______ 7. He *will need* a new coat in the fall.

______ 8. Abdul *has* already *left* for the movies.

______ 9. Please hurry, for they *are waiting* for us.

______ 10. We *will sell* tickets for the band concert next Wednesday at the mall.

EXERCISE 2 Identifying the Principal Parts of Verbs

On each line below, identify the principle part of the verb form shown. Write *base* for base form, *pres. part.* for present participle, *past* for past, or *past part.* for past participle.

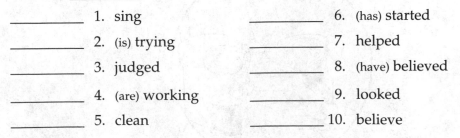

EX. pres. part. 1. (is) playing

______ 1. sing

______ 2. (is) trying

______ 3. judged

______ 4. (are) working

______ 5. clean

______ 6. (has) started

______ 7. helped

______ 8. (have) believed

______ 9. looked

______ 10. believe

REGULAR VERBS

18b A *regular verb* forms its past and past participle by adding *–ed* or *–d* to the base form.

Base Form	Present Participle	Past	Past Participle
wish	(is) wishing	wished	(have) wished
hop	(is) hopping	hopped	(have) hopped
happen	(is) happening	happened	(have) happened
move	(is) moving	moved	(have) moved

 **REFERENCE NOTE**: Most regular verbs that end in *e* drop the *e* before adding *–ing*. Some regular verbs double the final consonant before adding *–ing* or *–ed*. For a discussion of these spelling rules, see pages 293–299.

EXERCISE 3 Writing the Forms of Regular Verbs

The base form is given for each of the following verbs. Fill in the chart with the present participle, past, and past participle of each verb.

Base Form	Present Participle	Past	Past Participle
EX. 1. wish	(is) wishing	wished	(have) wished
1. look	(is)		(have)
2. select	(is)		(have)
3. shop	(is)		(have)
4. use	(is)		(have)
5. start	(is)		(have)

EXERCISE 4 Writing Sentences with Forms of Regular Verbs

Write a sentence, using the correct form of each italicized verb below.

EX. 1. past of *call* I called the jewelry store.

1. present participle of *hope* ______________________________

____

2. past participle of *enjoy* ______________________________

____

3. past of *drop* ______________________________

____

4. past participle of *raise* ______________________________

____

5. present participle of *slip* ______________________________

____

6. past participle of *talk* ______________________________

____

7. past of *ask* ______________________________

____

8. present participle of *answer* ______________________________

____

9. past of *follow* ______________________________

____

10. present participle of *laugh* ______________________________

____

IRREGULAR VERBS

18c An *irregular verb* forms its past and past participle in some other way than by adding *–d* or *–ed* to the base form.

If you are not sure about the principal parts of a verb, look in a dictionary. An entry for an irregular verb lists the principal parts of the verb. If the principal parts are not given in the dictionary entry, the verb is a regular verb.

COMMON IRREGULAR VERBS			
Base Form	**Present Participle**	**Past**	**Past Participle**
begin	(is) beginning	began	(have) begun
bite	(is) biting	bit	(have) bitten *or* bit
blow	(is) blowing	blew	(have) blown
break	(is) breaking	broke	(have) broken
bring	(is) bringing	brought	(have) brought
build	(is) building	built	(have) built
burst	(is) bursting	burst	(have) burst
catch	(is) catching	caught	(have) caught
choose	(is) choosing	chose	(have) chosen
come	(is) coming	came	(have) come
cost	(is) costing	cost	(have) cost
do	(is) doing	did	(have) done
draw	(is) drawing	drew	(have) drawn
drink	(is) drinking	drank	(have) drunk
drive	(is) driving	drove	(have) driven
eat	(is) eating	ate	(have) eaten
fall	(is) falling	fell	(have) fallen
feel	(is) feeling	felt	(have) felt
freeze	(is) freezing	froze	(have) frozen
get	(is) getting	got	(have) gotten *or* got

COMMON IRREGULAR VERBS			
Base Form	**Present Participle**	**Past**	**Past Participle**
give	(is) giving	gave	(have) given
go	(is) going	went	(have) gone
grow	(is) growing	grew	(have) grown
hurt	(is) hurting	hurt	(have) hurt
know	(is) knowing	knew	(have) known
lead	(is) leading	led	(have) led
lend	(is) lending	lent	(have) lent
lose	(is) losing	lost	(have) lost
make	(is) making	made	(have) made
meet	(is) meeting	met	(have) met
put	(is) putting	put	(have) put
ride	(is) riding	rode	(have) ridden
ring	(is) ringing	rang	(have) rung
run	(is) running	ran	(have) run
say	(is) saying	said	(have) said
see	(is) seeing	saw	(have) seen
sell	(is) selling	sold	(have) sold
send	(is) sending	sent	(have) sent
shrink	(is) shrinking	shrank *or* shrunk	(have) shrunk
sing	(is) singing	sang	(have) sung
sink	(is) sinking	sank *or* sunk	(have) sunk *or* sunken
speak	(is) speaking	spoke	(have) spoken
stand	(is) standing	stood	(have) stood
steal	(is) stealing	stole	(have) stolen
swim	(is) swimming	swam	(have) swum
take	(is) taking	took	(have) taken
tell	(is) telling	told	(have) told
throw	(is) throwing	threw	(have) thrown
wear	(is) wearing	wore	(have) worn
win	(is) winning	won	(have) won
write	(is) writing	wrote	(have) written

EXERCISE 5 Writing the Forms of Irregular Verbs

On the line in each of the following sentences, write the correct form (past or past participle) of the verb shown in italics.

EX. 1. *tell* Reggie ___told___ us about the work of the naturalist John Muir.

1. *write* Reggie and Ed have ________________ a play.
2. *win* As student playwrights, they have ________________ many awards.
3. *put* Last year, they ________________ on a play about John Muir's life.
4. *make* In his books and articles, John Muir ________________ many people aware of the beauty of the wilderness.
5. *know* Even a hundred years ago, Muir ________________ that the wilderness was endangered.
6. *choose* He ________________ to write about the wilderness in an effort to save it.
7. *come* Also, through his efforts, the Sierra Club ________________ into being.
8. *grow* Muir ________________ up on a farm in Wisconsin.
9. *get* He ________________ his education at the University of Wisconsin.
10. *lead* His studies of plants ________________ him to explore the woods for wildflowers.
11. *begin* John Muir ________________ his wilderness journeys as a young man.
12. *go* He ________________ on foot from Kentucky to Florida, collecting plants.
13. *write* As he walked, he ________________ in his journals about the plants he saw.
14. *give* These journals have ________________ many readers a guide to wildflowers.
15. *send* Muir's studies eventually ________________ him to California.

16. *see* In California, he ________________ the Yosemite Valley.

17. *say* In his writings, he ________________ that this valley is one of the United States' greatest treasures.

18. *draw* The beauty of the valley has ________________ many visitors over the years.

19. *build* People ________________ a dam to collect water in a huge lake there.

20. *take* Many hikers have ________________ the path that leads to Bridalveil Fall.

EXERCISE 6 Using Past and Past Participle Forms of Irregular Verbs to Write Interview Questions

A group of athletes has come to your school to train for the Olympics. You have been selected to interview the athletes. Your assignment is to find out facts about their backgrounds, training, skills, and hopes for winning gold medals. On your own paper, write ten questions that you might ask these athletes. In your questions, use the past or past participle forms of ten of the verbs on the list on pages 193 and 194. Underline each verb (including any helping verbs) that you use.

EX. 1. Why have you chosen to compete in the Olympics?

TENSE

18d The *tense* of a verb indicates the time of the action or of the state of being expressed by the verb.

Every verb has six tenses.

Tenses	Examples
Present	I see, you see, she sees
Past	I saw, we saw, they saw
Future	I will (shall) see, you will see, he will see
Present Perfect	I have seen, you have seen, she has seen
Past Perfect	I had seen, you had seen, he had seen
Future Perfect	I will (shall) have seen, she will have seen, they will have seen

This time line shows the relationship between the six tenses.

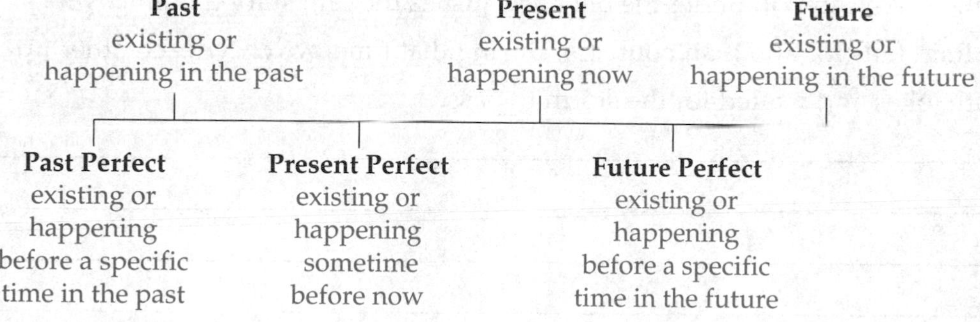

Past
existing or happening in the past
Present
existing or happening now
Future
existing or happening in the future
Past Perfect
existing or happening before a specific time in the past
Present Perfect
existing or happening sometime before now
Future Perfect
existing or happening before a specific time in the future

18e Do not change needlessly from one tense to another.

When writing about events that take place in the present, use verbs that are in the present tense. When writing about events that occurred in the past, use verbs that are in the past tense.

INCONSISTENT	As we **walk** through the park, we **met** Latrice. [*Walk* is in the present tense, and *met* is in the past tense.]
CONSISTENT	As we **walk** through the park, we **meet** Latrice. [Both *walk* and *meet* are in the present tense.]
CONSISTENT	As we **walked** through the park, we **met** Latrice. [Both *walked* and *met* are in the past tense.]

EXERCISE 7 Revising a Paragraph to Make Tenses of the Verbs Consistent

Many of the verbs in the paragraph below are inconsistent in tense. Rewrite the paragraph on the lines below. Change the verb forms to make their tenses consistent. Use your own paper if you run out of room.

EX. [1] We climbed the hill, and I see storm clouds.
[1] We climbed the hill, and I saw storm clouds.

[1] Odessa, Benny, and I are on a hike in the woods, and we got lost. [2] We start up a steep hill. [3] "Oh, no!" I shouted. [4] From the top of the hill, I see storm clouds. [5] A bad storm was rushing toward us. [6] Looking for cover, we run down the hill. [7] Then Benny finds a small cave in the side of the hill. [8] We climb in under the big rocks just as the rain started falling. [9] Rain falls for about an hour. [10] During that time, we cheer each other up with jokes and waited for the storm to pass.

SIT *AND* SET *AND* RISE *AND* RAISE

Sit and *Set*

18f The verb *sit* means "to be seated" or "to rest." *Sit* seldom takes an object. The verb *set* means "to place" or "to put (something)." *Set* usually takes an object. Unlike *sit, set* has the same form for the base form, past, and past participle.

Base Form	Present Participle	Past	Past Participle
sit	(is) sitting	sat	(have) sat
set	(is) setting	set	(have) set

EXAMPLES Melita and I **sat** in the back of the room. [no object]
Bobby Ray **set** the package on the table. [Bobby Ray set what? *Package* is the object.]

Brutus, my German shepherd, **is sitting** on the couch. [no object]
Jonah **is setting** his luggage on the cart. [Jonah is setting what? *Luggage* is the object.]

EXERCISE 8 Writing the Forms of *Sit* and *Set*

On the line in each of the sentences below, write the correct form of *sit* or *set*.

EX. 1. Last night I __sat__ in the kitchen and wrote a letter.

1. Elmore __________ the chairs around the table.
2. Come __________ by the fire and talk to me.
3. The cat is __________ on the new rug in the den.
4. __________ your rake down and rest for a while.
5. The chess players have __________ at their game tables all morning.

Rise and *Raise*

18g The verb *rise* means "to move upward" or "to go up." *Rise* almost never takes an object. The verb *raise* means "to lift (something) up." *Raise* usually takes an object.

Base Form	Present Participle	Past	Past Participle
rise	(is) rising	rose	(have) risen
raise	(is) raising	raised	(have) raised

EXAMPLES The sun **rose** at six o'clock this morning. [no object]
Franco **raised** his hand. [Franco raised what? *Hand* is the object.]

According to the report, the price of wheat **will rise** next year. [no object]
Melba **will raise** the curtain now. [Melba will raise what? *Curtain* is the object.]

EXERCISE 9 Identifying the Correct Forms of *Rise* and *Raise*

For each of the sentences below, underline the correct form of *rise* or *raise* in parentheses.

EX. 1. Everyone was silent as Iola (*rose, raised*) from her seat.

1. Should I (*rise, raise*) my voice so you can hear me more clearly?
2. We like to watch the drawbridge (*rise, raise*).
3. She explained that last summer she had (*rose, raised*) the price of her flowers.
4. Two weeks after she planted the seeds, little plants (*rose, raised*) from the ground.
5. As the heat was (*rising, raising*) during the summer, she watered the plants twice a day.

LIE *AND* LAY

18h The verb *lie* means "to recline," "to be in place," or "to remain lying down." *Lie* never takes an object. The verb *lay* means "to put (something) down" or "to place (something)." *Lay* usually takes an object.

Base Form	Present Participle	Past	Past Participle
lie	(is) lying	lay	(have) lain
lay	(is) laying	laid	(have) laid

EXAMPLES The dog **is lying** in the sun. [no object]
Ethel **is laying** the plates on the table. [Ethel is laying what? *Plates* is the object.]

Last night, I **lay** in bed and thought about our picnic. [no object]
Before class, I **laid** the book on the desk. [I laid what? *Book* is the object.]

EXERCISE 10 Identifying the Correct Forms of *Lie* and *Lay*

For each of the sentences below, underline the correct form of *lie* or *lay* in parentheses.

EX. 1. The Delaware River (*lies, lays*) on the western border of New Jersey.

1. Last night, we (*lay, laid*) our sleeping bags in the back of the station wagon.
2. You kids can (*lie, lay*) there and nap during our long trip to New Jersey.
3. Don't forget the map of New Jersey, which is (*lying, laying*) on the kitchen table.
4. Oh, no! I think the beach towels (*lay, laid*) in the washer all night.
5. (*Lie, Lay*) them over the kitchen chairs so that they will be dry before we leave.

EXERCISE 11 Writing the Forms of *Lie* and *Lay*

Complete each of the sentences below by filling in the blank with the correct form of *lie* or *lay*.

EX. 1. After the storm yesterday, deep puddles of water ___lay___ in the driveway.

1. Please ____________ your papers on my desk.
2. My sweater was covered with dog hair after the dog had ____________ on it.
3. Hans had ____________ your library books on the table in the hall.
4. Did you find the empty bowl that was ____________ on the shelf?
5. Morris had ____________ the garden tools somewhere in the garage.
6. Vietnam ____________ on the eastern coast of mainland Southeast Asia.
7. Giorgio has already ____________ compost on the new garden.
8. We had ____________ on the beach too long in the hot sun.
9. ____________ the tablecloth on the table while I get the plates and glasses.
10. Workers are ____________ a new surface on the northbound side of Route 95.

EXERCISE 12 Proofreading for the Correct Forms of *Lie* and *Lay*

Most of the sentences below contain errors in the use of *lie* and *lay*. If a sentence contains the wrong verb form, write the correct form on the line before the sentence. If a sentence is correct, write C on the line before it.

EX. ___lying___ 1. Empty soda cans were laying all over the field after the concert.

____________ 1. Do horses lay down to rest?

____________ 2. Before bed, he lay more wood on the fire.

____________ 3. Ernest was lying on the couch, reading the newspaper.

____________ 4. Barbara has lain the puzzle pieces out on the card table.

____________ 5. When he finished reading, Parvis lay his book on the shelf.

CHAPTER 18: USING VERBS CORRECTLY

CHAPTER REVIEW

A. Identifying the Correct Forms of *Sit* and *Set*, *Rise* and *Raise*, and *Lie* and *Lay*

For each of the sentences below, underline the correct form of the verb in parentheses.

EX. 1. When the man asked who wanted the extra tickets, I (*rose, raised*) my hand.

1. We were (*sitting, setting*) in the front row at the concert.
2. The lights dimmed as a platform (*rose, raised*) from beneath the stage.
3. Workers had (*sat, set*) that platform beneath a hidden trapdoor.
4. On the platform, they had (*lain, laid*) a red carpet, and on the carpet they had (*set, sat*) a couple of stools.
5. Even with the lights dimmed, we could see that someone was (*sitting, setting*) on one of the stools.
6. Suddenly, the lights (*rose, raised*) to full power.
7. Then Linda Ronstadt (*rose, raised*) her head and smiled.
8. A microphone was (*lying, laying*) on the stool beside her.
9. She began to sing as she (*sat, set*) there.
10. The audience (*rose, raised*) from their seats to join her as she sang "Desperado."

B. Proofreading a Paragraph for Correct Verb Forms

Most of the sentences in the following paragraph contain incorrect verb forms. If a sentence contains an error, draw a line through the wrong form of the verb. Write the correct form above the verb.

EX. [1] Ann Petry ~~growed~~ grew up in Connecticut.

[1] Ann Petry goed to college at the University of Connecticut.

[2] After graduating from college, she begun her career as a pharmacist.

[3] Later, she selled advertisements for a newspaper. [4] Eventually, she raised to the position of newspaper reporter. [5] Her newspaper career leads her to write novels and short stories. [6] In the past thirty years, she has wrote many novels and nonfiction books. [7] As she wrote those works, she used her own experiences and interests as background. [8] *The Street* telled a story about life in a Harlem ghetto. [9] *Harriet Tubman: Conductor on the Underground Railroad* gave readers valuable information about slavery in the United States. [10] Petry's books have became very popular with readers all over the world.

C. Using Regular and Irregular Verbs to Write a Letter

Choose an interesting place anywhere in the world that you would like to visit. Use an encyclopedia and other reference books to gather information about the place. What interesting sights might you see there? What historical events might you learn about during your visit? On your own paper, write a letter to tell a friend at home about your trip. In your letter, describe some of the sights that you have seen so far. Use at least five regular verbs and five irregular verbs in your letter. Proofread your finished letter for correct use of verb tenses. Underline the verbs that you use.

EX. Dear Joan,
I visited the Eiffel Tower in Paris yesterday. It was beautiful.

CASE OF PRONOUNS

19a *Case* is the form of a noun or pronoun that shows how it is used. There are three cases: *nominative, objective,* and *possessive.*

The form of a noun is the same for the nominative and the objective cases.

NOMINATIVE CASE The **teacher** asked a question. [noun used as subject]
OBJECTIVE CASE Bianca answered the **teacher**. [noun used as a direct object]

A noun changes its form only in the possessive case, usually by adding an apostrophe and an *s*.

POSSESSIVE CASE The **teacher's** question was about geography.

Unlike nouns, most personal pronouns have different forms for the nominative, objective, and possessive cases.

REFERENCE NOTE: For information about forming the possessive case of nouns, see page 283.

PERSONAL PRONOUNS		
Singular		
Nominative Case	**Objective Case**	**Possessive Case**
I	me	my, mine
you	you	your, yours
he, she, it	him, her, it	his, her, hers, its
Plural		
Nominative Case	**Objective Case**	**Possessive Case**
we	us	our, ours
you	you	your, yours
they	them	their, theirs

Some teachers prefer to call possessive forms of pronouns (such as *our, your,* and *their*) adjectives. Follow your teacher's instructions regarding possessive forms.

EXERCISE 1 Identifying Personal Pronoun Forms

Identify the case of each italicized pronoun in the following sentences. On the line before each sentence, write *nom.* for nominative, *obj.* for objective, and *poss.* for possessive.

EX. obj. 1. I showed *him* the mural on the school wall.

_____ 1. *My* mother carves wooden animals.

_____ 2. Did *you* read about the baseball player Hank Aaron?

_____ 3. Ms. Reyes told *us* to write two haiku poems each.

_____ 4. Sonya and *I* painted the doghouse purple.

_____ 5. It was *our* idea to have an international food festival.

_____ 6. Phillis Wheatley was one of the first African American poets to have *her* poems published.

_____ 7. That book is *his* to take home and study.

_____ 8. *They* wanted to start a school newspaper.

_____ 9. Did Antonio give *you* a tour of his home?

_____ 10. The watercolor painting in the hall is *mine*.

NOMINATIVE CASE PRONOUNS

19b The subject of a verb is in the nominative case.

A subject tells *whom* or *what* the sentence is about.

EXAMPLES **We** have a parakeet named Pícaro. [*We* is the subject of *have.*]
It is a beautiful bird. [*It* is the subject of *is.*]
She and **I** taught Pícaro to speak. [*She* and *I* are used together as the compound subject of *taught.*]

To help you choose the correct pronoun in a compound subject, try each form of the pronoun separately.

EXAMPLE My brother and (*I, me*) like Pícaro.
I like Pícaro.
Me like Pícaro.
ANSWER My brother and **I** like Pícaro.

EXAMPLE (*He, Him*) and (*I, me*) played with Pícaro.
He played with Pícaro.
Him played with Pícaro.
I played with Pícaro.
Me played with Pícaro.
ANSWER **He** and **I** played with Pícaro.

19c A predicate nominative is in the nominative case.

A ***predicate nominative*** follows a linking verb and identifies or explains the subject of the verb. A pronoun used as a predicate nominative usually identifies the subject and follows a form of the verb *be* (such as *am, are, is, was, were, be, been,* or *being).*

EXAMPLES The winner of the contest was **he.** [*He* follows the linking verb *was* and identifies the subject *winner.*]
The winners should have been **she** and **I.** [*She* and *I* follow the linking verb *should have been* and identify the subject *winners.*]

In informal, everyday conversation, people often use forms such as *It's me* and *That was her*. However, these forms are not standard, formal English.

EXERCISE 2 Choosing Pronouns Used as Subjects

In each sentence below, underline the pronoun or pair of pronouns that completes the sentence correctly.

EX. 1. Roberto and (*she, her*) collect stamps.

1. Yesterday, Roberto and (*me, I*) got together with our stamp albums.
2. For an hour or so, (*we, us*) traded stamps.
3. Then (*him and me, he and I*) read the advertisements in the latest issues of *Stamp Collecting* and *Stamp Digest*.
4. (*They, Them*) are two magazines for stamp collectors.
5. (*He, Him*) saw an advertisement for unusual stamps from Angola.

EXERCISE 3 Proofreading Sentences for Correct Use of Nominative Case Pronouns

Check each sentence carefully. If a sentence below contains the wrong form of a pronoun, write the correct form on the line before the sentence. If a sentence contains no errors, write C on the line.

EX. ___he___ 1. The person who wrote that poem might have been him.

_______ 1. Are your favorite poets Langston Hughes and her?

_______ 2. It was she who wrote the poem "Metaphor."

_______ 3. The best poets in our class are him and I.

_______ 4. The poems included in our program should have been them.

_______ 5. Among the poets in this book are Dorothy Parker and he.

OBJECTIVE CASE PRONOUNS

19d *Direct objects* and *indirect objects* of verbs are in the objective case.

A ***direct object*** follows an action verb and tells *whom* or *what* receives the action of the verb.

EXAMPLES Mrs. Delaney called **me** last night. [*Me* tells *whom* Mrs. Delaney called.]
Sam returned **them** to the library. [*Them* tells *what* Sam returned to the library.]

An ***indirect object*** comes between an action verb and a direct object. It tells *to whom* or *to what* or *for whom* or *for what* the action is done.

EXAMPLES The plants are dry; I'll give **them** some water. [*Them* tells *to what* I'll give water. *Water,* the direct object, tells *what* I'll give.]
Dr. Irwin bought **us** the tickets. [*Us* tells *for whom* Dr. Irwin bought the tickets. *Tickets,* the direct object, tells *what* he bought.]

To choose the correct pronoun in a compound object, try each form of the pronoun separately in the sentence.

EXAMPLE Bob invited Heta and (*she, her*). [*Bob invited she. Bob invited her.*]
ANSWER Bob invited Heta and **her**.

EXERCISE 4 Writing Pronouns Used as Direct Objects and Indirect Objects

Complete each sentence below by writing an appropriate pronoun on the line in the sentence. Use a variety of pronouns, but do not use *you* or *it*.

EX. 1. I met Ossie and ___her___ at the movies last night.

1. Please call __________ as soon as possible.
2. You should give __________ another chance.
3. Gina loaned __________ a pencil.
4. Tell __________ that joke you heard last night.
5. Our team beat __________ in the tournament.

EXERCISE 5 Identifying Correct Pronoun Forms

Each sentence below contains two pronouns in parentheses. Complete each sentence by underlining the correct pronoun.

EX. 1. The mayor gave (*we*, *us*) an award.

1. The city council nominated Rafael and (*I*, *me*) because we worked hard all summer to clean up the vacant lot.
2. Other students helped (*we*, *us*), too.
3. When the workers were finished, the boss presented (*they*, *them*) with a letter from the city.
4. Turning the lot into a park helped the city and (*we*, *us*).
5. People in the neighborhood loaned Melba and (*she*, *her*) rakes and brooms.

EXERCISE 6 Proofreading Sentences for Correct Use of Pronouns

If a sentence below contains an incorrect pronoun, write the correct pronoun on the line before the sentence. If the sentence contains no pronoun errors, write C on the line.

EX. ___me___ 1. Aunt Lois joined Tina and I at the auditorium.

_______ 1. Mr. Tamaka chose her and Philippe for the leading roles in the play.

_______ 2. The director called Sue and they for another audition.

_______ 3. Tina told Phoebe and I about the rehearsal schedule.

_______ 4. On Tuesday, my mother drove me to the rehearsal.

_______ 5. The dancers in the play gave Symon and she flowers after the performance.

PRONOUNS AS OBJECTS OF PREPOSITIONS

19e The *object of a preposition* is in the objective case.

A ***prepositional phrase*** is a group of words consisting of a preposition, a noun or a pronoun that serves as the object of the preposition, and any modifiers of that object.

EXAMPLES June waved at **us.** [*Us* is the object of the preposition *at*.]
The letter was addressed to **her** and **me.** [*Her* and *me* are the compound object of the preposition *to*.]

 **REFERENCE NOTE:** For a list of prepositions, see page 117. For more information on prepositional phrases, see pages 133–137.

EXERCISE 7 Choosing Correct Pronouns Used as Objects of Prepositions

Complete each sentence below by underlining the correct pronoun or pair of pronouns in parentheses.

EX. 1. The food was shared by (*he and she, him and her*).

1. Please pass the enchiladas to (*me, I*).
2. Enchiladas are rolled tortillas that have cheese or some other filling in (*they, them*).
3. Aunt Sofia gave this recipe for enchiladas to my brother and (*I, me*).
4. It is the best recipe for (*we, us*).
5. After softening the tortillas, put meat, cheese, or another filling in (*they, them*).
6. Roll up the tortillas and put grated cheese on top of (*they, them*).
7. Listen to (*him and I, him and me*) talk about the cooking directions.
8. Why don't you stay and eat dinner with (*us, we*)?
9. Just between you and (*I, me*), this will be one of the best meals you've ever tasted.
10. According to (*him, he*), we should eat enchiladas every day of the week.

EXERCISE 8 Using Pronouns as Objects of Prepositions

Each sentence below contains a noun or a phrase in italics. On the line before each sentence, write a pronoun that could be used to replace the italicized word or words.

EX. ___them___ 1. Hillary sent postcards to *Wanda and Sue.*

________ 1. An interesting man sat between my *sister and me* on the airplane.

________ 2. My sister stayed close to *Mom and Dad* as we walked through the airport.

________ 3. This was an exciting but scary experience for *my sister.*

________ 4. The steward on the plane gave snacks to *all the passengers.*

________ 5. In spite of *the crying baby,* we had a good flight.

________ 6. For *Dad,* this would be a business trip.

________ 7. While Dad worked, we stayed with *Aunt Isobelle* in Amsterdam.

________ 8. Aunt Isobelle toured the canals along with *my sister and me.*

________ 9. Everyone toured the house where Anne Frank had lived except *Aunt Isobelle.*

________ 10. Then we went to see paintings by *Vincent van Gogh* at a local museum.

WHO *AND* WHOM

19f The pronoun *who* has different forms in the nominative and objective cases. *Who* is the nominative form. *Whom* is the objective form.

In spoken English, the use of *whom* is becoming less common. In fact, when you are speaking, you may correctly begin any question with *who* regardless of the grammar of the sentence. In written English, however, you should distinguish between *who* and *whom*.

When you need to decide whether to use *who* or *whom* in a question, follow these steps:

Step 1: Rephrase the question as a statement.
Step 2: Decide how the pronoun is used in the statement—as a subject, a predicate nominative, an object of the verb, or an object of a preposition.
Step 3: Determine the case of the pronoun according to the rules of standard English.
Step 4: Select the correct form of the pronoun.

EXAMPLE (*Who, Whom*) are those men?
Step 1: The statement is *Those men are (who, whom).*
Step 2: The subject is *men*, the verb is *are*, and the pronoun is the predicate nominative.
Step 3: A pronoun used as a predicate nominative should be in the nominative case.
Step 4: The nominative form is *who.*
ANSWER **Who** are those men?

Peanuts reprinted by permission of UFS, Inc.

EXERCISE 9 Choosing *Who* or *Whom*

In each sentence below, underline the correct pronoun form.

EX. 1. (*Who*, *Whom*) did he choose?

1. (*Who*, *Whom*) is your coach?
2. The winners of the game were (*who*, *whom*)?
3. To (*who*, *whom*) did you loan my book?
4. (*Who*, *Whom*) have we forgotten to put on the list?
5. (*Who*, *Whom*) did you sit beside in math class?
6. (*Who*, *Whom*) is the present for?
7. For (*who*, *whom*) did you make that burrito?
8. In the fourth quarter, he passed the ball to (*who*, *whom*)?
9. With (*who*, *whom*) will you share your orange?
10. (*Who*, *Whom*) is your science teacher?

EXERCISE 10 Proofreading for Errors in the Use of *Who* and *Whom*

If a sentence below contains an error in the use of *who* or *whom*, write the correct pronoun on the line before the sentence. If a sentence contains no errors, write C on the line.

EX. Whom 1. Who have you invited to the party?

______ 1. Who called while I was in the shower?

______ 2. Whom will get your vote for class president?

______ 3. For who did Zeinab design that costume?

______ 4. With whom are we going to the movies?

______ 5. Whom wants another carrot stick?

PRONOUN APPOSITIVES AND REFLEXIVE PRONOUNS

PRONOUNS AS APPOSITIVES

Sometimes a pronoun is followed directly by a noun that identifies the pronoun. Such a noun is called an *appositive.*

EXAMPLE We **students** held a car wash. [The noun *students* is an appositive identifying the pronoun *we.*]

19g In deciding which pronoun to use before an appositive, omit the appositive, and try each form of the pronoun separately.

EXAMPLE Last night, (*we, us*) musicians had a concert. [*We had a concert. Us had a concert.*]

ANSWER Last night, **we** musicians had a concert.

EXAMPLE The police officer thanked (*we, us*) volunteers. [*The police officer thanked we. The police officer thanked us.*]

ANSWER The police officer thanked **us** volunteers.

EXERCISE 11 Choosing Correct Pronouns for Appositives

Complete each sentence below by filling in the blank with either the pronoun *we* or the pronoun *us*.

EX. 1. That was an exciting game for __us__ Cardinals.

1. ______ pet owners should take our animals to the veterinarian for regular checkups.
2. The store gave ______ clerks a large raise in our hourly pay.
3. Yesterday ______ Orioles fans were disappointed at the outcome of the game.
4. Sadly, ______ farmers have had very little rain for our crops this year.
5. Who will design the costumes for ______ chorus members?

REFLEXIVE PRONOUNS

A ***reflexive pronoun*** refers to the subject and directs the action of the verb back to the subject.

REFLEXIVE PRONOUNS	
First Person	myself, ourselves
Second Person	yourself, yourselves
Third Person	himself, herself, itself, themselves

19h The reflexive pronouns *himself* and *themselves* can be used as objects. Don't use the nonstandard forms *hisself* and *theirselfs* or *theirselves* in place of *himself* and *themselves.*

NONSTANDARD The farmer made hisself a shed for his tractor.
STANDARD The farmer made **himself** a shed for his tractor.

NONSTANDARD Of course, most candidates vote for theirselves.
STANDARD Of course, most candidates vote for **themselves**.

EXERCISE 12 Identifying Correct Pronoun Forms

For each of the sentences below, underline the correct pronoun in parentheses.

EX. 1. They helped (*themselves*, *theirselves*) to the lemonade.

1. Ansel Adams really enjoyed (*hisself, himself*) while taking pictures.
2. People who gossip should keep their words to (*themselves, theirselves*).
3. Virgil and his friends often keep to (*theirselves, themselves*) and rarely come to our meetings.
4. While preparing for the test, Elton asked (*hisself, himself*) many review questions.
5. All by (*himself, hisself*), John built a playhouse for his little brother.

CHAPTER REVIEW

A. Identifying Correct Pronoun Forms

For each of the sentences below, underline the correct pronoun in parentheses.

EX. 1. Frank sent Gina and (*she*, *<u>her</u>*) a letter.

1. John Lucas and (*he, him*) have become very successful coaches in the NBA.
2. They told (*theirselves, themselves*) not to be afraid on the roller coaster.
3. (*Who, Whom*) have you told about your experience in Milan?
4. The librarian was very helpful to Samantha and (*me, I*).
5. (*We, Us*) volunteers are always happy to help out in an emergency.

B. Correcting Errors in Pronoun Use

Most sentences in the following paragraph contain at least one error each in the use of pronoun forms. Correct each pronoun error by drawing a line through it and writing the correct pronoun form above it.

EX. 1 For ~~we~~ us athletes, Kenny Walker is an inspiration.

As a young child, Kenny Walker set a goal for hisself. He would not let deafness be a handicap. At school the other children and him played games at recess. Because Kenny was deaf, the team captains often picked he last. To they, Kenny was "different." However, Kenny and his mother told theirselves not to give up. Between him and she, they made a promise to work and train. By the time his friends and him were in high school, Kenny was a great football player. He went on to the University of Nebraska, where he became the defensive player of the year in the Big Eight. Whom is Kenny today? He is a defensive end for the

Denver Broncos. To us football fans, his story is one of courage and strength. Every time he runs out onto the playing field, Kenny Walker teaches an important lesson to you and I. Us players should always keep that lesson in mind. People can often succeed even when them are challenged. It seems to me that every person has problems and challenges special to him or she. Each of us people must work hard to deal with those problems and challenges. Kenny Walker believed in hisself. He showed you and I that dreams can come true if a person is willing to work hard. My favorite player is him, Kenny Walker.

C. Writing a Postcard

You are a news reporter. You and another reporter have been assigned to the news office in Israel. On your own paper, draw a postcard like the one below. Then, write to a friend in your hometown to tell him or her what you have seen and done since you've been in this country. Use encyclopedias and other reference books to find details you might include in your postcard. Be sure to use pronouns correctly.

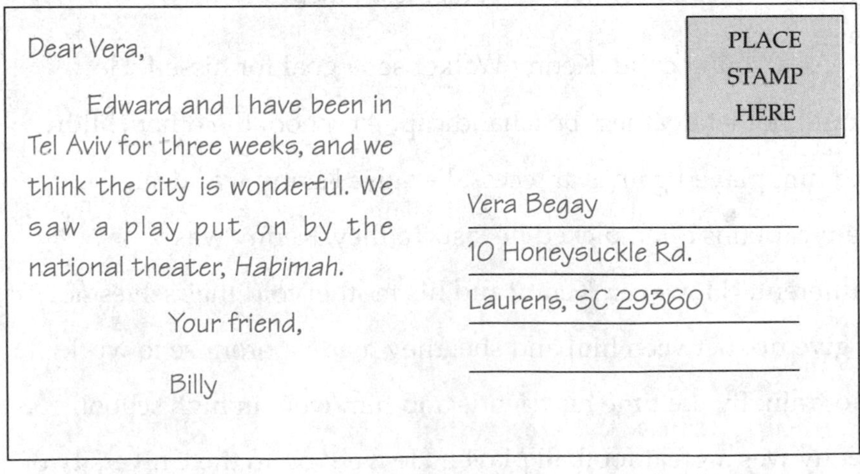

Dear Vera,

Edward and I have been in Tel Aviv for three weeks, and we think the city is wonderful. We saw a play put on by the national theater, *Habimah.*

Your friend,

Billy

PLACE STAMP HERE

Vera Begay
10 Honeysuckle Rd.
Laurens, SC 29360

COMPARISON OF ADJECTIVES AND ADVERBS

20a The three degrees of comparison of modifiers are the *positive,* the *comparative,* and the *superlative.*

(1) The *positive degree* is used when only one thing is being described.

EXAMPLES The water is **cold**.
Brad swam **swiftly** to shore.

(2) The *comparative degree* is used when two things are being compared.

EXAMPLES This water is **colder** than the water in Florida.
Tanya swam **more swiftly** than any of the other girls did.

(3) The *superlative degree* is used when three or more things are being compared.

EXAMPLES The water in Maine is the **coldest** of any water I've found.
Of all the racers, Brad swam the **most swiftly**.

REGULAR COMPARISON

Most one-syllable modifiers form their comparative and superlative degrees by adding *–er* and *–est*. Notice that both adjectives and adverbs form their degrees of comparison in the same way.

Positive	Comparative	Superlative
warm	warmer	warmest
thin	thinner	thinnest
straight	straighter	straightest
fast	faster	fastest

Some two-syllable modifiers form their comparative and superlative degrees by adding *–er* and *–est*. Other two-syllable modifiers form their comparative and superlative degrees by using *more* or *less* and *most* or *least*.

Positive	Comparative	Superlative
funny	funnier	funniest
tiny	tinier	tiniest
cheerful	more cheerful	most cheerful
often	more often	most often
sneaky	less sneaky	least sneaky
extreme	less extreme	least extreme

Modifiers that have three or more syllables form the comparative degree by using *more* or *less* and the superlative degree by using *most* or *least.*

Positive	Comparative	Superlative
difficult	less difficult	least difficult
important	more important	most important
thoughtfully	less thoughtfully	least thoughtfully
mysteriously	more mysteriously	most mysteriously

EXERCISE 1 Forming Degrees of Comparison of Modifiers

On the lines provided, write the forms for the comparative and superlative degrees of each of the following modifiers. Use a dictionary as necessary.

EX. 1. light ___lighter___ ___lightest___

1. soon ______ ______
2. independent ______ ______
3. wise ______ ______
4. lightly ______ ______
5. beautiful ______ ______
6. hungry ______ ______
7. cautiously ______ ______
8. hopeful ______ ______
9. nice ______ ______
10. shyly ______ ______

CHAPTER 20: USING MODIFIERS CORRECTLY

IRREGULAR COMPARISON

20b Some modifiers do not form their comparative and superlative degrees in the usual ways.

Positive	Comparative	Superlative
bad	worse	worst
far	farther	farthest
good	better	best
well	better	best
many	more	most

EXERCISE 2 Writing Comparative and Superlative Forms of Modifiers

On the line before each of the sentences below, write the correct form of the modifier in parentheses. Use a dictionary as necessary.

EX. ___best___ 1. Aunt Eliana makes the (*good*) enchiladas I have ever tasted.

_______ 1. Jeremy swam (*far*) than any of the other boys.

_______ 2. Joe has collected (*many*) sports cards than Tim.

_______ 3. In the state swimming meet, Kelly performed (*well*) than she ever had before.

_______ 4. Yori is (*good*) in math than in spelling.

_______ 5. The country with the (*many*) people is China.

_______ 6. The flooding is threatening to become (*bad*) than last month's flooding.

_______ 7. Pluto is the (*far*) planet from the sun.

_______ 8. This is the (*much*) money I have ever saved!

_______ 9. Hurricane Andrew was the (*bad*) storm to hit Florida in recent times.

_______ 10. After taking medicine for three days, he felt (*well*) than he had in two weeks.

EXERCISE 3 Using Comparative and Superlative Forms of Modifiers

In the blanks in the following paragraph, write appropriate modifiers from the list on page 221.

EX. [1] The ___worst___ act in the variety show was the one with the dancing poodles.

[1] Yesterday, we went to see a really ____________ show at the Grayson theater. [2] It was a variety show with ____________ funny, quirky, unusual acts. [3] Perhaps the ____________ bizarre of all the acts was the guy who played "The Battle Hymn of the Republic" by banging on a lot of plumbing fixtures. I enjoyed the folk singer from Chile. [4] She sang really ____________. However, my favorite act was the gospel singer. [5] Hers was the ____________ performance of the evening.

EXERCISE 4 Writing Sentences with Correct Forms of Modifiers

You are a movie reviewer. On your own paper, take notes about your two favorite or two least favorite movies. Write five complete sentences that use the comparative and superlative forms of modifiers. Circle the comparative and superlative degrees of modifiers. Some topics you may want to discuss in your review are each movie's plot, action, characters, dialogue, actors, and ending.

EX. 1. The (funniest) movie I have ever seen is Home Alone. Macaulay Culkin is (quicker) than the crooks and (better) than they are at setting traps.

FRANK & ERNEST ® by Bob Thaves

Frank & Ernest reprinted by permission of NEA, Inc.

SPECIAL PROBLEMS IN USING MODIFIERS

20c Use *good* to modify a noun or a pronoun. Use *well* to modify a verb.

EXAMPLES Julio enjoys reading a **good** mystery story. [*Good* modifies the noun *story*.]
The dinner that you made was a **good** one. [*Good* modifies the pronoun *one*.]
His broken leg is healing **well.** [*Well* modifies the verb phrase *is healing*.]

Good should not be used to modify a verb.

NONSTANDARD Lydia speaks Spanish good.
STANDARD Lydia speaks Spanish **well**.

20d Use adjectives, not adverbs, after linking verbs.

A linking verb is often followed by a predicate adjective. The adjective modifies the subject.

EXAMPLE Kadeem looked **nervous** on stage. [The predicate adjective *nervous* modifies the subject *Kadeem*.]

Some linking verbs can also be used as action verbs. As action verbs, they may be modified by adverbs.

EXAMPLE Kadeem looked **nervously** at the audience. [*Nervously* modifies the action verb *looked*.]

REFERENCE NOTE: For a list of linking verbs, see page 109.

EXERCISE 5 Using Adjectives and Adverbs Correctly

On the line before each sentence, write the correct adjective or adverb from the pair in parentheses.

EX. ___sad___ 1. Jerry felt (*sad, sadly*) about losing the race.

_______ 1. Cynthia had a fever and didn't look (*good, well*).

_______ 2. The flowers grew (*quick, quickly*) in the garden.

_______ 3. If you like scary movies, you will think that this is a (*good, well*) one.

_______________ 4. Please stay (*quiet, quietly*) during the play.

_______________ 5. That camera takes (*good, well*) pictures.

_______________ 6. The tortillas smell (*fresh, freshly*).

_______________ 7. That plant will not grow (*strong, strongly*) without water and sun.

_______________ 8. The band practiced all week and sounds (*well, good*) now.

_______________ 9. Rebecca writes poetry (*good, well*).

_______________ 10. The dog smells his food (*careful, carefully*) before eating it.

EXERCISE 6 Finding and Correcting Misused Modifiers in a Paragraph

In the paragraph below, there are ten misused modifiers. Draw a line through each mistake and write the correct form above it.

EX. [1] I ~~sure~~ surely enjoyed the movie.

[1] I could tell that summer was coming quick. [2] And I am happily that it is almost summer. [3] According to the weather forecaster, it will be a well summer with lots of sun. [4] When I go to the beach this summer, I have to be carefully that I do not get a sunburn. [5] The cold water at the beach feels well on a hot day. [6] I always run into the waves and get wet quick. [7] Some of my friends ease in slow. [8] If the wind blows good, we fly a kite at the water's edge. [9] Sometimes I walk along the high-water mark and look close for interesting shells or stones. [10] I know I will feel sadly when summer is over.

DOUBLE COMPARISONS

20e Avoid double comparisons.

A ***double comparison*** is the use of both *–er* and *more* (less) or *–est* and *most* (least) to form a comparison. When you make a comparison, use only one form, not both.

NONSTANDARD Dad's old car had a more smoother ride than his new one has.
STANDARD Dad's old car had a **smoother** ride than his new one has.

NONSTANDARD This is the most quickest way to the airport.
STANDARD This is the **quickest** way to the airport.

20f Avoid the use of double negatives.

A ***double negative*** is the use of two negative words to express one negative idea.

Common Negative Words			
barely	never	none	nothing
hardly	no	no one	nowhere
neither	nobody	not (–n't)	scarcely

NONSTANDARD Shing didn't have none of his allowance left.
STANDARD Shing had **none** of his allowance left.

NONSTANDARD She couldn't find a seat nowhere else on the train.
STANDARD She could find a seat **nowhere** else on the train.
STANDARD She could**n't** find a seat anywhere else on the train.

EXERCISE 7 Eliminating Double Comparisons and Double Negatives

Revise the following sentences to eliminate the double comparisons and double negatives.

EX. 1. Math seems more easier this year than last year.
Math seems easier this year than last year.

1. Jon had not never been out of the country. ______________________

2. Penny won't never forget her best friend. ______________________

____

3. Traffic is most heaviest around five o'clock in the afternoon. ________

____

4. Ted isn't going to the meeting neither. ______________________

____

5. The baby was more quieter than a mouse. ______________________

____

6. Are you working more longer than you used to? ________________

____

7. I am not doing nothing tonight. ____________________________

____

8. Hasn't James never seen the ocean? __________________________

____

9. Dominique couldn't never be mean to anyone. ____________________

____

10. Of all the members of the basketball team, Antonio is the most shortest. ____

____

EXERCISE 8 Revising to Correct Double Comparisons and Double Negatives

On your own paper, rewrite the paragraph below, correcting nonstandard use of modifiers.

EX. [1] The Mbuti live in Zaire in one of the world's most richest forests.
1. *The Mbuti live in Zaire in one of the world's richest forests.*

[1] The Mbuti don't use nothing but leaves and branches to build a village. [2] A woman starts building a hut by making a dome from the more younger trees in a clearing. [3] Leaves cover this dome, keeping out the most worst rain and winds. [4] The Mbuti never live hardly more than two months in one place. [5] They move on to make a new village where food sources are more closer.

PLACEMENT OF MODIFIERS

20g Place modifying phrases and clauses as close as possible to the words they modify.

Notice how the meaning of these sentences changes when the position of the phrase *across the street* changes.

EXAMPLES The woman **across the street** opened a clothing shop for children. [The phrase modifies *woman*.]
The woman opened a clothing shop for children **across the street.** [The phrase modifies *children*.]
Across the street, the woman opened a clothing shop for children. [The phrase modifies *opened*.]

A ***prepositional phrase*** is a group of words consisting of a preposition, a noun or pronoun that serves as the object of the preposition, and any modifiers of that object. A prepositional phrase used as an adjective should be placed directly after the word it modifies.

MISPLACED The dog ran up to Julie **with long, shaggy hair**.
CLEAR The dog **with long, shaggy hair** ran up to Julie.

A prepositional phrase used as an adverb should be placed near the word it modifies.

MISPLACED Janet read about a lost kitten **in that magazine**.
CLEAR **In that magazine**, Janet read about a lost kitten.

Avoid placing a prepositional phrase so that it seems to modify either of two words. Place the phrase so that it clearly modifies the word you intend it to modify.

MISPLACED Rico said **on Friday** he had found a missing wallet. [Does the phrase modify *said* or *found*?]
CLEAR Rico said that he had found a missing wallet **on Friday**.
CLEAR **On Friday**, Rico said that he had found a missing wallet.

EXERCISE 9 Revising Sentences with Misplaced Prepositional Phrases

The meaning of each of the following sentences is not clear because the modifying phrase is misplaced. Decide where the phrase belongs. Then write the revised sentence on the line.

EX. 1. Willis gave a speech to explain how to look for a job at the new civic center.

Willis gave a speech at the new civic center to explain how to look for a job.

1. The girl is jogging around the park from next door. ____________

____

2. The boy was riding on a bicycle in blue polka-dot shorts. ____________

____

3. She gave the gift to the boy with the pink wrapping paper. ____________

____

4. I heard a report that a bad storm is coming on the radio. ____________

____

5. The train arrived after we had lunch from San Diego. ____________

____

EXERCISE 10 Placing Prepositional Phrases Correctly

On your own paper, rewrite each of the following sentences by adding the prepositional phrase given in parentheses. Be careful to place each prepositional phrase near the word or words it modifies.

EX. 1. Many paintings show strange, fantastical scenes. (by Marc Chagall)

1. Many paintings by Marc Chagall show strange, fantastical scenes.

1. Elaine put the shirt on the baby. (with green stripes)
2. The monkey was chattering at the children. (in the tree)
3. The girl is making a dress. (with pigtails)
4. We learned that a big blizzard was coming. (from Aunt Melanie)
5. The boy was walking the dog. (with the red boots)

PLACEMENT OF PARTICIPIAL PHRASES

20h A *participial phrase* consists of a verb form—either a present participle or a past participle—and its related words. A participial phrase modifies a noun or a pronoun. Like a prepositional phrase, a participial phrase should be placed as close as possible to the word that it modifies.

EXAMPLES **Listening to the radio**, she heard her favorite song. [The participial phrase modifies *she*.]

Greg's violin, **bought at a secondhand store**, is actually a valuable antique.[The participial phrase modifies *violin*.]

A participial phrase that is not placed next to the noun or pronoun that it modifies is a ***misplaced modifier***.

MISPLACED Lying on the back seat of the car, Jon found his guitar.

CLEAR Jon found his guitar **lying on the back seat of the car**.

A participial phrase that does not clearly and sensibly modify a word in the sentence is a ***dangling participle***.

DANGLING Visiting the city's animal shelter, the perfect puppy was found.

CLEAR **Visiting the city's animal shelter**, we found the perfect puppy.

20i An *adjective clause* modifies a noun or a pronoun. Most adjective clauses begin with a relative pronoun—*that, which, who, whom,* or *whose.*

MISPLACED My brother Len works for a paint company who is trying to grow a beard.

CLEAR My brother Len, **who is trying to grow a beard**, works for a paint company.

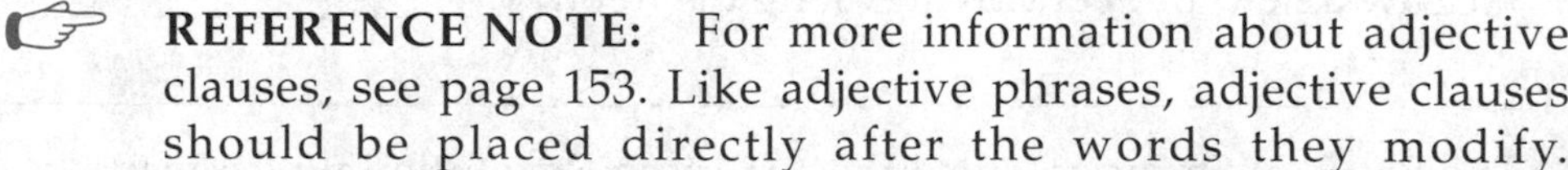

REFERENCE NOTE: For more information about adjective clauses, see page 153. Like adjective phrases, adjective clauses should be placed directly after the words they modify.

EXERCISE 11 Revising Sentences to Correct Errors in the Use of Modifiers

On the lines below, revise the sentences to correct the errors in the placement of modifiers. [Hint: You will need to add, delete, or rearrange some words.]

EX. 1. The band began to play for the huge audience marching down the football field.
Marching down the football field, the band began to play for the huge audience.

1. Deirdre has earned a scholarship whose record is outstanding. ________

2. Listening to the words, tears suddenly came to my eyes. ________

3. The dress does not fit me that you made. ________

4. Played by the band, I heard some of my favorite songs. ________

5. The man hurried through the store wearing a raincoat and boots. ________

6. Ms. Cuomo saw two owls camping at the river. ________

7. Sitting under that shady tree, some of my best poems are written. ________

8. We saw a herd of deer driving along the freeway. ________

9. The Battle of Saratoga saved the American Revolution which was fought in 1777. ________

10. I found a book at the library that was written by Amy Tan. ________

CHAPTER REVIEW

A. Correcting Misplaced and Dangling Modifiers

Each of the following sentences contains a dangling or misplaced modifier. On the lines after each sentence, rewrite the sentence so that it is clear and correct.

EX. 1. The car was driven by the man with new paint and white sidewall tires.
The man drove the car with new paint and white sidewall tires.

1. He told us that he had saved his allowance for a year to buy the bike at the party. ____________________

____

2. Hurtling through space, some scientists think asteroids will someday hit the earth. ____________________

____

3. Driving to the mall, a shortcut was discovered. ____________________

____

4. An orange lay on the table that had been peeled. ____________________

____

5. I got a dog from the pet shop that is only six weeks old. ____________________

____

B. Identifying and Correcting Errors in the Use of Modifiers

On your own paper, rewrite the following paragraph to eliminate the errors in the use of modifiers.

EX. [1] There aren't hardly any tigers left in one of India's national parks.
1. There are hardly any tigers left in one of India's national parks.

[1] Some people believe that tigers are the most beautifulest of all the animals. [2] In the past, tourists who wanted to see tigers couldn't find no better place than this park. [3] The tigers here seemed more friendlier. [4] The chances to see a tiger here were well. [5] This

situation was due to the fact that the tigers were protected so good by the park system. [6] Today, though, you can't scarcely find a tiger in the park. [7] In 1991, the larger number of tigers counted was forty-five. [8] In 1992, the count was smallest; there were only seventeen tigers left. [9] Much tigers have been killed by poachers. [10] Other tigers may have grown tiredly of having humans around, and so they may have left the park.

C. Using Modifiers Correctly

Choose one of the pairs of topics below, and compare the two topics. Use at least two comparative and two superlative forms of modifiers to compare the topics. Write your answers on the lines below.

videocassette movies and movies in a theater
soccer and football
Mexican food and Italian food

EX. Sitting on the couch in my living room, I like to watch movies on video. Movies in the theater are more recent, but I can't stop the film in the middle to go to the kitchen for a snack.

ACCEPT / AS (LIKE)

The lessons on the next few pages contain a ***glossary***, or alphabetical list, of common problems in English usage. You will notice that a number of examples used in this glossary are labeled *standard* or *nonstandard*. ***Standard English*** is used in *formal* situations, such as speeches and compositions for school. It is also used in *informal* situations, such as conversations and everyday writing. ***Nonstandard English*** does not follow the rules and guidelines of standard English.

accept, except *Accept* is a verb that means "to receive." *Except* may be either a verb or a preposition. As a verb, it means "to leave out." As a preposition, it means "excluding."

EXAMPLES Jerome **accepted** the award. [verb]
Because she is not feeling well, Meredith will be **excepted** from play rehearsal. [verb]
Everyone **except** Lucinda attended the concert. [preposition]

ain't Avoid this word in speaking and writing. It is nonstandard English. Use *is not*, *am not*, or *are not*.

all right Used as an adjective, *all right* means "satisfactory" or "unhurt." Used as an adverb, *all right* means "well enough." *All right* should always be written as two words. (*Alright* is nonstandard English.)

EXAMPLES The weather looks **all right** for a picnic. [adjective]
Howie did **all right** in the spelling contest. [adverb]

a lot *A lot* should always be written as two words.

EXAMPLE There is **a lot** of food left over from Jon's birthday party.

already, all ready *Already* means "previously." *All ready* means "completely prepared."

EXAMPLES Everyone in our group was **already** on the bus by the time Mr. Lo arrived.
I practiced for a long time, and I'm **all ready** for my piano recital tonight.

among See **between, among**, page 235.

as See **like, as**, page 237.

EXERCISE 1 Identifying Correct Usage

Underline the correct word or words in parentheses in each of the sentences below.

EX. 1. All the boys are in line (*accept, except*) Michael.

1. Ruth Bader Ginsburg (*accepted, excepted*) the nomination to become a Supreme Court justice.
2. Seth had a bad cold, but he's (*all right, alright*) now.
3. Suzi is packed and (*already, all ready*) to leave for vacation.
4. Because of the large crowd, there (*ain't, aren't*) many empty seats.
5. No school council members will be (*accepted, excepted*) from today's meeting.
6. By the time the waitress brought Rico's lasagna, I had (*already, all ready*) finished eating my lunch.
7. The store sold every copy of Amy Tan's latest book (*accept, except*) one.
8. Because I don't have to do (*alot, a lot*) of homework, I can go to the concert with you.
9. Did Franklin (*accept, except*) the nomination for class officer?
10. Theresa read (*alot, a lot*) of Mariana's poems.

Beetle Bailey reprinted with special permission of King Features Syndicate, Inc.

BETWEEN / HAD OUGHT

between, among Use *between* when referring to two people or things at a time. They may be part of a group consisting of more than two. Use *among* when referring to a group rather than to separate individuals.

EXAMPLES I divided the work **between** Abdul and Jamie.
There isn't much difference **between** these four brands of soap. [Although there are more than two brands, each one is being compared with the others separately.]
The job of preparing and printing the programs was divided **among** six students. [The six students are thought of as a group.]

bring, take *Bring* shows action directed *toward* the speaker or writer. *Take* shows action directed *away from* the speaker or writer. Think of *bring* as related to *come* and *take* as related to *go*.

EXAMPLES **Bring** the microphone to me.
Please **take** the piano stool with you.

bust, busted Avoid using these words in place of *burst* or *break*.

EXAMPLES A balloon **bursts** when stuck with a pin. [not busts]
His glasses **broke** when he dropped them. [not busted]

could of Do not write *of* with the helping verb *could*. Write *have* instead. Also avoid *ought to of, should of, would of, might of*, and *must of*.

EXAMPLE Tito's band could **have** performed all night. [not of]

except See **accept, except**, page 233.

fewer, less *Fewer* is used with plural words. *Less* is used with singular words. *Fewer* tells "how many," and *less* tells "how much."

EXAMPLES Sam told **fewer** jokes than he had planned.
There was **less** applause last night.

good, well *Good* is always an adjective. Never use *good* to modify a verb; use *well*, which is an adverb.

NONSTANDARD Marjorie and Paco sang their duet good.
STANDARD Marjorie and Paco sang their duet **well**.

Feel good and *feel well* mean different things. *Feel good* means "to feel happy or pleased." *Feel well* means "to feel healthy."

EXAMPLES Performing makes me feel **good**.
After eating the large meal, Paula did not feel **well**.

had ought, hadn't ought The verb *ought* should never be used with the verb *had*.

NONSTANDARD The director had ought to give clearer directions to the cast.
STANDARD The director **ought** to give clearer directions to the cast.

EXERCISE 2 Revising Sentences by Correcting Errors in Usage

The sentences below contain errors in usage. On your own paper, revise each sentence, using standard English. [Note: A sentence may contain more than one error.]

EX. 1. No one wanted to try the soup accept Willard.
1. No one wanted to try the soup except Willard.

1. Mark would of come to the show, but he caught the flu and doesn't feel good.
2. As I was getting into my costume, the zipper busted.
3. David hadn't ought to lift that piece of stage scenery by himself.
4. Will you take the magician's rabbit over here to us?
5. Mrs. Adriana divided the pizza between the six of us.
6. Sam felt well because he had less tests on Tuesday than Paula did.
7. I wish I could of brought the dog on our trip.
8. I have less sponsors than you for the Walk for Hunger.
9. You had ought to clean your room before Mom gets home.
10. He busted out laughing when I told him the joke I had just heard.

HISSELF / TRY AND

hisself, theirself, theirselves These words are nonstandard English. Use *himself* and *themselves*.

EXAMPLES Yoshi was proud of **himself** for finishing the race. [not *hisself*]
The girls gave **themselves** extra time to get ready. [not *theirselves*]

its, it's *Its* is a personal pronoun in the possessive case. *It's* is a contraction of *it is* and *it has*.

EXAMPLES Please feed the cat because **it's** ready for **its** dinner. [*It's* is the contraction of *it is*. *Its* is a possessive pronoun.]
It's been snowing since yesterday. [*It's* is the contraction of *it has*.]

kind, sort, type The words *this, that, these,* and *those* should agree in number with the words *kind, sort,* and *type*. *This* and *that* are singular. *These* and *those* are plural.

EXAMPLES **That kind** of bird is rarely seen in this part of the country.
Those kinds of cars are very reliable.

learn, teach *Learn* means "to acquire knowledge." *Teach* means "to instruct" or "to show how."

EXAMPLES Danielle is **learning** how to play chess.
Mr. Haddad is **teaching** Bobby how to play the guitar.

less See **fewer, less**, page 235.

like, as *Like* is a preposition; therefore, it introduces a prepositional phrase. In informal English, *like* is often used as a conjunction meaning "as." In formal English, *as* is always preferred.

EXAMPLES **Like** my mother, I order sushi when we go out to eat. [*Like* introduces the phrase *Like my mother*.]
Shahla added one cup of milk, **as** the recipe directed. [*As the recipe directed* is a clause and needs the conjunction *as*, not the preposition *like*, to introduce it.]

might of, must of See **could of**, page 235.

real In informal English, the adjective *real* is often used as an adverb meaning "very" or "extremely." In formal English, *real, very,* and *extremely* are often overused and should be avoided.

INFORMAL Their new house is real bright because of the large windows.
FORMAL Their new house is **quite** bright because of the large windows.

this here, that there The words *here* and *there* are not needed after *this* and *that*.

EXAMPLES Mia can ride **this** horse. [not *this here*]
That one might be too playful for her. [not *that there*]

try and In informal English, *try and* is often used for *try to*. In formal English, *try to* is preferred.

INFORMAL Let's try and win a prize.
FORMAL Let's **try to** win a prize.

EXERCISE 3 Revising Sentences by Correcting Errors in Usage

The sentences below contain twenty errors in usage. On your own paper, revise each sentence, using standard English.

EX. 1. The young children weren't acting like they should have.
1. The young children weren't acting as they should have.

1. Will you learn me how to cook these kind of authentic Mexican dishes, Mrs. Rodríguez?
2. They must of looked at pictures of theirselves in the photo album no less than ten times.
3. Saburo tried and taught hisself some magic tricks real quickly.
4. Should we try and finish our report by this here Wednesday?
5. Sabrina might of decided to study piano like her mother did.
6. That there wolf taught it's cubs to hunt for theirself.
7. Its too bad; your cousin might of won.
8. These sort of hand-woven rugs are imported real often from Afghanistan.

WELL / YOUR, YOU'RE

well See **good, well**, page 235.

when, where Do not use *when* or *where* incorrectly in writing a definition.

NONSTANDARD "Occasional" is when something happens now and then.
STANDARD "Occasional" means something happens now and then.

where Do not use *where* for *that*.

EXAMPLE I read on a map **that** two of the countries bordering China are India and North Korea. [not *where*]

who, which, that The relative pronoun *who* refers to people only. *Which* refers to things only. *That* refers to people or things.

EXAMPLES Li is the student **who** is collecting money for the field trip. [person]
Here are the concert tickets, **which** were a gift from my aunt. [things]
The waiter brought me the empanada **that** I ordered. [thing]
Ms. Yee wanted to reward the boy **that** returned her wallet. [person]

whose, who's *Whose* is the possessive form of *who*. *Who's* is a contraction of *who is* or *who has*.

EXAMPLES **Whose** jacket is on the floor? [possessive pronoun]
Who's at the door? [contraction of *who is*]
Who's finished reading the chapter? [contraction of *who has*]

without, unless Do not use the preposition *without* in place of the conjunction *unless*.

EXAMPLE Don't use your computer **unless** Paul first shows you how. [not without]

would of See **could of**, page 235.

your, you're *Your* is the possessive form of *you*. *You're* is a contraction of *you are*.

EXAMPLES **Your** brother answered the phone.
You're just in time for dinner.

EXERCISE 4 Identifying Correct Usage

Underline the correct word or words in parentheses in each of the sentences below.

EX. 1. (*Whose, Who's*) been to Ellis Island in New York?

1. Myrtilla Miner was the person (*who, which*) opened an African American girls' school in Washington, D.C., in 1851.
2. I believe (*your, you're*) sitting in my seat.
3. A synonym is (*a word that, when a word*) has the same or nearly the same meaning as another word.
4. Did you forget (*your, you're*) jacket on the bus?
5. Sara was the first person (*who, which*) answered the phone.
6. There is the boy (*whose, who's*) pen I borrowed.
7. I read in our textbook (*that, where*) February 5 is the day people in Mexico celebrate Constitution Day.
8. The bus driver won't leave (*unless, without*) all the students are seated.
9. From this far away, Sabrina can't see (*good, well*) without her glasses.
10. (*Who's, Whose*) going to have some of these *buñuelos* with me?

EXERCISE 5 Using Words Correctly

On your own paper, write a sentence to demonstrate any five of the glossary entries below.

well (good)
when, where
who, which, that
whose, who's
without, unless
would of (could of)
your, you're

EX. 1. Did she give you your books?

CHAPTER REVIEW

A. Identifying Correct Usage

Underline the correct word or words in parentheses in each of the sentences below.

EX. 1. Marian Anderson was (*between*, *among*) this country's greatest opera singers.

1. I read (*that*, *where*) a famous conductor said Ms. Anderson had the kind of voice that is heard only "once in a hundred years."
2. Because she was African American, Marian Anderson was not always (*accepted*, *excepted*) by U.S. audiences of the 1920s and 1930s.
3. By that time, she was (*already*, *all ready*) well known in Europe.
4. In 1939, the Daughters of the American Revolution felt Marian Anderson (*hadn't ought to*, *shouldn't*) sing in Constitution Hall.
5. Eleanor Roosevelt, (*who*, *which*) was First Lady, found Ms. Anderson a place to sing.
6. She didn't want anything to stop Ms. Anderson from coming to Washington, D.C., to (*bring*, *take*) her music to the people.
7. Try (*and*, *to*) imagine what it was like on that cold afternoon at the Lincoln Memorial.
8. Ms. Anderson must (*of*, *have*) been amazed to see seventy-five thousand people in the audience.
9. She sang (*a lot*, *alot*) of beautiful songs.
10. Marian Anderson, (*whose*, *who's*) voice thrilled audiences everywhere, died in 1993.

B. Revising Sentences to Correct Errors in Usage

Some of the following sentences contain errors in usage. Rewrite the sentences correctly on your own paper. Write *C* for those sentences that are correct.

EX. 1. I'd like to buy this here belt.
   1. I'd like to buy this belt.

1. Melissa is a shy person who doesn't like alot of attention.
2. During the extremely cold weather, our water pipes froze, and then they busted.

3. Will Wanda be at the sports banquet to except her trophy?
4. Please bring me a glass of water.
5. They sold less tickets to the play than they had hoped.
6. Those type of watches are no longer being made.
7. Salvador tried to wipe hisself off after falling in the mud.
8. With her head tucked into her green jacket, the little girl looked like a turtle.
9. I can't believe that your moving so far away.
10. Mrs. Olivero should of told us that we were having an English quiz today.

C. Using Words Correctly in Writing

The year is 2100. You are a new crew member of an underwater research laboratory. You may send letters home only once a month. On your own paper, write a letter to a friend to describe what you have seen and to explain how you feel in your new assignment. In your letter, use at least five of the words or expressions that were covered in this chapter. Underline the words or expressions you use.

EX. Dear Martha,

It's been a month since I've written. I would have written sooner, but we can send letters only once a month. I feel very good about my decision to work on the AquaStation, which now has a crew of fifteen. We wear gill suits when we conduct our experiments outside the AquaStation. I got your letter last month. Thanks for sending it.

Your friend,
Alfred

THE PRONOUN I AND PROPER NOUNS

22a Capitalize the pronoun *I*.

EXAMPLE Perhaps **I** can help you.

22b Capitalize proper nouns.

A ***proper noun*** is a specific name for a particular person, place, thing, or idea. It is always capitalized. A ***common noun*** names a type of person, place, thing, or idea. A common noun is not capitalized unless it begins a sentence or is part of a title.

Proper Nouns	Common Nouns
Brazil	country
August	month
Santha Rama Rau	author
Sequoia National Park	park
USS *Nautilus*	submarine

 **REFERENCE NOTE:** For information about using capital letters in abbreviations, see the chart on page 257.

Some proper nouns consist of more than one word. In these names, short prepositions (those of fewer than five letters) and articles (*a, an,* and *the*) are not capitalized.

EXAMPLES Declaration **of** Independence
Eric **the** Red

 **REFERENCE NOTE:** For more information about proper nouns, see page 97.

EXERCISE 1 Identifying Correct Capitalization

For each of the following pairs of phrases, write *C* on the line before the phrase that is capitalized correctly.

EX. ______ 1. a. visit a Museum
C b. visit the Museum of Science

_____ 1. a. in late September
_____ b. in late september

_____ 2. a. the Empire State Building
_____ b. a Building in New York City

_____ 3. a. my parents and i
_____ b. my parents and I

_____ 4. a. a famous movie director
_____ b. a director named steven spielberg

_____ 5. a. a clown named Rufus The Red
_____ b. a clown named Rufus the Red

EXERCISE 2 Correcting Errors in Capitalization

For each sentence below, correct all errors in capitalization. Write your corrections on the line after each sentence. Separate your answers with semicolons.

EX. 1. In 1992, my parents and i went to peru.
I; Peru

1. Our flight left miami, florida, early in the Morning.

____

2. We traveled on faucett airlines and flew over puerto rico.

____

3. The flight attendant could see that i was really excited about my first trip outside the united states.

____

4. We landed in lima, the capital city of peru.

____

5. Then we took a Taxi to the gold museum.

____

PLACES AND PEOPLE

22c Capitalize geographical names.

Type of Name	Examples
continents	North America, Asia
countries	Canada, Poland
cities, towns	Mexico City, Greenfield
states	Texas, North Dakota
islands	Oak Island, Galveston
bodies of water	Sea of Japan, Persian Gulf
streets, highways	North Michigan Avenue, Skyline Drive
parks and forests	Turkey Swamp County Park, Stokes Forest
mountains	Rocky Mountains, Swiss Alps
sections of the country	the Midwest, the South

In a hyphenated street number, the second part of the number is not capitalized.

EXAMPLE East Twenty-third Street

Words such as *east, west, north,* or *south* are not capitalized when the words merely indicate directions.

EXAMPLES That street ends **south** of here. [direction]
These legends are told throughout the **West**. [section of the country]

22d Capitalize the names of planets, stars, and other heavenly bodies.

EXAMPLES Saturn, Betelgeuse, Milky Way

22e Capitalize the names of persons.

EXAMPLES Mai Tranh, Ravi Satas, Red Deer, Maria Lorca

EXERCISE 3 Correcting Errors in Capitalization

For each sentence below, correct the errors in capitalization. Either change capital letters to lowercase letters or change lowercase letters to capital letters. Write your corrections on the line after each sentence. Separate your answers with a semicolon.

EX. 1. Someday I'd love to visit the Etosha National park in namibia.
Etosha National Park; Namibia

1. The country of tunisia is in the northern part of africa.

2. The city of boston sits by the atlantic ocean in the eastern part of massachusetts.

3. The novelist rosario ferré was born in puerto rico in 1942.

4. In science class we watched a film by astonomer carl sagan about the beginnings of the solar system.

5. To get to times square, go north on fifth avenue to Forty-Second street.

6. Many famous writers in the united states were born in the south.

7. The island known as key west is located in the gulf of mexico.

8. The colorado river flows through grand canyon national park.

9. Just a few miles West of washington, d.c., are the blue ridge mountains.

10. Through a telescope, our teacher, Mr. Jiménez, showed us the planets saturn and jupiter.

CHAPTER 22: CAPITAL LETTERS

GROUPS, ORGANIZATIONS, AND RELIGIONS

22f Capitalize the names of organizations, teams, businesses, institutions, and government bodies.

Type of Name	Examples
organizations	Academy of American Poets
teams	Minnesota Vikings
businesses	General Motors Corporation
institutions	Internal Revenue Service

Do not capitalize words such as *hotel, theater,* and *middle school* unless they are part of the name of a particular building or institution.

EXAMPLES Jefferson Middle School
your middle school

22g Capitalize the names of nationalities, races, and peoples.

EXAMPLES French, Egyptian, Navajo, Hispanic

The words *Black* and *White* may or may not be capitalized when they refer to races.

EXAMPLE Both Blacks and Whites [*or* blacks and whites] worked to end slavery.

22h Capitalize the names of religions and their followers, holy days, sacred writings, and specific deities.

Type of Name	Examples
religions and followers	Islam, Christian, Hindu
holy days	Ramadan, Rosh Hashana
sacred writings	Koran, Upanishads, Bible
specific deities	God, Jehovah, Allah, Vishnu

The word *god* is not capitalized when it refers to a god of ancient mythology. The names of specific gods are capitalized.

EXAMPLE The Roman god of war was named Mars.

EXERCISE 4 Proofreading Sentences for Correct Capitalization

For each sentence below, correct the errors in capitalization. Either change capital letters to lowercase letters or change lowercase letters to capital letters. Write your corrections on the line after each sentence. Separate your answers with a semicolon.

EX. 1. My brother went to the university of michigan for one year.
University of Michigan

1. woodman middle school is the oldest school in the city.
____

2. The american automobile association will be closed on christmas.
____

3. Have you called the chamber of commerce about the parade?
____

4. Sara Donham is the minister at the congregational church.
____

5. When you visit Washington, D.C., be sure to see the united states senate.
____

EXERCISE 5 Identifying Correct Capitalization

For each of the pairs of phrases below, write the letter C on the line before each phrase that is capitalized correctly.

EX. __C__ 1. a. Stay at the Shore Hotel.
_____ b. Stay at the shore hotel.

_____ 1. a. the New York Yankees
_____ b. the Dallas cowboys

_____ 2. a. a jewish temple
_____ b. Catholicism

_____ 3. a. French bread
_____ b. a mexican dinner

_____ 4. a. a large, nineteenth-century bible
_____ b. a large, nineteenth-century Bible

OBJECTS, EVENTS, STRUCTURES, AND AWARDS

22i Capitalize the brand names of business products.

EXAMPLES Healthy Choice soups, Canon copier [Notice that the names of the types of products are not capitalized.]

22j Capitalize the names of historical events and periods, special events, and calendar items.

Type of Name	Examples
historical events and periods	Thirty Years War, The Dark Ages
special events and holidays	Cinco de Mayo, Election Day
calendar items	Flag Day

Do not capitalize the name of a season unless it is part of a proper name.

EXAMPLES the spring rains
the Spring Writing Conference

22k Capitalize the names of ships, trains, airplanes, and spacecraft.

Type of Name	Examples
ships	*Titanic, Seawise Giant*
trains	the *General, Wabash Cannonball*
airplanes	the *Spirit of St. Louis,* Concorde
spacecraft	*Ranger 4, Challenger*

22l Capitalize the names of buildings and other structures.

EXAMPLES New York Public Library, Golden Gate Bridge

22m Capitalize the names of monuments and awards.

TYPE OF NAME	EXAMPLES
Monuments	Vietnam Veterans Memorial
Awards	Academy Award

EXERCISE 6 Proofreading Sentences for Correct Capitalization

For each sentence below, correct the errors in capitalization. Either change capital letters to lowercase letters or change lowercase letters to capital letters. Write your corrections on the line after each sentence. Separate your answers with a semicolon.

EX. 1. My favorite holiday is cinco de mayo.
Cinco de Mayo

1. General Radwell awarded Carl the purple heart.

2. There will be fireworks and a picnic on the fourth of july.

3. The washington monument is over 555 feet high and is partly made of white marble.

4. For lunch I had some swiss cheese and some carrot sticks.

5. My favorite Winter month is december.

6. Near the ice-skating rink was a sign announcing an upcoming event: the rockport winter carnival.

7. The white house is near the lincoln memorial.

8. The Fall leaves are quite beautiful, especially in the month of october.

9. One of Agatha Christie's novels took place on a train, the *orient express.*

10. The poet Gwendolyn Brooks won the pulitzer prize in 1950.

TITLES

22n Capitalize titles.

(1) Capitalize the title of a person when the title comes before the name.

EXAMPLES Reverend Martin Luther King, Jr., Madame Curie

REFERENCE NOTE: For more information about abbreviations, see page 257.

(2) Capitalize the title used alone or following a person's name only when you want to emphasize the title of someone holding a high office.

EXAMPLES The Mayor herself marched with us.
Perhaps Yori, who was vice-president last year, can help.

A title used by itself in a direct address is usually capitalized.

EXAMPLES Please explain, Captain.
Could you take us to the beach, Uncle?

(3) Capitalize a word showing a family relationship when the word is used before or in place of a person's name.

EXAMPLES Ask if Uncle Horace will be there.
I sent Mother a nice card.

Do not capitalize a word showing a family relationship when a possessive such as *Bob's* or *your* comes before the word.

EXAMPLE Can Bob's sister and your cousin Clara ride together?

(4) Capitalize the first and last words and all important words in titles of books, magazines, newspapers, poems, short stories, movies, television programs, works of art, and musical compositions.

Unimportant words in titles include:

- articles (*a, an, the*)
- coordinating conjunctions (*and, but, for, nor, or, so, yet*)
- prepositions of fewer than five letters (such as *by, for, on, with*)

Type of Name	Examples
books	*Listen to the Crows*
magazines	*National Geographic*
newspapers	the *Baltimore Sun*
poems	"Another Mountain"
short stories	"The Gift of the Magi"
movies	*Back to the Future, Part I*
television programs	*Home Improvement*
works of art	*The Last Supper*
musical compositions	"The Star-Spangled Banner"

The article *the* before a title is not capitalized unless it is the first word of the title. For more about italics, see page 277.

EXAMPLES Here's the *Sumter County Journal.*
Yes, I own *The Book of Lists.*

EXERCISE 7 Using Capital Letters in Titles

For each sentence below, correct the errors in capitalization. Either change capital letters to lowercase letters or change lowercase letters to capital letters. Write your corrections on the line after each sentence. Separate your answers with a semicolon.

EX. 1. This latest issue of the national geographic world is interesting.
National Geographic World

1. Yes, Professor, my sister donna was in your drawing class.

______

2. A review of that book, *the helen keller story,* appeared in a newspaper, *the beacon.*

______

3. My painting, called *the cattle driver,* is based on that old song "ghost riders in the sky."

______

4. Tomorrow grandfather Matsuda will speak on the topic "bridges in the garden."

______

FIRST WORDS, PROPER ADJECTIVES, SCHOOL SUBJECTS

22o Capitalize the first word in every sentence.

EXAMPLES Those lilies look beautiful.
My sister grew them.

The first word of a direct quotation should begin with a capital letter, whether or not the quotation starts the sentence.

EXAMPLE Dezba announced, "We found your key!"

☞ **REFERENCE NOTE:** For more information about using capital letters in quotations, see page 279.

Traditionally, the first word of every line of poetry begins with a capital letter.

EXAMPLE I wonder if an orchard grieves
To see the falling of its leaves.

Some modern poets do not follow this style. If you are quoting lines from a poem, be sure to follow the capitalization that the poet uses.

22p Capitalize proper adjectives.

A ***proper adjective*** is formed from a proper noun and is always capitalized.

Proper Nouns	Proper Adjectives
China	Chinese art
Shakespeare	Shakespearean theater
Rome	Roman statues
Texas	Texas chili

22q Do not capitalize the names of school subjects, except course names followed by a number and languages.

EXAMPLES art, science, Mathematics 101, Typing II, German, Spanish

EXERCISE 8 Using Capital Letters Correctly

On the lines below, rewrite the following passage to correct all errors in the use of capital letters.

[1] In english we read a poem by an American poet. [2] The poem was about chinese porcelain. [3] according to the poet, pieces of beautiful, old porcelain sometimes wash up on the beach. [4] After we read this poem, I tried writing my own poem. Here are a few lines:

the sea so like a mystery
reveals the pieces of history.
from restless depths for me to see
an ancient world so new to me.

[5] As my friend Marieka said, "it's interesting to think that these fragments came all the way across the ocean."

CHAPTER REVIEW

A. Correcting Errors in Capitalization

For each sentence below, correct the errors in capitalization. Either change capital letters to lowercase letters or change lowercase letters to capital letters. Write your corrections on the line after each sentence. Separate your answers with a semicolon.

EX. 1. The name of our School football team is the patriots.
school; Patriots
____

1. The Doctor wrote an article that appeared in *contact* magazine.

____

2. Next year i can take biology 1, which is taught by mrs. López.

____

3. This year the bancroft science fair will be held at holder auditorium.

____

4. We asked Carl's Sister to bring in her model of a hawaiian canoe.

____

5. The film *A Night To Remember* was about the sinking of the *titanic.*

____

6. Did aunt Kate go to the same College in the midwest that your father went to?

____

7. Is the planet venus named after the roman goddess?

____

8. I think the African-American institute is on forty-seventh street.

____

9. How many flags did the red, white, and blue company send us for our labor day parade?

____

10. Did nikki giovanni write the poem "Knoxville, tennessee"?

____

B. Proofreading a Paragraph for Correct Capitalization

In the following paragraph, all capital letters have been omitted. On your own paper, rewrite the paragraph, and add the necessary capital letters.

[1] last week the students at granville t. woods middle school celebrated international day. [2] one student, imani dobbey, sang nigerian folk songs. [3] another student sang songs from the appalachian mountains. [4] my cousin ruben brought in a poster showing the taj mahal, and mr. totsi showed us how to make sand paintings. [5] a reporter from the *daily word* visited our school and then wrote a story called "students celebrate the world."

C. Writing a Travel Log

The year is 1843, and you and a friend are traveling the Oregon Trail. Traveling in a covered wagon that has left Omaha, Nebraska, you are trying to reach Portland, Oregon.

1. Use an atlas or other reference book to make notes about your trip. You might include details about the following topics: rivers, cities, and mountains that you see; people that you encounter; the dates that you travel; and the holidays that you celebrate.
2. On your own paper, use your notes to write ten sentences for a travel log of your journey. Be sure to capitalize correctly. [Note: You may want to work with a partner.]

EX. April 1—Devon and I crossed the Platte River somewhere near Fremont. We headed west.

CHAPTER 23: PUNCTUATION

END MARKS AND ABBREVIATIONS

An ***end mark*** is a mark of punctuation placed at the end of a sentence. *Periods, question marks,* and *exclamation points* are end marks.

23a Use a period at the end of a statement.

EXAMPLE A chef's salad contains meat, cheese, tomatoes, and greens**.**

23b Use a question mark at the end of a question.

EXAMPLE Did you call Kaloma yet**?**

23c Use an exclamation point at the end of an exclamation.

EXAMPLE What a wonderful dancer you are**!**

23d Use either a period or an exclamation point at the end of a request or a command.

EXAMPLES Please hold the door**.** [a request]
Open the door this instant**!** [a command]

23e Use periods after most abbreviations.

Abbreviations with Periods	
Personal Names	E**.** B**.** White, Livie I**.** Durán
Titles Used with Names	Mrs**.**, Ms**.**, Mr**.**, Dr**.**, Jr**.**, Sr**.**
Organizations and Companies	Co**.**, Inc**.**, Assoc**.**
Addresses	St**.**, Rd**.**, Ave**.**, P**.**O**.** Box
Times	A**.**M**.**, P**.**M**.**, A**.**D**.**
Abbreviations without Periods	
Government Agencies	IRS, CIA, FBI
State Abbreviations Followed by ZIP Code	Seattle, WA 98009
Units of Measure	kg, mm, cm, pt, gal, lb
Certain Widely Used Abbreviations	NW, SE, IQ, FM

Inch(es) is abbreviated ***in.*** to avoid confusing it with ***in***, the preposition. If you are not sure whether to use periods with abbreviations, look in a dictionary.

EXERCISE 1 Adding End Marks to Sentences

Write the end mark that should appear at the end of each sentence below.

EX. 1. Are you taking the bus or walking**?**

1. How brave those firefighters were
2. What authors do you like best
3. The art teacher will show us how to make dyes from natural ingredients like roots
4. Hold this bandage against the wound and press firmly
5. Will Nayati enter the marathon again this year
6. Who was that on the telephone
7. The Fourth of July fireworks are fantastic
8. Tomorrow my mother is taking me to the game
9. When is the bus coming
10. Wow, what a great movie that was

EXERCISE 2 Proofreading for the Correct Use of Abbreviations

Add periods where needed in the exercises below. On the line before each name or phrase, write C if the phrase needs no periods.

EX. 1. Dr**.** T**.** I**.** Livingstone

_____ 1. Ms E A Rodríguez

_____ 2. Parker Toy Co , Inc

_____ 3. at 4:30 P M ,

_____ 4. 5 ft 10 in tall

_____ 5. turn NW after two blocks

_____ 6. weighing 1 lb 4 oz

_____ 7. at 13185 Mill Stone Dr

_____ 8. outside the CIA building

_____ 9. Lake Pleasant, NY 12108

_____ 10. Sam Dole, Sr

COMMAS IN A SERIES

End marks are used to separate complete thoughts. *Commas*, however, are used to separate words or groups of words within a complete thought.

23f Use commas to separate items in a series.

A series is a group of three or more items written one after another. The items in a series may be words, phrases, or clauses.

Words in a Series
Bread**,** cheese**,** and carrot sticks are in the basket. [nouns] The audience laughed**,** cried**,** and whistled. [verbs] Her trip was long**,** productive**,** and satisfying. [adjectives]
Phrases in a Series
They learned to draw**,** to paint**,** and to sculpt. [infinitive phrases] People sat on tables**,** on chairs**,** and on the floor to hear him speak. [prepositional phrases] Dropped in cement**,** lost in high weeds**,** and run over by a truck**,** my lucky penny has seen some pretty hard times. [participial phrases]
Clauses in a Series
I searched**,** I found**,** and I rejoiced. [short independent clauses]

23g Use a comma to separate two or more adjectives that come before a noun.

To see whether a comma is needed, insert *and* between the adjectives. If *and* sounds awkward, don't use a comma.

EXAMPLES Your apartment is a cheerful**,** sunny place.
The letter was illustrated with small **stick figures**. [not *small, stick figures*]

 **REFERENCE NOTE:** When an adjective and a noun are closely linked, they may be considered one word. Such a word is called a *compound noun*. For more about compound nouns, see page 97.

EXERCISE 3 Proofreading Sentences for the Correct Use of Commas

Add or delete commas to correct the sentences below. On the line before the sentence, write *C* if the sentence is correct.

EX. _____ 1. Rafael owns the record, the tape, and the CD.

_____ 1. Yori Bob and I enjoyed watching the rodeo last Sunday.

_____ 2. The actors wore large colorful masks made of wood.

_____ 3. My favorite vegetables include corn, tomatoes, and spinach.

_____ 4. Be sure to bring your bathing suit and a dry towel.

_____ 5. Several teachers volunteered to cook to serve and to clean up after the dinner.

_____ 6. The bus drove through Arkansas through Oklahoma and across Texas.

_____ 7. The trees bent over, the telephone poles cracked, and the fence blew away during the hurricane.

_____ 8. Someone extinguished the campfire covered it with sand and drenched it with water.

_____ 9. My father used to carry an old black lunch pail to school.

_____ 10. The Japanese gymnast was young strong and graceful.

_____ 11. I want to learn to speak French, Spanish, and Japanese.

_____ 12. Hard work dedication and funding have made our project a success.

_____ 13. The costumes they wore were long flowing dresses.

_____ 14. The clerk needs to know who you are where you live and when you moved here.

_____ 15. We need new erasers, and more chalk.

_____ 16. Have you been to her cool peaceful garden?

_____ 17. I found ants in the drawers, on the counter tops, and under the cabinet.

_____ 18. The horse had a long, blond mane.

_____ 19. In this river you can fish for bass trout or sunfish.

_____ 20. Where is a store that sells televisions stereos and VCRs?

COMMAS WITH COMPOUND SENTENCES

23h Use a comma before *and, but, for, or, nor, so,* and *yet* when they join independent clauses in a compound sentence.

EXAMPLE Julius Lester rewrote the stories**,** and his publisher liked them.

When independent clauses are very short, the comma before *and, but,* or *or* may be omitted.

EXAMPLES Chuck left but I stayed.
The winds blew and the rain began.

So is often overused. If possible, try to reword a sentence to avoid using *so.*

EXAMPLES We stopped to eat, **so** we were late.
Because we stopped to eat, we were late.

Don't be confused by a simple sentence with a compound verb. A simple sentence has only one independent clause.

SIMPLE SENTENCE WITH COMPOUND VERB I **put** gas in the car and then **checked** the oil.

COMPOUND SENTENCE I put gas in the car**,** and then I checked the oil. [two independent clauses]

EXERCISE 4 Correcting Compound Sentences by Adding Commas

For each of the following sentences add commas where they belong. On the line before the sentence, write C if the sentence is correct.

EX. _____ 1. Electronic mail is not new yet few people use it.

_____ 1. The contest will not take place until June but we already have four entries.

_____ 2. Tree swallows can fly out of their nests and catch insects in midair.

_____ 3. They brought no meat or fish nor did they miss either one.

_____ 4. The bear sleeps during the winter and then comes out in the spring.

_____ 5. Our cabin was simple but it had three rooms.

_____ 6. People knew about the tomato yet they were afraid to eat it.

_____ 7. Early Arab people used these numbers and they taught the numbers to other people.

_____ 8. The wind shifted, and it blew the rain in through our window.

_____ 9. Janell drew the pictures but another artist wrote the words.

_____ 10. We rested for an hour for we had hiked to the top.

EXERCISE 5 Combining Sentences

On your own paper, rewrite each pair of sentences below as a single compound sentence. Use a comma and *and, but, or, for, but, so,* or *yet.*

EX. 1. The sun was hot. The breeze was cool.
1. The sun was hot, but the breeze was cool.

1. I had plenty to eat. I still wanted fruit salad for desert.
2. My brother practices his violin every day. He is a wonderful musician.
3. I made dinner for my mother. My sister brought her flowers.
4. Janice plays soccer after school. She still does her homework.
5. You could walk in the park. You could walk on the beach.
6. Close the windows tightly. This evening is supposed to bring wind and showers.
7. My class will pick up trash from the schoolyard. We will return bottles for recycling.
8. Kieshia could enter her painting in the art show. She could enter her photographs.
9. The summer is going to be hot. I should go to the town pool often.
10. The restaurant was crowded Friday night. The service was still excellent.

COMMAS WITH SENTENCE INTERRUPTERS

23i Use commas to set off an expression that interrupts a sentence.

Two commas are needed if the expression to be set off comes in the middle of the sentence. One comma is needed if the expression comes first or last.

EXAMPLES Thomas Hart Benton**,** the artist**,** lived there.
You know my cousin**,** of course.

23j Use commas to set off nonessential participial phrases and nonessential subordinate clauses.

A ***nonessential*** (or ***nonrestrictive***) phrase or clause adds information that isn't needed to understand the meaning of the sentence.

NONESSENTIAL PHRASE The messenger arrived late**, breathing rapidly**.
NONESSENTIAL CLAUSE My necklace**, which you admired last week,** is made from porcupine quills and beads.

Do not set off ***essential*** (or ***restrictive***) phrases or clauses. Since such a phrase or clause tells *which one(s)*, it cannot be omitted without changing the meaning of the sentence.

ESSENTIAL PHRASE The dog **lurking near our garage** belongs to Tina. [*Which* dog?]
ESSENTIAL CLAUSE Tyrone returned the ring **that I lost**. [*Which* ring?]

A clause beginning with *that* is usually essential.

EXERCISE 6 Using Commas Correctly

On the line before each of the following sentences, write *e.* if the italicized phrase or clause is essential. Write *n.e.* if the phrase or clause is nonessential. Insert commas where necessary.

EX. n.e. 1. Washington, D. C., *our nation's capital*, is an interesting city.

_____ 1. The Empire State Building *which is featured in that movie* is in New York City.

_____ 2. The book *that I liked best* is by Sandra Cisneros.

_____ 3. The Monadnock Building *in Chicago* is a beautiful example of nineteenth-century public architecture.

_____ 4. Massachusetts *a small state in the Northeast* had the first public schools in the American colonies.

_____ 5. The plant *that is in my room* doesn't need much water.

_____ 6. Mark Juneau *who works on North Street* is a talented hairdresser.

_____ 7. The White Mountains *which are located in New Hampshire* are beautiful.

_____ 8. The bird *that you saw by the pond* was a snowy egret.

_____ 9. The bus driver *who drives Bus 48* found my folder.

_____ 10. Mt. Everest *which is located on the border of Tibet and Nepal* is the highest peak in the world.

_____ 11. The highway *that I talked about* is closed.

_____ 12. My car *which is ten years old* still runs well.

_____ 13. Edgar Allan Poe *who wrote many horror stories* died at an early age.

_____ 14. Is it the woman on my right *who is governor*?

_____ 15. The dress *that you sent* fits me.

_____ 16. This matter *which is very private* should not be discussed.

_____ 17. The athlete *who won the race* was Gwen Torrence.

_____ 18. Emma Willard *who founded the first women's school in the United States* is an interesting subject for research.

_____ 19. The team's mascot *which is a bear* attends almost every game.

_____ 20. Those *who lost their tickets* must wait outside.

CHAPTER 23: PUNCTUATION

OTHER USES OF THE COMMA

23k Use commas to set off appositives and appositive phrases that are nonessential.

An ***appositive*** is a noun or a pronoun used to explain or identify another noun or pronoun.

EXAMPLES Mel, **our family lawyer,** is also an old friend.
Parts of Windsor Castle, **one of the royal houses**, can be visited by tourists.

Do not use commas to set off an appositive that is essential to the meaning of a sentence.

ESSENTIAL My partner **Lorenzo** finished the race first. [The speaker has more than one partner and must give a name to identify which partner.]

NONESSENTIAL My partner, **Lorenzo**, finished the race first. [The speaker has only one partner and is giving his name as added information.]

EXERCISE 7 Proofreading Sentences for the Correct Use of Commas and Appositives

For each of the following sentences, underline the appositive phrase. Add commas where needed. [Hint: Not all of the appositives will require commas.]

EX. 1. The tree, a sequoia, is more than two hundred feet tall.

1. I asked Mr. Hatzidais my next-door neighbor about his hobby.
2. Did you know that Sophia my aunt used to have a beautiful tree in her yard?
3. The tree an American elm died of some disease.
4. Mr. Finkle a biologist told me about the disease.
5. Did you know that Dutch elm disease a fungus can spread from tree to tree?

23l Use commas to set off words that are used in direct address.

EXAMPLES **Akiva**, here is a test tube.
Let's see, **Elton**, where your seat is.
I know you can do it, **Ron**.

23m Use commas to set off parenthetical expressions.

A ***parenthetical expression*** is a side remark that adds information or that relates ideas.

EXAMPLES This baseball glove, **I believe**, is Jonah's.
For example, I donated six games to the toy drive.

EXERCISE 8 Correcting Sentences by Adding Commas

On the lines before each of the sentences below, write the parenthetical expressions. Include the needed commas.

EX. ___, by the way,___ 1. Penicillin by the way is a kind of mold.

________ 1. Today Louise we know the value of penicillin.

________ 2. By 1940 however this mold became a new medicine.

________ 3. Alexander Fleming I believe was the man who discovered the mold used in making penicillin.

________ 4. To tell the truth I don't know why he even noticed it.

________ 5. However the mold had ruined one of Fleming's experiments.

________ 6. Frank many scientists would have thrown out an experiment like this.

________ 7. In fact the mold had killed the bacteria in his dish.

________ 8. Nevertheless Fleming took a second look.

________ 9. This second look in my opinion showed his true genius.

________ 10. On the other hand perhaps any hard-working scientist would have done the same.

MORE USES OF THE COMMA

23n Use a comma after *yes, no,* or any mild exclamation, such as *well* or *why,* when it begins a sentence.

EXAMPLES **Yes,** your answer is correct.
Why, you are just the person I was looking for.

23o Use a comma after an introductory participial phrase.

EXAMPLE **Starting next week,** Mario will be the monitor.

23p Use a comma after two or more introductory prepositional phrases.

EXAMPLE **At the end of the story,** there was a small note about the character.

Use a comma after a single introductory prepositional phrase only when the comma is necessary to make the meaning of the sentence clear.

EXAMPLES After the movie we went home. [clear without a comma]
After the movie, stars lit up the sky. [The comma is needed so that the reader doesn't read "After the movie stars."]

23q Use a comma after an introductory adverb clause.

An adverb clause that comes at the end of a sentence does not usually need a comma.

EXAMPLES **Before you leave,** please feed the dog.
Please feed the dog **before you leave**.

23r Use commas to separate items in dates and addresses.

A comma separates the last item in a date or an address from the words that follow it. However, a comma does not separate a month and a day (*December 5*), a state and its ZIP Code (*Utah 84767* or *UT 84767*), or a house number and its street name (*63 Willow Street*).

EXAMPLES On **December 5, 1993,** we left for Canada.
I have lived at **63 Willow Street, Chico, California 95928,** for eight years.

EXERCISE 9 Adding Commas with Introductory Elements

On the line before each sentence below, write the word before each missing comma, and add the comma. Write C if the sentence is correct.

EX. ____store,____ 1. In the store aisles were crammed with bargains.

________ 1. Shopping for the weekend I noticed many sales.

________ 2. Well most people pay more attention to nutrition now.

________ 3. In the chapter were many facts about food.

________ 4. When the weather is stormy our animals roam freely in the barn.

________ 5. At the end of one aisle I noticed a shelf of free pamphlets.

________ 6. The package from 101 Fifteenth Street Bradenton Florida 34206 must be from my uncle's store.

________ 7. During the week of January 3 1995 the owner gave free balloons to her customers.

________ 8. Because the bananas were soft Ollie decided to make banana bread.

________ 9. You can bring your dog along if you want to.

________ 10. Around this time of day I get very hungry.

EXERCISE 10 Using Commas Correctly

In the sentences below, insert commas wherever they are needed.

EX. 1. Nellie Ross was elected governor of Wyoming on November 4, 1924.

1. On May 24 1883 the Brooklyn Bridge opened.
2. You may write to me at 700 West State Street Burley ID 83318.
3. The Panama Canal first opened for shipping on August 15 1914 after years of hard work by many individuals.
4. We stopped in San Francisco California on our way to Hawaii.
5. It wasn't until November 11 1918 that World War I finally ended.

CHAPTER 23: PUNCTUATION

REVIEW EXERCISE

A. Proofreading Sentences for the Correct Use of Commas

In the sentences below, insert commas where they are needed.

EX. 1. We see, we hear, and we learn.

1. This book Marta is one that you should read.
2. It's about a doctor who worked in the country in several cities and on the battlefield.
3. Elizabeth Blackwell whom I admire was the doctor's name.
4. She must have been an intelligent determined woman.
5. She wanted to be a doctor but most schools would not train her.
6. Well it was hard for a woman to get a medical education then.
7. She went to medical school in Geneva New York in the 1840s.
8. She and Emily her sister both became doctors.
9. A doctor's life is varied challenging and rewarding.
10. If you would like to read about an interesting person choose a book about Elizabeth Blackwell the first woman doctor.

B. Proofreading a Paragraph for Correct Use of Commas

In the following paragraph, insert commas where they are needed.

EX. [1] The Cardiff Giant, you know, was a statue.

[1] On an ordinary day in 1869 a large stone man was discovered in Cardiff New York. [2] Several workers had been digging a well and they discovered the statue. [3] William Newell the owner of the property erected a tent; then he began charging admission. [4] People came from all over to see this statue which was called the Cardiff Giant. [5] Doctors historians and neighbors wondered where it had come from. [6] Newell sent the giant on tour to Albany Syracuse Boston and New York. [7] Then the truth came out. [8] Professor Othniel Marsh a well-known scholar reported that the statue had

been carved out of gypsum a material that would have dissolved in a few years. [9] If you want to see it however you can. [10] It now rests in the Farmer's Museum in Cooperstown New York.

C. Writing Notes for an Article

The new Time Travel Amusement Park is opening in your city. Your local paper wants you to write a feature article about the opening day. As you walk through the park, you listen to people talking. On your own paper, write down their comments and impressions about the exhibits. Be sure to write down your own thoughts about the exhibits.

1. Think about what exhibits might fill the Time Travel Amusement Park. Research or invent locations and dates of the exhibits.
2. Create at least five sentences about the park. You might want to include things that you overhear and your thoughts about what you see. Include sentences with introductory words and phrases, interrupters, appositives, direct address, or parenthetical expressions.
3. Be sure that your sentences include all necessary commas.

EX. 1. For opening day, crowds of people lined up inside the park gate.
2. Look, there's a moon rocket and a skywalk!

SEMICOLONS

A *semicolon* looks like a combination of a period and a comma, and that is just what it is. A semicolon separates complete thoughts as a period does. A semicolon also separates items within a sentence as a comma does.

23s Use a semicolon between independent clauses if they are not joined by *and, but or, nor, for, so,* or *yet.*

EXAMPLES Maya looked outside and sighed; rain was still falling.
The train pulled into the station; only one person got out.

23t Use a semicolon rather than a comma before a coordinating conjunction to join independent clauses that contain commas.

CONFUSING I brought lettuce, tomatoes, and carrots, but bread, milk, and cheese were donated.

CLEAR I brought lettuce, tomatoes, and carrots; but bread, milk, and cheese were donated.

Semicolons are most effective when they are not overused. Sometimes it is better to separate a compound sentence or a heavily punctuated sentence into two sentences rather than to use a semicolon.

ACCEPTABLE The wind blows the sand around and causes the grains to rub against each other; the constant rubbing gradually shapes each grain, making it rounder as time goes on.

BETTER The wind blows the sand around and causes the grains to rub against each other. The constant rubbing gradually shapes each grain, making it rounder as time goes on.

EXERCISE 11 Using Semicolons Correctly

On the lines before each of the sentences below, write the words before and after the missing semicolon. Insert a semicolon between these words.

EX. elephants; ivory 1. Not all ivory comes from elephants ivory also comes from other animals.

____________ 1. Ivory comes from animals' tusks a lot of ivory comes from walruses.

____________ 2. Look at these carvings they were made by artists hundreds of years ago.

____________ 3. Some carvings combined two materials this artist used soapstone and wood.

____________ 4. Carvers did not begin to carve right away first they held the material and looked at it.

____________ 5. They thought the ivory already contained a shape thus, they believed in waiting to discover it.

____________ 6. One carver found the shape of a fish inside the ivory another carver found the shape of a flower.

____________ 7. Some Inuits carved fossil ivory this was very old ivory that had been buried for years.

____________ 8. Other carvings were beautiful however they were not made out of ivory.

____________ 9. These carvings were made out of soapstone this substance looks darker than ivory.

____________ 10. I have seen carvings of a bear, a duck, and a walrus they were all carved out of soapstone.

COLONS

23u Use a colon before a list of items, especially after expressions such as *the following* or *as follows.*

EXAMPLES Please bring these items to camp: bedding, a pillow, a flashlight, and a folding cup.
Every room comes equipped with the following items: a bed, a mattress, a dresser, and a lamp.

Never use a colon directly after a verb or a preposition. Omit the colon, or reword the sentence.

INCORRECT In the next exhibit, look at: the pond, the shore, the high grass, and the sand.
CORRECT In the next exhibit, look at these areas: the pond, the shore, the high grass, and the sand.

23v Use a colon between the hour and the minute.

EXAMPLE It is now 3:30 P.M. We will leave at 6:00 A.M.

23w Use a colon after the salutation of a business letter.

EXAMPLE Dear Dr. Gaetano: Dear Reference Librarian:

23x Use a colon between chapter and verse in referring to passages from the Bible.

EXAMPLE Matthew 6:9–15 Ruth 2:9–10

EXERCISE 12 Using Colons and Commas Correctly

On the line after each of the following word groups, write a complete sentence by adding the information suggested in brackets to the word group. Insert colons and commas where they are needed. [Hint: before a list of items, you might need to add words such as *the following*.]

EX. 1. My favorite show begins at [*time*].
My favorite show begins at 8:00 P.M.

1. We have shopped at these stores [*list*].

___

2. I go to bed at [*time*].

____

3. "[*salutation*]" is the greeting line of this business letter.

____

4. I am going to the park to play, and I'll be home at [*time*].

____

5. Jennifer gave invitations to [*list*].

____

6. Today I am going to read [*Bible, chapter, and verse*].

____

7. The baseball game starts at [*time*].

____

8. This summer vacation, I am going to [*list*].

____

9. I go jogging every day at [*time*].

____

10. The activities that I enjoy are [*list*].

____

CHAPTER 23: PUNCTUATION

CHAPTER REVIEW

A. Proofreading Sentences for the Correct Use of Commas

For each of the sentences below, add commas where needed.

EX. 1. Well, I just heard a strange story.

1. Look at all the ostriches Raoul.
2. There are ostrich farms in Arizona Arkansas California and Texas.
3. These birds are large powerful animals.
4. On September 12 1882 a New York newspaper wrote a story about ostrich feathers.
5. Anaheim California was the location of the first ostrich farm in the United States.
6. The first baby ostrich which belonged to Billie Frantz was born on July 4 1883.
7. By the end of 1911 there were more than six thousand ostriches in the United States.
8. Feathers which are clipped not plucked are harvested every eight or nine months.
9. Ostrich feathers which are used as decoration are in demand.
10. They decorate hats fans feather dusters and several other items.

B. Using End Marks, Commas, Semicolons, and Colons Correctly in a Paragraph

The sentences in the following paragraph need end marks, commas, semicolons, or colons. Add the missing punctuation.

My family lived in Japan for two years and I loved every minute of it My mother works for a computer company which sent her there We moved to Japan on March 5 1990 While we were there we lived in three different cities Tokyo Yokohama and Asaka Which city do you think was my favorite Tokyo was it Tokyo has parks and gardens that are outstanding There were numerous restaurants to try sports exhibitions to see and museums to visit Also Tokyo you know has many museums These include the following choices a clock museum a haiku museum a toy museum and a kite museum The toy museum was certainly my favorite Mom however liked the haiku museum best.

C. Proofreading a Letter

Some parts of the letter below need end marks, commas, semicolons, or colons. Add the missing punctuation marks.

710 Lakeport Drive
Stony Point NY 10980
August 22 1994

Dr Emil Valdez
3486 Wichita Place
Haverstraw NY 10927

Dear Dr Valdez

My school Jefferson Junior High has a science fair every year This year it will be held on October 10 1994 at the Warren Auditorium Fair entries include the following four categories the heavens our planet water and machines What a wonderful crowd we had last year This year however we'd like to make the fair even better This desire to improve our fair is why I am writing to you Dr Valdez

Last month my uncle Lokela heard you speak about diets and young people He thought you were an excellent speaker and he found the topic fascinating Well my class wants you for its speaker Would you give the speech at our science fair We would schedule a time between 1 30 and 3 30 P M We could pick you up at the airport drive you to the fair and take you back to the airport We would also include your name on our list of sponsors I hope you will accept our offer Please let us know before September 8 1994

Sincerely
Irma Lukas

UNDERLINING (ITALICS)

24a Use underlining (italics) for titles of books, plays, periodicals, films, television programs, works of art, long musical compositions, ships, aircraft, and spacecraft.

Type of Name	Examples
Books	*The Hobbit, A Tale of Two Cities*
Plays	*The Hitchhiker, Lost in Yonkers*
Periodicals	*Newsweek*, the *Atlanta Journal*
Films	*Back to the Future, Dances with Wolves*
Television Programs	*Jeopardy, A Different World*
Works of Art	*The Blue Boy, The Thinker*
Long Musical Compositions	*Swan Lake, Appalachian Spring*
Ships	the *Lusitania*, the USS *Constitution*
Aircraft	the *Spirit of St. Louis, Hindenburg*
Spacecraft	*Discovery, Challenger*

The article *the* is often written before a title but is not capitalized unless it is part of the official title. The official title of a book is found on the title page. The official title of a newspaper or periodical is found on the masthead, which usually appears on the editorial page.

EXAMPLE I agreed with the editorial in *The Denver Post*.

24b Use underlining (italics) for words, letters, and figures referred to as such.

EXAMPLES The word ***mask*** has several meanings.
Do you know a word that contains the vowels ***a, e, i, o,*** and ***u***?
Write an *8* in the last column.

EXERCISE 1 Using Underlining (Italics) Correctly

For each sentence below, underline each word or item that should be italicized.

EX. 1. Willy has the lead role in Fiddler on the Roof.

1. I read the last chapter of Barrio Boy for homework.
2. A popular television show in the 1950s was I Love Lucy.
3. Yesterday, the San Francisco Examiner had an informative article about electric cars.
4. Annie misspelled the word license in her report.
5. Winslow Homer's painting Snap the Whip hangs in a museum in Youngstown, Ohio.
6. In English class, we watched the film To Kill a Mockingbird.
7. Mozart composed the score for the opera The Marriage of Figaro.
8. Is there one p in the name Mississippi?
9. The play Raisin in the Sun was written by Lorraine Hansberry.
10. In 1989, the spacecraft Galileo took pictures of the planet Venus.

EXERCISE 2 Proofreading a Paragraph for the Correct Use of Underlining (Italics)

In the paragraph below, underline each word or item that should be italicized.

EX. [1] We went to the space museum and saw an exhibition about the Challenger.

[1] Darryl and I looked through The Boston Globe and the North Shore Record. [2] This weekend we could see the play Our Town or the ballet version of Romeo and Juliet. [3] I had read a book called The Art of Thornton Wilder about Our Town's writer. [4] Of course, we could stay home and watch the great episode of The Cosby Show that is on television tonight. [5] We finally decided to take a ride on a ship called the Appledore III in Rockport, MA.

QUOTATION MARKS

24c Use quotation marks to enclose a direct quotation—a person's exact words.

Be sure to place quotation marks both before and after a person's exact words.

EXAMPLES In *Poor Richard's Almanac*, Ben Franklin advised his readers, "Early to bed and early to rise, makes a man healthy, wealthy, and wise."
"Do you know what you would do," asked the guide, "if you came face to face with a big bear?"

24d A direct quotation begins with a capital letter.

EXAMPLES Emilio said, "Last summer I went on an expedition into the Volcán Santiago National Park in Nicaragua."
In a book about the early history of the Americas, the author states, "People made clay popcorn poppers two thousand years ago."

24e When the expression identifying the speaker interrupts a quoted sentence, the second part of the quotation begins with a small letter.

EXAMPLES "The village," explained Kali, "is surrounded by rice fields and farmland."
"When you leave the house," added Chris, "lock the door."

A quoted sentence that is divided in this way is called a *broken quotation*. Notice that each part of a broken quotation is enclosed in a set of quotation marks. When the second part of a divided quotation is a sentence, it begins with a capital letter.

EXAMPLE "Sit down," directed Kitty. "The concert is about to begin."

24f A direct quotation is set off from the rest of the sentence by a comma, a question mark, or an exclamation point, but not by a period.

EXAMPLES Shane said, "We're studying rain forests."
"Everyone should learn about them, " suggested Alexis.
"Why are they so important?" asked Jalene.
"Rain forests teem with life!" exclaimed Vince.

24g A period or a comma should always be placed inside the closing quotation marks.

EXAMPLES Alan replied, "My appointment is next week."
"I'm going for my yearly checkup today," said Gilda.

24h A question mark or an exclamation point should be placed inside the closing quotation marks when the quotation itself is a question or an exclamation. Otherwise, it should be placed outside.

EXAMPLES "Where is the trail?" asked the hiker. [The quotation is a question.]
Who said, "Drafts cause colds"? [The sentence, not the quotation, is a question.]

When both the sentence and a quotation at the end of the sentence are questions (or exclamations), only one question mark (or exclamation point) is used. It is placed inside the closing quotation marks.

EXAMPLE Did Kayla ask, "How do I get to Central Park from here?"

EXERCISE 3 Punctuating Quotations

For each sentence below, insert quotation marks and other marks of punctuation where needed.

EX. 1. "This year," said Chen, "is going to be the Year of the Dragon."

1. Lim Sing is looking forward to the Festival of Lanterns said her father
2. Chen replied I received calendars from relatives in Hong Kong
3. If you look closely at them he explained you can see each day's lunar date written in Chinese.
4. Will you help me cook the special roasted seeds and dried fruits Mother bought for the New Year's meal asked Lim Sing
5. Aunt Jun steamed a whole fish exclaimed Chen now she is cooking my favorite pork dish.

24i When you write dialogue (conversation), begin a new paragraph every time the speaker changes.

EXAMPLE Louis smiled and said, "You can be the stepmother, Bernice. You'll be perfect for the part. I will be the prince because I am the tallest and the most handsome."

"What about me?" asked Megan. "What part can I play?"

"Why you—you can be Cinderella!"

"Oh, dear," said Megan, "I always have to be something dull like that. I wish I could be the stepmother or at least one of Cinderella's stepsisters."

24j When a quotation consists of several sentences, put quotation marks only at the beginning and the end of the whole quotation.

EXAMPLE "Where are your manners, my little friend? Just look at your hands! You must wash them before coming to my table," scolded Mr. Plessas.

24k Use single quotation marks to enclose a quotation within a quotation.

EXAMPLE Seth explained, "The photographer said, 'You must observe the world around you very closely.'"

24l Use quotation marks to enclose the titles of short works such as short stories, poems, articles, songs, episodes of television programs, and chapters and other parts of books.

EXAMPLES Don Marquis' poem "the lesson of the moth" is quite funny.
Will you sing "America the Beautiful" at the assembly?

EXERCISE 4 Punctuating Quotations

Insert quotation marks where needed in each of the following sentences.

EX. 1. "Read the chapter 'Edge of the Sea' for homework," said Mrs. Zayas.

1. Did you know that the city of Santa Barbara sponsors an Old Spanish Days fiesta in August? asked Mario.
2. Last night I read the story The Last Leaf to my sister, said Nora.
3. Marian Anderson once sang America at the Lincoln Memorial.
4. Who said, An apple a day keeps the doctor away? asked Meli.

5. Our sun is just an ordinary star! exclaimed Floyd. It's neither the biggest nor the brightest. However, it's the star nearest earth.
6. Rachel Field wrote a poem called Snow in the City.
7. Mr. Ryder said, The last chapter in *Anne of Avonlea* is A Wedding at the Stone House.
8. Read the article called Saving the Coast in the school newspaper.
9. Sarah said, This will be a busy weekend. We are planting beach grass on the dunes to hold the sand in place. The grass will also help the dunes grow higher.
10. Didn't the teacher say, Use your calculator? asked Bruce.

EXERCISE 5 Punctuating Paragraphs

On your own paper, rewrite the paragraph below, using quotation marks and other marks of punctuation wherever necessary. Remember to begin a new paragraph each time the speaker changes. [Note: The punctuation marks that are already included in the exercise are correct.]

EX. [1] You want fish again for supper! exclaimed Mr. Brooks.
 1. "You want fish again for supper!" exclaimed Mr. Brooks.

[1] You have had fish every night this week, Mr. Brooks reminded his son. [2] I thought that you didn't like fish." [3] I don't replied Felix but we're having a big social studies test next week. [4] What has that got to do with eating fish asked his father, as he stood at the sink, peeling potatoes. [5] Well answered Felix my friend Ben said Fish is brain food. [6] If you eat enough fish, you'll become smarter. [7] Mr. Brooks turned and faced his son. [8] Felix, fish is no better for your brain than any other food. [9] You'll be better off worrying less about your diet and spending more time studying. [10] I was afraid of that Felix replied gloomily.

APOSTROPHES

The ***possessive case*** of a noun or a pronoun shows ownership or relationship.

Ownership	Relationship
Lenny's desk	a **week's** pay
the **player's** score	**our** parents
her sweater	**cat's** paw
everyone's test	two **cents'** worth

24m To form the possessive case of a singular noun, add an apostrophe and an *s*.

EXAMPLES the man**'s** shirt — Georgia**'s** painting
a friend**'s** house — Gary**'s** idea

A proper noun ending in *s* may take only an apostrophe to form the possessive case if the addition of *'s* would make the name awkward to say.

EXAMPLES Mr. Barnes' coat — Athens' location — Ruiz' party

24n To form the possessive case of a plural noun ending in s, add only the apostrophe.

EXAMPLES friends' names — two years' practice — two enemies' plans
wolves' tracks — the Ryans' cottage — artists' paintings

24o To form the possessive case of a plural noun that does not end in *s*, add an apostrophe and an *s*.

EXAMPLES women**'s** suits — people**'s** faces — children**'s** books
deer**'s** tails — geese**'s** wings — moose**'s** antlers

Do not use an apostrophe to form the plural of a noun. Remember that the apostrophe shows ownership or relationship.

INCORRECT Two girls' have red coats.
CORRECT Two **girls** have red coats.
CORRECT The two **girls'** coats are red.

24p Do not use an apostrophe with possessive personal pronouns.

EXAMPLES Is that dog **theirs**?
Is the pen **his** or **hers**?

EXERCISE 6 Using Apostrophes for Singular Possessives

In each sentence in the paragraph below, underline the word that needs an apostrophe, and insert the apostrophe.

EX. [1] The Spanish galleon was one of the <u>world's</u> greatest ships.

[1] A sailors life on a galleon was hard and uncomfortable. [2] The captains orders had to be obeyed without question. [3] On a voyage, a seamans strength and courage were put to the test. [4] A single days work left all on board exhausted. [5] Sailors raised the galleons sails by pulling on heavy ropes. [6] If the wind picked up, the sails had to be lowered without a moments delay. [7] While the ship rolled violently, sailors climbed the masts rigging. [8] In rough seas, the ships timbers moved. [9] Often, the hulls seams opened, letting in a flood of water. [10] Because the crews sleeping quarters were below the waterline, sailors often had to sleep in wet, smelly bunks.

EXERCISE 7 Writing Possessives

Rewrite each of the expressions below by using the possessive case. Be sure to insert apostrophes in the right places.

EX. 1. the records of the singer ___the singer's records___

1. the tools of the carpenters ________________
2. the tails of the mice ________________
3. the towel that belongs to Fatima ________________
4. the office of the coach ________________
5. the toys of the children ________________

OTHER USES OF THE APOSTROPHE

A *contraction* is a shortened form of a word, a number, or a group of words.

24q Use an apostrophe to show where letters, numbers, or words have been omitted (left out) in a contraction.

Common Contractions	
I am..........................I'm	they had....................they'd
1994 ....'94	where is ....where's
let us.....................let's	we are ....we're
of the clock ......o'clock	he is .... he's
she would ....she'd	you will......................you'll

The word *not* can be shortened to *n't* and added to a verb, usually without any change in the spelling of the verb.

EXAMPLES is not..............is**n't** has not................has**n't**
does not....does**n't** would not......would**n't**

EXCEPTIONS will not........wo**n't** cannot..................ca**n't**

Be careful not to confuse contractions with possessive pronouns.

Contractions	Possessive Pronouns
It's your book. [It is]	**Its** tail is long and bushy.
You're early. [You are]	**Your** dinner is ready.
They're here. [They are]	**Their** name is Yahada.
There's Mom. [There is]	That book is **theirs**.

24r Use an apostrophe and an *s* to form the plurals of letters, of numerals, and of words referred to as words.

EXAMPLES I sometimes write *g*'**s** for *q*'**s**.
The winning number had two *4*'**s** and three *7*'**s** in it.
Don't use so many *and*'**s** and *well*'**s** when you speak.

EXERCISE 8 Using Apostrophes in Contractions Correctly

For each of the sentences below, underline the word or words requiring an apostrophe, and insert the apostrophe. On the line before the sentence, write *C* if the sentence is correct.

EX. _____ 1. You can't believe everything you read or hear.

_____ 1. Should you drink water while youre exercising?

_____ 2. Some people think they shouldnt drink any liquids.

_____ 3. They think water will bloat them, and they won't be able to run fast.

_____ 4. You musnt pay any attention to these people because theyre wrong.

_____ 5. Now well find out why.

_____ 6. When you're running or exercising hard, your body loses water very quickly.

_____ 7. Youll get sick or even faint if you lose too much water.

_____ 8. Lets use some common sense.

_____ 9. Dont forget to replace the missing liquids.

_____ 10. The next time youre playing hard, drink some water.

EXERCISE 9 Writing Contractions

On the line before each sentence, write a contraction for each italicized word or word pair.

EX. we're 1. In biology class *we are* studying life in the oceans.

__________ 1. Sunlight *cannot* reach the depths of the ocean.

__________ 2. Because *there is* no light near the ocean floor, many animals that live in the deep ocean create their own light, like fireflies.

__________ 3. *What is* the strangest creature in the deep ocean?

__________ 4. *I am* convinced that the oddest of them all is the angler fish.

__________ 5. *It is* able to attract prey using a dorsal fin that dangles above its mouth.

CHAPTER REVIEW

A. Proofreading for the Correct Use of Apostrophes, Quotation Marks, and Underlining (Italics)

Rewrite each of the following sentences so that apostrophes, quotation marks, and underlining are used correctly. [Note: A sentence may contain more than one error.]

EX. 1. Dont mix up the words symbol and cymbal, said Jesse.
"Don't mix up the words symbol and cymbal," said Jesse.

1. What does the word symbol that begins with an s mean? asked Leroy. ______________________________

2. "Did you know that a, b, c, and d are symbols? asked Jesse. All letters stand for sounds. ______________________________

3. Numbers are symbols, too," added Cora. When you write 5s and 7s and 9s, youre writing symbols. ______________________________

4. "Countries also have symbols, said Jesse. The United States' has lots of symbols. Uncle Sams one of them." ______________________________

5. "Youve probably seen him, added Cora. "Hes a tall, skinny cartoon character in a red-white-and-blue suit. ______________________________

6. The first cartoon's of Uncle Sam didnt appear until the 1830s, added Jesse. But a book titled The Adventures of Uncle Sam had appeared in 16. ______________________________

7. One clever cartoon of him appeared on the cover of The Saturday Evening Post in 1927, said Cora. ______________________________

____

8. He was wearing a pilots helmet, explained Jesse, in honor of Charles Lindbergh's flight across the Atlantic in the Spirit of St. Louis. ______________________________

____

____

9. "Didn't Uncle Sam say, I Want YOU?" asked Leroy. I think that the government used Uncle Sam to get people to join the armed forces." ______________________________

____

____

10. Im feeling patriotic! exclaimed Jesse. Lets sing Yankee Doodle! ________

____

____

B. Writing a Dialogue

On your own paper, create a new dialogue based on the comic strip below. Write the dialogue in sentence form. Be sure to use quotation marks and other marks of punctuation correctly. In addition to punctuation marks, you will have to add dialogue tags to identify who is speaking (*asked Leroy, exclaimed Jessie*).

Peanuts reprinted by permission of UFS, Inc.

CHAPTER 25: SPELLING

THE DICTIONARY

A dictionary entry is divided into several parts. Study the parts of the following sample dictionary entry:

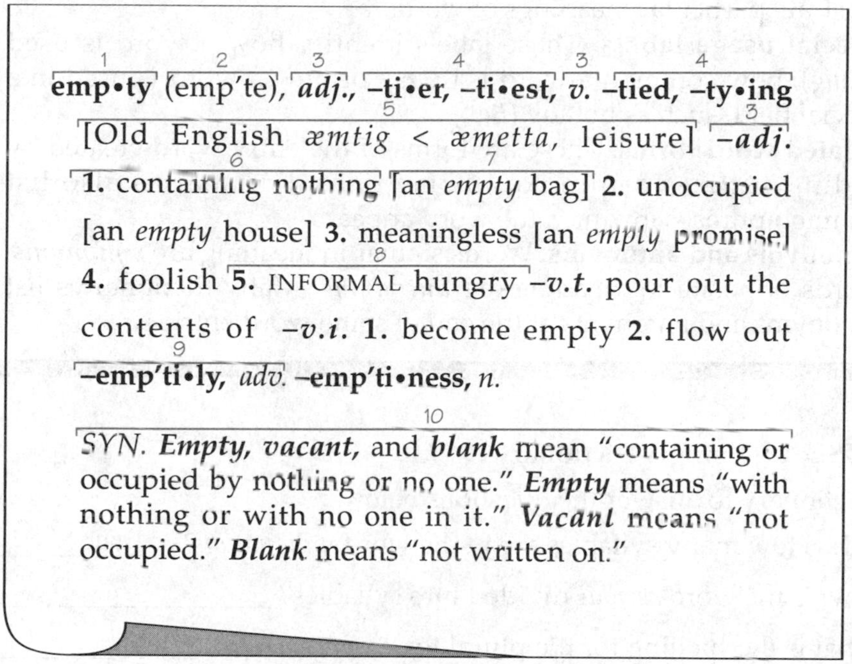

> **emp•ty** (emp′te), ***adj.,*** **–ti•er, –ti•est,** ***v.*** **–tied, –ty•ing** [Old English *æmtig* < *æmetta,* leisure] ***–adj.*** **1.** containing nothing [an *empty* bag] **2.** unoccupied [an *empty* house] **3.** meaningless [an *empty* promise] **4.** foolish **5.** INFORMAL hungry ***–v.t.*** pour out the contents of ***–v.i.*** **1.** become empty **2.** flow out **–emp′ti•ly,** *adv.* **–emp′ti•ness,** *n.*
>
> *SYN.* ***Empty, vacant,*** and ***blank*** mean "containing or occupied by nothing or no one." ***Empty*** means "with nothing or with no one in it." ***Vacant*** means "not occupied." ***Blank*** means "not written on."

1. **Entry word.** The entry word shows the correct spelling of the word. An alternate spelling may also be shown. The entry word shows how the word should be divided into syllables and may also show if the word should be capitalized.
2. **Pronunciation.** The pronunciation is shown using accent marks, phonetic symbols, or diacritical marks. Each ***phonetic symbol*** represents a specific sound. ***Diacritical marks*** are special symbols placed above letters to show how those letters sound.
3. **Part-of-speech labels.** These labels are usually abbreviated and show how the entry word should be used in sentences. Some words may be used as more than one part of speech. In this case, a part-of-speech label is also given before the set of definitions that matches each label.
4. **Other forms.** Sometimes a dictionary shows spellings of plural forms of nouns, tenses of verbs, or the comparative forms of adjectives and adverbs.

5. **Etymology.** The ***etymology*** tells how a word (or its parts) entered the English language. The etymology also shows how the word has changed over time.
6. **Definitions.** If there is more than one meaning, definitions are numbered or lettered.
7. **Sample usage.** Some dictionaries include sample phrases to illustrate particular meanings of words.
8. **Special usage labels.** These labels identify how a word is used (*Slang*), how common a word is (*Rare*), or how a word is used in a special field, such as botany (*Bot.*).
9. **Related word forms.** These are forms of the entry word created by adding suffixes or prefixes. Sometimes dictionaries also list common phrases in which the word appears.
10. **Synonyms and antonyms.** Words similar in meaning are ***synonyms***. Words opposite in meaning are ***antonyms***. Many dictionaries list synonyms and antonyms at the end of some word entries.

EXERCISE 1 Using a Dictionary

Use a dictionary to answer the questions below.

EX. 1. How many syllables are in the word *indignation*? four

1. How is the word *serious* divided into syllables? ____________
2. What is the spelling for the plural form of *armadillo*? ____________
3. What are three different meanings for the word *peck*? ____________

____
4. What is the past tense of *awake*? ____________
5. When should the word *cupid* be capitalized? ____________

EXERCISE 2 Writing Words with Alternate Spellings

Write the alternate spelling for each of the words below on the line after the word.

EX. 1. pickax pickaxe

1. enroll ____________
2. catalog ____________
3. hurrah ____________
4. whiz ____________
5. judgment ____________

CHAPTER 25: SPELLING

SPELLING RULES

ie and *ei*

25a Write *ie* when the sound is long *e*, except after *c*.

EXAMPLES field, belief, grief, thief, receipt, ceiling
EXCEPTIONS neither, either, seize, leisure, weird

Write *ei* when the sound is not long *e*, especially when the sound is long *a*.

EXAMPLES neighbor, vein, eight, reign, height, foreign
EXCEPTIONS pie, tie, friend, mischief

EXERCISE 3 Writing Words with *ie* and *ei*

On the line in each word, write the letters *ie* or *ei* to spell each word correctly. Use a dictionary as needed.

EX. 1. br *ie* f

1. sh_____ld
2. fr_____ght
3. p_____r
4. sl_____gh
5. y_____ld
6. p_____ce
7. rev_____w
8. w_____ght
9. rec_____ve
10. fr_____nd

FRANK & ERNEST ® by Bob Thaves

Frank & Ernest reprinted by permission of NEA, Inc.

–cede, –ceed, **and** *–sede*

25b The only word ending in *–sede* is *supersede*. The only words ending in *–ceed* are *exceed, proceed,* and *succeed*. All other words with this sound end in *–cede*.

EXAMPLES re**cede**, con**cede**, inter**cede**, pre**cede**

EXERCISE 4 Proofreading a Paragraph to Correct Spelling Errors

The paragraph below contains ten spelling errors. Underline the misspelled words. Write the correct spelling above each misspelled word.

EX. [1] Everyone in Pepita's nieghborhood (neighborhood) was looking forward to *Carnaval*.

[1] The sight on the street exceded the vision she remembered, and Pepita could hardly believe her eyes. [2] For a breif moment, she thought she was back in Trinidad. [3] The street was crowded with people dressed in thier colorful masks and costumes. [4] They liesurely strolled around, waiting for the parade to begin. [5] Pepita beleived that she recognized the steel band on a platform halfway down the street. [6] She knew several of the musicians, who were from iether Trinidad or Barbados. [7] Sheilding her eyes from the late-afternoon sun, Pepita paused and listened to the calypso beat. [8] She had to conceed that the band sounded as good as any group back home on the island. [9] Suddenly, a freind seized her hand. [10] "Here," said Marita, "try a peice of this fish."

CHAPTER 25: SPELLING

PREFIXES AND SUFFIXES

A *prefix* is a letter or a group of letters added to the beginning of a word to change its meaning. A *suffix* is a letter or a group of letters added to the end of a word to change its meaning.

25c When adding a prefix to a word, do not change the spelling of the word itself.

EXAMPLES mis + place = **mis**place dis + satisfy = **dis**satisfy
un + happy = **un**happy im+ mortal = **im**mortal

25d When adding the suffix *–ness* or *–ly* to a word, do not change the spelling of the word itself.

EXAMPLES thick + ness = thick**ness** dry + ness = dry**ness**
week + ly = week**ly** soft + ly = soft**ly**

EXCEPTION For most words that end in *y,* change the *y* to *i* before *–ly* or *–ness.*

EXAMPLES sloppy + ness = slopp**iness** easy + ly = eas**ily**

25e Drop the final silent *e* before a suffix beginning with a vowel.

Vowels are the letters *a, e, i, o, u,* and sometimes *y.* All other letters of the alphabet are *consonants.*

EXAMPLES large + est = larg**est** write + ing = writ**ing**
like + able = lik**able** slice + er = slic**er**

EXCEPTION Keep the silent *e* in words ending in *ce* and *ge* before a suffix beginning with *a* or *o.*

EXAMPLES service + able = servic**eable**
outrage + ous = outrag**eous**

25f Keep the final *e* before a suffix beginning with a consonant.

EXAMPLES use + less = use**less** nine + ty = nine**ty**
peace + ful = peace**ful** safe + ly = safe**ly**

EXCEPTIONS argue + ment = argu**ment** true + ly = tru**ly**

EXERCISE 5 Spelling Words with Prefixes and Suffixes

On the line after each partial word equation, write the word with the given prefix or suffix that completes the word problem.

EX. 1. cheerful + ly cheerfully

1. new + ness ________
2. real + ly ________
3. un + clear ________
4. over + spend ________
5. final + ly ________
6. loud + ness ________
7. over + ripe ________
8. playful + ness ________
9. friendly + ness ________
10. ir + regular ________
11. mis + spell ________
12. im + perfect ________
13. heavy + ness ________
14. dis + able ________
15. in + formal ________
16. joyful + ly ________
17. steady + ly ________
18. in + complete ________
19. last + ly ________
20. shy + ness ________

EXERCISE 6 Spelling Words with Suffixes

On the line after each partial word equation, write the word with the given suffix that completes the word problem.

EX. 1. plenty + ful plentiful

1. noisy + ly ________
2. believe + ing ________
3. hope + ful ________
4. strange + est ________
5. graze + ing ________
6. pave + ment ________
7. polite + ness ________
8. waste + ful ________
9. adore + able ________
10. busy + ly ________
11. amaze + ing ________
12. hasty + ly ________
13. measure + ment ________
14. courage + ous ________
15. drive + er ________
16. angry + ly ________
17. brave + er ________
18. little + est ________
19. change + able ________
20. care + ful ________

SUFFIXES

25g For words ending in *y* preceded by a consonant, change the *y* to *i* before any suffix that does not begin with *i*.

EXAMPLES merry + ment = merr**iment** worry + ing = worry**ing**
hasty + ly = hast**ily**

Words ending in *y* preceded by a vowel do not change their spelling before a suffix.

EXAMPLES obey + ed = obe**yed** play + ful = play**ful**
EXCEPTIONS pay + ed = pa**id** day + ly = da**ily**

25h Double the final consonant before adding *–ing, –ed, –er,* or *–est* to a one-syllable word that ends in a single consonant preceded by a single vowel.

EXAMPLES hot + est = ho**tt**est sad + er = sa**dd**er
drip + ed = dri**pp**ed

With a one-syllable word ending in a single consonant that is not preceded by a single vowel, do not double the consonant before adding *–ing, –ed, –er,* or *–est.*

EXAMPLES hard + er = har**d**er quick + est = quic**k**est
bump + ing = bum**p**ing start + ed = star**t**ed

EXERCISE 7 Spelling Words with Suffixes

On the line after each partial word equation, write each word, with the given suffix that completes the word problem.

EX. 1. swim + er swimmer

1. dizzy + ness ____________
2. grin + ing ____________
3. skid + ed ____________
4. fresh + er ____________
5. rusty + est ____________
6. key + ed ____________
7. multiply + ing ____________
8. cheer + ed ____________
9. lazy + er ____________
10. stay + ed ____________

EXERCISE 8 Identifying Incorrect Spelling in a Paragraph

The paragraph below contains ten spelling errors. Underline the incorrect words. Then write the correct spelling above the incorrect word.

hottest

EX. [1] I think Saturday must have been the hotest day of the year so far.

[1] The temperature was ninety-five and still riseing. [2] My fruit juice icy melted and driped on my shorts faster than I could eat it. [3] Even though it was unusualy hot, we started to bike to the town pool. [4] Suddenly we heard sirens, so I slammed on my brakes and skided in the dust. [5] Three firetrucks went raceing by. [6] My friend cryed out, "Look at the flames!" [7] Smoke was begining to appear above the trees. [8] Worryed about our safety, we stood far from the edge of the forest. [9] During Fire Prevention Week at school, we learnned that hot, dry weather makes forest fires more likely. [10] The fire was put out, but a firefighter later said, "Somebody was careless with a campfire, so the trees and animals payed the price."

PLURALS OF NOUNS I

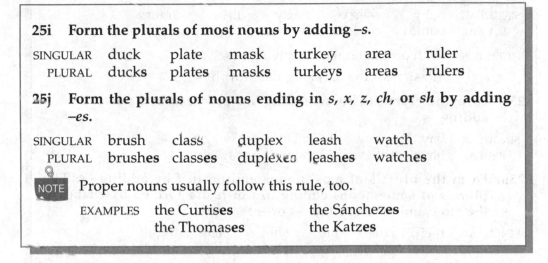

25i Form the plurals of most nouns by adding *–s*.

SINGULAR	duck	plate	mask	turkey	area	ruler
PLURAL	ducks	plates	masks	turkeys	areas	rulers

25j Form the plurals of nouns ending in *s, x, z, ch,* or *sh* by adding *–es.*

SINGULAR	brush	class	duplex	leash	watch
PLURAL	brushes	classes	duplexes	leashes	watches

NOTE Proper nouns usually follow this rule, too.

EXAMPLES the Curtises the Sánchezes
the Thomases the Katzes

EXERCISE 9 Spelling the Plurals of Nouns

On the line after each noun, write its correct plural form.

EX. 1. tax taxes

1. dish ______
2. pillow ______
3. reflex ______
4. Pérez ______
5. ranch ______
6. wish ______
7. field ______
8. monkey ______
9. guess ______
10. closet ______
11. bench ______
12. flash ______
13. Martínez ______
14. ax ______
15. dance ______
16. idea ______
17. chimney ______
18. harness ______
19. Jones ______
20. dash ______
21. candle ______
22. kiss ______
23. waltz ______
24. rocket ______
25. stitch ______

25k Form the plurals of nouns ending in *y* preceded by a consonant by changing the *y* to *i* and adding *–es*.

SINGULAR	baby	cherry	daisy	lily	surgery
PLURAL	babies	cherries	daisies	lilies	surgeries

EXCEPTION With proper nouns, simply add *–s*.

EXAMPLES the Barkleys, the Murphys

25l Form the plurals of nouns ending in *y* preceded by a vowel by adding *–s*.

SINGULAR	bay	valley	Monday	toy	guy
PLURAL	bays	valleys	Mondays	toys	guys

25m Form the plurals of most nouns ending in *f* by adding *–s*. The plurals of some nouns ending in *f* or *fe* are formed by changing the *f* to *v* and adding either *–s* or *–es*.

SINGULAR	reef	chief	life	shelf	leaf	gulf
PLURAL	reefs	chiefs	lives	shelves	leaves	gulfs

NOTE When you are not sure how to spell the plural of a noun ending in *f* or *fe*, look in a dictionary.

25n Form the plural of compound nouns consisting of a noun plus a modifier by making the modified noun plural.

SINGULAR	sister-in-law	sea horse	Chief of State
PLURAL	sisters-in-law	sea horses	Chiefs of State

EXERCISE 10 Spelling the Plurals of Nouns

On the line after each noun below, write its correct plural form.

EX. 1. company companies

1. pen pal ________
2. library ________
3. handkerchief ________
4. mystery ________
5. wife ________
6. coat-of-arms ________
7. victory ________
8. scarf ________
9. staff ________
10. subway ________
11. country ________
12. Brodsky ________
13. journey ________
14 melody ________
15. goal post ________
16. half ________
17. boy ________
18. Sunday ________
19. galaxy ________
20. elf ________

CHAPTER 25: SPELLING

PLURALS OF NOUNS II

25o Form the plurals of nouns ending in *o* preceded by a vowel by adding –*s*. The plurals of many nouns ending in *o* preceded by a consonant are formed by adding –*es*.

SINGULAR	radio	studio	echo	potato
PLURAL	radios	studios	echoes	potatoes
EXCEPTIONS	tuxedo		hello	
	tuxedos		hellos	

Form the plurals of most musical terms ending in *o* by adding –*s*.

SINGULAR	cello	tango	piccolo	piano
PLURAL	cellos	tangos	piccolos	pianos

NOTE To form the plurals of some nouns ending in *o* preceded by a consonant, you may add either –*s* or –*es*.

SINGULAR	volcano	cargo	tornado
PLURAL	volcanos	cargos	tornados
	or	*or*	*or*
	volcanoes	cargoes	tornadoes

25p The plurals of a few nouns are formed in irregular ways.

SINGULAR	woman	goose	child	mouse	fish
PLURAL	women	geese	children	mice	fish

EXERCISE 11 Spelling the Plurals of Nouns

On the line after each of the following nouns, write its correct plural form.

EX. 1. tomato tomatoes

1. igloo ________
2. zero ________
3. sombrero ________
4. ox ________
5. foot ________
6. deer ________

7. motto ______________ 9. tooth ______________

8. trio ______________ 10. patio ______________

EXERCISE 12 Identifying Incorrect Spelling in a Paragraph

The paragraph below contains several errors in spelling. Underline the incorrect words. Write the correct spelling above each misspelled word. If the sentence has no errors, write *C* above the sentence. [Hint: One sentence contains two errors.]

women

EX. [1] Our entire family, both men and woman, have always liked music.

[1] When my brother and I were young childs, we began enjoying music. [2] We had radioes in our rooms, and we would tune in whenever we could. [3] I enjoyed pianoes more than any other instrument. [4] My brother liked to listen to stringed instruments, like celloes and banjoes. [5] Our father preferred to hear the high notes of the flutes and piccoloes. [6] For my mother, the sound of drums was the best, and drummers were her heros. [7] Our grandparents, on the other hand, listened to operas every chance they could. [8] At any time of the day, the family loved to hear musical echos throughout the house. [9] Now, whenever there are family gatherings on holidaies, we have some kind of music and song. [10] Everyone joins in, sopranoes and tenors alike.

CHAPTER REVIEW

A. Correcting Spelling Errors in Sentences

Underline the misspelled word in each sentence below. Then write the misspelled word correctly on the line before the sentence.

EX. ___their___ 1. Bicycle riders used to push against the ground with thier feet.

_______________ 1. Bicycles today look very different from models that preceeded them.

_______________ 2. The front wheels of some early bicycles were largeer than the rear wheels.

_______________ 3. On one model, the hieght of the wheel was five feet.

_______________ 4. Obviously, a rider could not climb on the seat easyly.

_______________ 5. Many riders had to have stitchies as the result of falls.

_______________ 6. Nonetheless, these bicycles were a familiar sight along the highwayes in the 1870s.

_______________ 7. One turn of the pedal would move the bicycle forward an amazeing distance.

_______________ 8. As the front wheels became smaller, bicycles became safer for adults and childs.

_______________ 9. Instead of siting on top of the large wheel, a rider could sit between the wheels.

_______________ 10. Still, the rider had to watch out for wet, slippery leafs on the sidewalk.

B. Proofreading a Paragraph to Correct Spelling Errors

The following paragraph contains twenty spelling errors. For each sentence, underline the misspelled word or words. Write the correct spelling above each misspelled word.

EX. [1] A coral reef is home to many liveing (living) creatures.

[1] Many mysteryous creatures live on beautyful coral reeves.

[2] Sponges come in many shapes and sizes and are sometimes the color of lemmons or potatos. [3] Provideing homes for small creatures, they anchor themselfs to rocks or other objects under the water. [4] These creatures get food from the water that passes through the sponges' bodys. [5] Coral reefs are formed by skeletons of billions of tiney animals caled coral polyps. [6] One sea animal you may find thier will not be noticable. [7] For example, octopuss can change color to match their surroundings. [8] Most of these animales measure only several inchs in length. [9] Because they are bonless, they can easyly squeeze through small openings. [10] To confuse their enemys, they shoot out inky liquid and then hastyly procede to safety.

C. Writing Sentences

You are a student living in Japan. You have been asked to talk to your Japanese classmates about the spelling rules of English. Discuss three rules from this chapter. On your own paper, write ten sentences that you might use in your presentation. Be sure to include examples of spelling rules in your explanation.

EX. To form plurals of nouns ending in o preceded by a vowel, you must add –s. For example, the plural of radio is radios.